Theology, Rhetoric, and Politics
in the Eucharistic Controversy, 1078–1079

THE LAST SUPPER

Fresco, the church of Sant'Angelo in Formis, near Capua.

The church was built in the period 1072–1086 by Abbot Desiderius of Monte Cassino and contains his name in the dedicatory inscription over the west door and his portrait in the central apse. The figure of Judas (among the apostles, the fifth from the right) reminds the viewer that in our treatise (chapters 7 and 16), in two citations from a sermon of St. John Chrysostom, Judas is invoked as the type of those who partook of the Eucharist with their lips but not with their hearts (*ore sed non corde*). This theme in the treatise is used to characterize the author's opponents.

Theology, Rhetoric, and Politics in the Eucharistic Controversy, 1078–1079,

Alberic of Monte Cassino Against Berengar of Tours

CHARLES M. RADDING
FRANCIS NEWTON

COLUMBIA UNIVERSITY PRESS
New York

Columbia University Press

Publishers Since 1893
New York Chichester, West Sussex

Copyright © 2003 Columbia University Press
All rights reserved

ISBN 0–231–12684–0 (cloth); ISBN 0–231–12685–9 (pbk.)
LC number: 2002073646

Complete CIP data is on file with the Library of Congress.

∞
Columbia University Press books are printed
on permanent and durable acid-free paper.

Printed in the United States of America

c 1 3 5 7 9 10 8 6 4 2
p 1 3 5 7 9 10 8 6 4 2

CONTENTS

PREFACE

ingentis, genitos diversis partibus orbis, / inter se coiisse viros.
Virgil, Aen. 12. 708–9[1]

On 5 January 1088 Berengar of Tours died, deeply mourned by his close followers.[2] It had been almost nine years since the day, at a synod in Rome in February 1079, when he was forced publicly to repudiate the interpretation of the Eucharist with which his name is linked. On this occasion, he subscribed under oath to a *credo* which stated that in the Mass the elements of the communion were changed "in substance" (*substantialiter*) into the body and blood of Christ. The 1079 synod marked (it so stipulated) the end of Berengar's public teaching on the Eucharist. But Berengar had not forgotten, and in those last nine years he wrote and left behind him a document in which he accused Alberic of Monte Cassino, whom he called "that not-monastic-but-DEMONastic" (*non monachus sed daemoniacus*), of having betrayed him in the debate and of having been largely responsible for the adverse outcome. In the same document Berengar refers in a dark and riddling fashion to Alberic's actions as having been designed to serve the interests of certain "victors," and this reference to "victors" in the struggle is repeated in the same bitter vein, in another late Berengarian document.

A different source also affirms that Alberic played a major role in the 1079 synod. The *Chronicle* of Monte Cassino relates, as part of the account of the accomplishments of the abbey's most renowned teacher

---

1. "[he marveled] that [two] mighty heroes, born in different parts of the world, had met in conflict. . . ."
2. See, for example, the poetic lament of his brilliant student, Hildebert of Le Mans, which begins,

    Quem modo miratur, semper mirabitur orbis,
      ille Berengarius non obiturus obit.

    [He whom the world now views with wonder and always shall,
      that famous Berengar who will never die, has died.]

    The text of this ode is quoted from the critical edition of A. Brian Scott, *Hildeberti Cenomanensis Episcopi Carmina Minora* (Leipzig, 1969), pp. 7–9.

in the late eleventh century, that when the participants in the synod were unable to come to an agreement on the validity of Berengar's interpretation, Alberic composed a little treatise, backed by opinions of the Fathers, "in which he utterly destroyed all his [Berengar's] doctrine." This work of Alberic's has been considered lost by modern scholars, and its loss has been mourned for the light that it undoubtedly could shed on the resolution of the Eucharistic crisis.

It is the goal of this monograph to demonstrate that Alberic's treatise, far from being lost, is in fact a text that can be identified and that has been known to scholars for seventy years. Our study includes a fresh edition and translation of this libellus with thorough discussion of the evidence for Alberic's authorship. As occasionally happens, the text we present as Alberic's and to which we invite the attention of other scholars is not the kind of text that most of us had previously envisioned in our conceptions of the working-out of the Controversy. The authors of this study are as surprised as anyone at the unexpected results of the identification of Alberic's treatise. Now we can see not only Alberic's role—which remains most important—in a new light but the role of Alberic's superior, Abbot Desiderius of Monte Cassino, and the Lenten synod of 1079 itself must be viewed in a new way as well. It is for this reason that we have found it necessary to reconstruct afresh the events of the synod of 1079 in an extended discussion and to return to, among other evidence, the two key documents of Berengar's, mentioned above, in which he discusses his experiences in Rome in 1078–1079.

The present collaboration began in Naples and continued at the American Academy in Rome. Thanks are due as well to the National Endowment for the Humanities, the Duke University Research Council, and the Institute for Advanced Study, and to Giles Constable of the Institute's School for Historical Studies; to Dr. Colin McLaren, keeper of the manuscripts, and Dr. Dorothy Johnston of the Department of Manuscripts and Archives, Aberdeen University Library, for the generous assistance during two visits paid to the library by Francis Newton; to Edward Mahoney for bibliographical advice; to Don Francesco Duonnolo, priest of S. Angelo in Formis, for access and consultation on the church's frescoes; to Don Faustino Avagliano, prior and archivist of Monte Cassino, and his assistant Don Mariano Dell'Omo, for discussions of aspects of the Controversy; and to

R. B. C. Huygens, and to the editor and referees of *Speculum* for many valuable comments. At different times, Carmela Franklin, John Howe, Stephen Jaeger, Carol Lanham, Robert Lerner, Ann Matter, Paul Meyvaert, Robert Somerville, and Ronald Witt, and the anonymous readers for Columbia University Press, have read all or part of our draft, and provided us with valuable criticism and suggestions. At the Press we record our gratitude to Wendy Lochner and her colleagues, and in the production process to Peter Strupp and his colleagues at Princeton Editorial Associates. We were also aided in production of our manuscript by Jenna Golnik of Duke University; Stefan Hagel of the Austrian Academy of Sciences helped us use the Classical Text Editor for the edition and translation. We owe special thanks to Francis Newton's research assistants: to Benjamin Morris for his bibliographical help, and to Steven Turner, whose assistance infinitely lightened the burden of creating the edition. Responsibility for errors and omissions, and for conclusions that these readers may not share, of course, remains ours alone. The debt that is greatest is that to Maureen Flanagan and to Louise Newton.

ABBREVIATIONS

The following abbreviations are used throughout the notes and bibliography:

CC	*Corpus Christianorum*
CCCM	*Corpus Christianorum, Continuatio Mediaevalis*
CSEL	*Corpus Scriptorum Ecclesiasticorum Latinorum*
MGH	*Monumenta Germaniae Historica*
Briefe	*Briefe der deutschen Kaiserzeit*
Epp. sel.	*Epistolae Selectae*
Schriften	*Schriften der MGH*
SS	*Scriptores*
PL	Migne, *Patrologia Latina*

Theology, Rhetoric, and Politics
in the Eucharistic Controversy, 1078–1079

ONE

Berengar of Tours and the Eucharistic Controversy

Introduction

The Eucharistic Controversy of the eleventh century is of importance not just for the ideas at stake, crucial as they were for the central rite in Christian religious practice, but as a key episode in the process by which an intellectual and scholarly community took shape.[1] Although the issues themselves were not new, having first been raised and debated in the ninth century, they were pursued with an unprecedented

1. A detailed survey of the history of the Eucharistic Controversy is provided by J. de Montclos, *Lanfranc et Bérenger. La controverse eucharistique du XIe siècle* [Spicilegium Sacrum Lovaniense. Études et documents, 37] (Louvain, 1971). More information on the earlier stages is given in Margaret Gibson, *Lanfranc of Bec* (Oxford, 1978), pp. 63–97, and, for the theological debates, in Brian Stock, *Implications of Literacy* (Princeton, 1983), pp. 272–315, which provides a detailed examination of individual works produced in the course of the Controversy. Gary Macy, *The Theologies of the Eucharist in the Early Scholastic Period. A Study of the Salvific Function of the Sacrament According to the Theologians c. 1080–c. 1220* (Oxford, 1984), discusses the eleventh-century debate briefly as a background to later developments; see especially pp. 35–43 and the bibliography cited there. A similar perspective is adopted in Miri Rubin, *Corpus Christi* (Cambridge, 1991); see especially pp. 13–17. Older studies of the two principals in the Controversy include R. W. Southern, "Lanfranc of Bec and Berengar of Tours," in *Studies in Medieval History Presented to Frederick Maurice Powicke*, ed. R. W. Hunt, W. A. Pantin, and R. W. Southern, (Oxford, 1948), pp. 27–48; and A. J. MacDonald, *Berengar and the Reform of Sacramental Doctrine* (London, 1930). A brief overview of the later stages of the dispute, with some especially valuable observations on the events of 1078–1079, may be found in Robert Somerville, "The Case Against Berengar of Tours—A New Text," *Studi Gregoriani* 9 (1972): 55–75. The most recent overview of all of these issues is provided by the collection of papers given at the conference held at Wolfenbüttel to commemorate the 900th anniversary of Berengar's death: *Auctoritas und Ratio. Studien zu Berengar von Tours*, ed. Peter Ganz, R. B. C. Huygens, and Friedrich Niewöhner [Wolfenbütteler Mittelalter-Studien, bd. 2] (Wiesbaden, 1990). In addition to these works and the bibliography cited in them, the student of the South Italian connection can profit from H. E. J. Cowdrey, *The Age of Abbot Desiderius* (Oxford, 1983), pp. 90–95.

vigor for thirty years, ending only with the Roman council of Lent, 1079. This long period afforded both sides ample opportunity to develop their own positions, and to respond, sometimes awkwardly, to the arguments being offered by their opponents. Although the problems raised during the controversy were genuinely difficult, so much so that many of them lingered into the thirteenth century,[2] this tentativeness also reflects the condition of learning in the mid-eleventh century, when scholars still expected ancient authorities to provide the answers to most questions. In the case of the Eucharist, however, that expectation was dramatically disappointed: the relevant patristic sources were vague, off the point, and (as events amply demonstrated) susceptible to various interpretations. In northern France, this experience with the ambiguity of texts would give rise to a study of logic and language that would last well into the twelfth century and mark generations of medieval philosophy and theology.

But the Eucharistic Controversy was not and could not be a struggle that was waged only at the level of scholarship. Defining eucharistic doctrine was the business of church councils, whose actions marked out the key periods in the course of the controversy and determined the issues to be taken up next. Such councils were inevitably dominated by abbots, archbishops, and bishops, not all of whom necessarily grasped

---

Important new documentary evidence has been brought forth in recent decades, with interpretive conclusions, by P. Meyvaert, "Bérenger de Tours contre Albéric du Mont-Cassin," *Revue Bénédictine* 70 (1960): 324–32; by Rudolf Maurer, "Berengarii ut videtur De eucharistia (Wiederauffindung eines seit Mabillon verschollenen Fragmentes)," *Wiener Studien* 103 (1990): 199–205, which contains a fresh edition of the fragmentary statement of Berengar found by Mabillon; and Somerville, "The Case Against Berengar of Tours," with first edition of the important Poitiers Council text of 1075. There is now an essential new edition of Berengar's principal work, once called the *De Sacra Coena:* Beringerius Turonensis, *Rescriptum contra Lanfrannum*, ed. R. B. C. Huygens (Turnhout, 1988) [*CCCM*, no. 84 and 84a]; vol. 84a is a complete facsimile of the unique and contemporary Wolfenbüttel MS, Cod. Guelf. Weissenburg 101, with introduction by W. Milde. It is interesting to note that the text (as opposed to the heading) of the Aberdeen treatise, which we discuss here, uses a spelling close to that which Huygens regards as correct: Beringarius (see vol. 84, p. 9 and n. 2). Huygens collects a number of relevant texts in *Serta Medievalia. Textus varii saeculorum X–XIII* Tractatus et epistulae [*CCCM*, no. 171] (Turnhout, 2000), which supersedes his earlier editions published as articles.

2. See especially the work of Gary Macy, *Theologies*, and "Berengar's Legacy as Heresiarch," in *Auctoritas und Ratio*, pp. 47–67; Ludwig Hödl, "Die theologische Auseinandersetzung mit Berengar von Tours im frühscholastischen Eucharistietraktat *De corpore Domini*," also in *Auctoritas und Ratio*, pp. 69–88; and for some of the more general concerns the essays of M.-D. Chenu collected in *La théologie au douzième siècle*, 3rd ed. (Paris, 1976) [partially translated in *Nature, Man, and Society in the Twelfth Century*, ed. and trans. Jerome Taylor and Lester K. Little (Chicago, 1968)].

the philosophical and theological issues involved; and although councils had never failed to condemn Berengar, they varied widely in the wording of their decrees and of the oaths they insisted that Berengar swear on the occasions when he was present. Having as an audience this wider ecclesiastical community inevitably worked to give shape to the scholarly debate itself, forcing both sides to seek formulations of their positions that would attract the widest possible support.

This monograph of ours concerns the concluding period of the controversy: the Roman councils of 1078 and 1079. But the intellectual issues, and even the politics, of that brief period cannot be understood apart from the earlier stages of the controversy, the course of whose discussions had defined the issues that the judgment in Rome was intended to resolve. Unfortunately for modern historians, the evidence for the first decades of the controversy is no more tractable than that for its ending. Many works, especially those of Berengar, are lost, and it has been difficult to establish the dates, authors, or audience for many of those works that do survive. The result has been that many details of the history of the controversy remain under discussion, even after the intensive research of recent decades. It will not be possible in the brief survey appropriate for our purposes for us to discuss all these questions; fortunately, understanding the precise course of earlier events—as opposed to the main outlines—only rarely impinges on the questions surrounding the events of 1078–1079.

The Carolingian Background
and the Eleventh-Century Debate

Although the commemoration of the Last Supper had been the central Christian ritual since the earliest days, it was not until the ninth century that the bread and wine of the Mass became a subject of sustained discussion. The first treatise on the topic was written in 831–833 by Pascasius Radbertus, a monk of Corbie, in response to a request from the abbot of Corbie's daughter monastery, Corvey; in 843 or 844 Pascasius, then abbot of Corbie, gave a revised copy of his work to Charles the Bald, king of west Francia.[3] In this work, Pascasius main-

---

3. The recent works dealing with the Carolingian controversy include Celia Chazelle, *The Crucified God in the Carolingian Era. Theology and Art of Christ's Passion* (Cambridge, 2001), chapter 6,

tained that the body of Christ consumed in the mass was identical to the historical body of Christ that was born of Mary, sacrificed on the cross, and resurrected from the tomb. It was the true body, he argued, not a figure of it; and it is no more to be wondered at that the substance of the bread and wine (*panis ac vini substantia*) would be changed invisibly to the flesh and blood of Christ, without alteration of external appearance or flavor, than it is that the Holy Ghost could create, without generative seed, Christ the man in the womb of the Virgin.[4] To the obvious question of how this transformation could occur without changing the appearance of the bread and wine, Pascasius replied—as would many in the eleventh century—that nothing was impossible to God, and that nature itself was nothing except the will of God.[5]

The other Carolingian works on the Eucharist are difficult to date, and it was perhaps not until the 850s that there was much wider discussion of the issues that Pascasius had raised. Pascasius found little support for his views except from Hincmar of Reims, with most of those who wrote opposing his insistence on the physical identity of the Eucharist with Christ's body. Hrabanus Maurus and Gottschalk of Orbais both wrote against the view that Christ was physically present in the consecrated bread, although we know of Hrabanus's work only because he mentions it in one of his letters.[6] But the most important treatise was that written by Ratramnus of Corbie.[7] Having been asked by Charles the Bald to address the question whether the body of Christ received by the faithful is present in truth or in mystery, Ratramnus both insisted that there was a "true" presence of Christ while refuting the idea that this meant an identity of substance. "For the bread is not substantially [*substantialiter*] Christ, nor is the vine Christ, nor are

which also cites much useful, earlier work; and David Ganz, *Corbie in the Carolingian Renaissance* (Sigmaringen, 1990).

4. "Unde nec mirum Spiritus Sanctus qui hominem Christum in utero virginis sine semine creavit, etiam si ipse panis ac vini substantia carnem Christi et sanguinem invisibili potentia cotidie per sacramenti sui sanctificationem operatur, quamvis nec visu exterius nec gustu saporis conpraehendatur," *De Corpore et Sanguine Domini,* ed. B. Paulus [*CCCM,* 16] (Turnhout, 1969) p. 27, ll. 82–87. In addition to the works already cited, see also the discussion of Pascasius in J. Geiselmann, *Die Eucharistielehre der Vorscholastik* (Paderborn, 1926), pp. 144–70.

5. *De Corpore,* pp. 13–17.

6. Chazelle, *Crucified God,* pp. 225–32, including a discussion of John the Scot's references to the issue in several works.

7. *Ratramnus De Corpore et sanguine Domini. Texte original et notice bibliographique,* ed. J. N. Bakhuizen van den Brink [Verhandlingen der Koninklijke Nederlandse Akademie van Wetenschappen, Afd. Letterkkunde, nieuwe reeks, deel. 87](Amsterdam/London, 1974).

apostles the branches."[8] (The last reference is to John 15:5.) The bread
and wine, he continues, retain their appearance, flavor, and scent, so
that there is nothing through which a transformation can be known.
Since Pascasius never argued that consecration altered the outward appearance of the eucharistic elements, and Ratramnus does not mention him by name, some scholars have suggested that this treatise was
directed against other opponents.[9] But Ratramnus's argument clearly
extends to the position laid out by Pascasius, for he insists that the eucharistic meal is spiritual not corporeal. Substituting the Augustinian
concept of "figure" for Charles's term "mystery," Ratramnus argued
that the eucharistic elements became Christ's body both figurally and
in truth. In effect, he took the position that it is the spiritual rather
than the physical identity that is truly important.

Active discussion of the Eucharist dropped off sharply after the initial flurry of activity, never arriving at any agreement. References to the
subject in tenth- and early eleventh-century texts show that the questions were not forgotten, but the evidence is too scattered for us to
trace the process by which Pascasius's views—which had won little
support from his contemporaries—gained wide acceptance in the ecclesiastical community. By the end of the tenth century, Heriger of
Lobbes could assert that Ambrose, Augustine, Jerome, and Gregory all
agreed that the bread and wine were the body and blood of Christ.[10]
In this context, Berengar's open defense of Ratramnus's treatise (which
he attributed to John the Scot) struck many of his contemporaries as
a dangerous departure from patristic teachings and accepted doctrine.

The eleventh-century controversy proceeded at two levels: the intellectual contest among scholars and the ecclesiastical debate within
church councils. Whereas participants in the Carolingian debate rarely
addressed each other's views directly, leaving us even in doubt concerning the extent to which Ratramnus intended his treatise as a refutation of Radbertus, the eleventh-century debate saw a sequence of attack and counterattack as Berengar answered his critics and they him.

---

8. "Nam substantialiter nec panis christus, nec vitis christus, nec palmites apostoli." p. 44, ll. 29–30.

9. Jean-Paul Bouhot, *Ratramne de Corbie. Histoire littéraire et controverses doctrinales* (Paris, 1976),
   pp. 85–88; C. Chazelle, "Figure, Character, and the Glorified Body in the Carolingian Eucharistic Controversy," *Traditio* 47 (1992): 1–36 at pp. 5–9.

10. Heriger of Lobbes, *Libellus de Corpore et Sanguine Domini*, PL 139: 179–88; the edition erro-
    neously attributes the work to Gerbert.

This change reflects an intellectual world in which masters were more numerous than in the ninth century and also more accustomed to defending and developing their ideas. The same pattern can be seen in eleventh-century glosses to the liberal arts, where the views of various masters—sometimes including Lanfranc—were collected and presented side by side.

Interacting with the theological debate were efforts to use church councils to define what constituted acceptable teachings on the Eucharist. In 1050, immediately after Berengar's views first became known,[11] councils in Rome and Vercelli acted to condemn his teaching.[12] Although these condemnations took place *in absentia* and did nothing to dissuade Berengar from his position, they illustrate another aspect of this period: the ongoing interaction between the Berengarian controversy and the papal reform movement. Thus, both the Rome and Vercelli councils were presided over by Pope Leo IX, then in the early stages of his campaign against simony. Papal legate Hildebrand, the future Gregory VII, presided over a 1054 council at Tours where Berengar was permitted to swear a compromise oath that he had written himself. A fourth council before Pope Nicholas II at Rome in 1059 ended in Berengar being forced to swear an oath, drafted by Cardinal Humbert of Silva Candida (another prominent reformer), that Berengar found truly repellent.[13]

After the Roman council of 1059, the world of ecclesiastical governance may have considered the issue settled. Only two councils of the 1060s showed enough interest in Berengar's ideas to condemn them— the 1062 council at Angers and the 1064 council at Lisieux. But Berengar himself certainly did not accept this judgment, for upon his return to France he published a (now lost) book attacking the decision of the 1059 Roman council and the role of his principal adversary Humbert. Berengar was then answered by Lanfranc of Bec, in his *Liber de corpore et sanguine Domini* of ca. 1063, and later, in the 1070s, by Lanfranc's student Guitmund, a Norman monk who later became bishop of Aversa

11. On the possibility of open discussions as early as 1047, see the remarks of O. Capitani, "L'«affaire bérengarienne» ovvero dell'utilità delle monografie," *Studi medievali* 3rd ser., 16 (1975): 353–78, at 369–71.
12. On these councils, and the stance of Leo IX toward Berengar, see H. E. J. Cowdrey, "The Papacy and the Berengarian Controversy," in *Auctoritas und Ratio*, pp. 109–36, at pp. 112–14.
13. See Macy, *Theologies*, p. 38, with citations of earlier literature.

in Southern Italy. Both Lanfranc and Guitmund were concerned not only with refuting Berengar but also with defending the council of 1059 and the specific oath that Berengar had been forced to swear.

Although Berengar's response to Lanfranc is our principal source for his ideas, that work evidently did not circulate. His continued recalcitrance must nonetheless have been widely known and in the 1070s the public debate reopened. The turning point may have come in 1073 when Cardinal Deacon Hildebrand was chosen pope: rightly or wrongly—the issue is still debated—Berengar regarded him as sympathetic to his views, and he may have been emboldened in pressing his opinions. In 1075, however, Berengar's views were condemned at a council in Poitou that he attended in his capacity as a cleric of Tours and Anjou. In 1078 Berengar made a final journey to Rome seeking vindication, only to be condemned again following months of discussion at a council in Lent 1079. It is that event, and the role of Alberic of Monte Cassino in it, that is the focus of this monograph. But before we can begin to discuss Alberic's role, and the significance of the treatise he wrote against Berengar, it is first essential to sketch in broad strokes the issues around which the controversy revolved prior to 1078.

Berengar's Theology of the Eucharist

When the Eucharistic Controversy arose in the late 1040s, Berengar was a mature scholar of middle age. He had studied at Chartres under its famous teacher—Bishop Fulbert (d. 1025), and in the 1030s he apparently taught as a member of the cathedral chapter of Saint-Martin of Tours, a church where his uncle and brother were already canons. By 1040 he had added the position of archdeacon of Angers to his responsibilities at Tours, serving further as treasurer of the cathedral for a few years in the late 1040s; during this period he was a key adviser to Bishop Eusebius Bruno of Angers and Count Geoffrey Martel of Anjou, composing letters issued under the names of both. Berengar evidently lost some influence following his condemnation in 1059 and Count Geoffrey's death in 1060, for he ceased to witness as archdeacon and apparently returned to Tours.[14]

---

14. For the evidence on Berengar's career, see Margaret Gibson, "Letters and Charters Relating to Berengar of Tours," in *Auctoritas und Ratio*, pp. 5–23; and Montclos, pp. 31–37.

Recent scholars have explained the intellectual quality of the Eucharistic Controversy by noting the increasingly expert attention being paid to the study of the liberal arts in northern France. R. W. Southern, in particular, taught us to see Berengar as a grammarian devoted to new speculative theories of language and as a pioneer in the new learning that would reshape European intellectual life in the early twelfth century—an interpretation repeated by many historians.[15] But a reconsideration of the evidence suggests a very different picture.[16] Although Berengar certainly would have been exposed to the basic texts of the liberal arts while studying with Fulbert of Chartres, nothing in Fulbert's literary remains or in the works later written by his students suggests that instruction in these fields was particularly sophisticated or detailed. Fulbert's real interest appears to have been in scripture and theology. He himself left some short treatises and many sermons, including one on the Eucharist, and it was Fulbert's instruction in scripture and the Fathers that Adelmann of Liège recalled to his former schoolmate Berengar at the beginning of the controversy.[17]

Berengar's own learning did not greatly depart from this model. Huygens's fine new edition of Berengar's main surviving work, his *Rescriptum* against Lanfranc of Bec, makes it possible to see that Berengar's own learning was far more profound in patristics and scripture than it was in the trivium. Berengar invokes the liberal arts only rarely and in brief peripheral passages: Huygens's index of works cited, for example, lists only a bare handful of references to texts of the liberal arts, most of which were not original with Berengar but rather were contained in excerpts from Lanfranc's book that Berengar quoted in order to refute them. But beyond this, even his assertion of the importance of *ratio* in sacred matters appears to have rested on Augus-

---

15. Southern, "Lanfranc of Bec and Berengar of Tours"; Southern's ideas are repeated in his two biographies of Saint Anselm [*Saint Anselm and His Biographer. A Study of Monastic Life and Thought 1059–c.1130* (Cambridge, 1963); and *Saint Anselm. A Portrait in a Landscape* (Cambridge, 1990)], and have been widely taken up elsewhere, for example, Montclos, *Lanfranc et Bérenger* and Gibson, *Lanfranc*.

16. C. M. Radding, "The Geography of Learning in Early Eleventh-Century Europe: Lanfranc of Bec and Berengar of Tours Revisited," *Bullettino dell'Istituto Storico Italiano per il Medio Evo e Archivio Muratoriano* 98 (1992): 145–72.

17. Adelmann of Liège, *Ep. ad Berengarium*, in R. B. C. Huygens, "Textes latins du XIe au XIIIe siècle," *Studi medievali* 3rd s. 8 (1967): 476–89, now in *Serta Mediaevalia. Textus varii saeculorum x–xiii* [=*CCCM* 171], pp. 166–201.

tine rather than on Aristotle.[18] As Henry Chadwick has recently observed, "a reading of the *Rescriptum* as a whole does not suggest that Berengar was dominated by either logic or grammar, but by his patristic readings."[19] Indeed, the main innovations toward bringing the liberal arts to bear on theological issues were the modest steps made in this direction by Lanfranc, who had acquired the basic elements of dialectic in his earlier education in northern Italy.[20]

But if Berengar's reading was less oriented toward grammar and logic than Southern supposed, French schools of the early eleventh century were departing from early medieval models in other ways. To begin with, it was precisely in this region between the Loire and the Rhine that masters were becoming an increasingly professional group who could move from one teaching position to another instead of making their careers in a single monastery or cathedral. Berengar himself was one of the first to follow this career path, holding positions at Tours and Angers; but his example was not unique even before 1050, and in the last half of the century it would become common. This professionalism, moreover, was accompanied by a more systematic style of instruction than appears to have been practiced previously. Line-by-line exposition of authoritative texts, with an emphasis on noting definitions and explicating specific passages, had always been the usual form of medieval instruction, but eleventh-century French scholars were beginning to raise *quaestiones* and address broader doctrinal problems;[21] not only are the glosses that survive from the later eleventh century more technical and sophisticated than those from the tenth

---

18. André Cantin, "Bérenger, lecteur du *De ordine* de saint Angustin, ou, comment se préparait, au milieu du XIe siècle, une domination de la *ratio* sur la science sacrée," in *Auctoritas und Ratio,* pp. 89–107.

19. Henry Chadwick, "Symbol and Reality: Berengar and the Appeal to the Fathers," in *Auctoritas und Ratio,* pp. 25–45, at p. 35.

20. Radding, "Geography"; for additional comments on Lanfranc's learning see Suzanne J. Nelis, "What Lanfranc Taught, What Anselm Learned," *Haskins Society Journal* 2 (1990): 75–82. H.E.J. Cowdrey, "The Enigma of Archbishop Lanfranc," *Haskins Society Journal* 6 (1994): 129–52, at pp. 130–32.

21. For glimpses of earlier instruction, see, in addition to marginal glosses, two codices that appear to contain the results of such teaching: Laon manuscript 468, described by Suzanne Martinet, "Les arts libéraux à Laon au IXe siècle," in *Enseignement et vie intellectuelle (IXe–XVe siècle)* [Actes du 95e Congrès national des sociétés savantes] (Reims, 1970), pp. 55–62; and Bonn Univ. Bib. S. 218, studied in detail in Rainer Reiche, *Ein Rheinisches Schulbuch aus den 11. Jahrhundert* [Münchener Beiträge zur Mediävistik und Renaissanceforschung, 24] (Munich, 1976).

century, but masters now often developed their analyses through long digressions that took them into issues not specifically addressed in their texts. Finally, one must note the new custom—and one that certainly contributed to the vigor with which the Eucharistic Controversy was fought—by which masters noted the opinions of their contemporaries and undertook to defend their own.[22] Although this practice was to flourish in the twelfth century to the extent that it can seem typical of medieval education, it was not widespread earlier than 1050. The Eucharistic Controversy itself thus coincides with the formative moment of this educational environment, and the proud and contentious Berengar stands as one of the first of a new type of master.

Berengar's position on the Eucharist defies easy description, a consequence both of the complexity of his views and of the fact that his most important surviving work—the *Rescriptum contra Lanfrannum*—was a comparatively late treatise that did not circulate in his own lifetime. This work, written in response to Lanfranc's book against Berengar's earlier *Opusculum*, comes down to us in a single manuscript that may contain autograph notes, Wolfenbüttel Herzog August Bibliothek MS Weissenburg 101. The precise date when Berengar wrote it is uncertain, because there are few clues, apart from the fact that it answered Lanfranc's 1063 treatise. MacDonald suggested a date before 1070,[23] and Gibson preferred a date close to 1065 despite the fact that, as Huygens observed, if the treatise had been written that early it must never have been circulated because no mention of the *Rescriptum* appears in the later treatises against Berengar (such as those of Guitmund of Aversa or, we may now add, Alberic).[24]

---

22. Typical of both tendencies is the commentary on Priscian known as the *Glosule;* it is discussed in R. W. Hunt, "Studies on Priscian in the Eleventh and Twelfth Centuries," *Medieval and Renaissance Studies* 1 (1941–43): 194–231; 2 (1950) 1–56; and M. Gibson, "The Early Scholastic 'Glosule' to Priscian, 'Institutiones Grammaticae': the Text and Its Influence," *Studi Medievali* 20,1 (1979): 235–54. See also the broader discussion in C. M. Radding and William W. Clark, *Medieval Architecture, Medieval Learning. Builders and Masters in the Age of Romanesque and Gothic* (New Haven, 1992), pp. 20–33. In Italy, the translation of Nemesius *Peri Anthropou Physeos*—with its long array of the opinions of the ancients on the nature of the soul—by Alfanus of Salerno may reflect the same interest. There is a Teubner edition by Burkhard (Leipzig, 1917).

23. *Berengar,* p. 162.

24. Gibson, "Letters and charters," pp. 15–16; Huygens, "A propos de Bérenger et son traité de l'eucharistie," *Revue Bénédictine* 76 (1966): 133–39. Guitmund's treatise, *De Corpore et Sanguine Christi,* is printed in PL 149: 1427–1508; for an Italian translation of the text and a commentary on it, see Luciano Orabona, *Guitmondo di Aversa. La «Verità» dell'Eucaristia* [Chiese del Mezzogiorno. Fonti e Studi, 6] (Naples, 1995). Guitmund's career and the dating of the treatise are discussed in Somerville, "Case," pp. 70–71. See also below at notes 67–75.

Although the *Rescriptum* is indispensable for understanding both Berengar's views and the learning on which they were based, its value for understanding the course of the debate is less certain. The views expressed in the *Rescriptum* had been refined and elaborated during the twenty or so years of debate. One cannot, therefore, simply read the *Rescriptum* back into the world of 1050, or assume that his adversaries were aware of all the ideas found there. Berengar's core position, however, remained remarkably consistent from his earliest surviving writings—his letters to Ascelin the Breton and to Adelmann of Liège—down to the *Rescriptum:* that is (as he wrote to Ascelin in 1050) "the words themselves said in consecration of the bread prove that the matter of the bread does not depart from the sacrament" [convincere ipsa verba in consecrationem panis instituta non decedere sacramento materiam panis].[25] Ten years later, in his treatise against Humbert and the council of 1059, Berengar wrote: "by consecration at the altar the bread and wine are made into religious sacraments, not so that they cease to be that which they were, but so that they are that which is changed into something else, as the blessed Ambrose says in his book On Sacraments" [per consecrationem altaris fiunt panis et vinum sacramenta religionis, non ut desinant esse quae erant, sed ut sint quae in aliud commutentur, quod dicit beatus Ambrosius in libro De sacramentis].[26] And the same position is upheld, at tortuous length, throughout the *Rescriptum* itself: "as attested by all of the Scriptures, the bread and wine are converted by consecration into the flesh and blood of Christ, and it is agreed that everything that is consecrated, and everything blessed by God, is not diminished, not taken away, not destroyed but remains and is of necessity exalted into something better than it was" [panis autem et vinum, attestante hoc omni scriptura, per consecrationem convertuntur in Christi carnem et sanguinem, constatque omne quod consecretur, omne cui a deo benedicatur, non absumi, non auferri, non destrui, sed manere et in melius quam erat necessario provehi].[27]

Berengar's first line of defense for this proposition lay in the "reasons of all nature" (*omnis naturae rationes*):[28] the fact that the physical characteristics of the bread and wine remained unchanged after con-

25. *Serta Mediaevalia*, p. 148, ll. 33–35.
26. *Rescriptum* p. 101, ll.1–4, quoting the earlier work.
27. *Rescriptum*, p. 183, ll.3015–20.
28. *Serta Mediaevalia*, p. 148, ll. 20–21.

secration was, he argued, an indication that the substance of the bread must have survived as well. This argument appears as early as his correspondence from the 1050s, as when he wrote Ascelin that the persistence of the matter of the bread "is so plain that even a boy still in school, who has some active knowledge of the force that resides in the joining of words, can understand and demonstrate this" [ita planum est ut sufficiat hoc sentire et convincere etiam puerulus in schola constitutus, qui vim iuncturae[29] verborum non instrenue calleat].[30] Later, in the *Rescriptum*, he answered opposing contentions that nature was nothing other than the will of God by replying that, although God certainly had the power to alter natural law, this occurred only "manifestly." As he wrote to Lanfranc,

> In truth you with your learning should have regarded it as completely obvious that the cases of Moses' staff and the waters of Egypt have absolutely no resemblance to the change in the bread and the wine at the Lord's table, and that those actions have nothing to do with these that are carried out with the bread and the wine by consecration at the altar, because the staff was only a thing in Moses' hand, and the serpent to be created out of that had never existed and the staff obviously by corruption of the subject was going to cease to be a staff, and the serpent by generation of the subject (the staff being cast upon the ground) then for the first time had to begin to be, while the bread and the wine of the altar undergo no corruption of the subject but instead take on consecration.

> ―――――

> [Revera manifestissimum habere debuit eruditio tua rem gestam de Moysi virga et de aquis Egipti nulla prorsus similitudine convenire cum conversione panis et vini mensae dominicae, nulla similitudine res gestas illas ea, quae de pane et vino per consecrationem geruntur altaris, contingere, quia solum quiddam in manu Moysi virga erat, serpens de ea faciendus numquam extiterat, virga manifeste per corruptionem subiecti desitura erat esse virga, serpens per generationem subiecti, virga in terram proiecta, tunc primo incipere esse habebat, panis autem atque vinum altaris nullam patitur corruptionem subiecti sed potius consecrationem suscipit.][31]

―――――

29. Hor. *AP* 47–48 callida . . . iunctura.
30. *Serta Mediaevalia*, p. 148, ll. 37–39.
31. *Rescriptum*, p. 126, ll. 936–46.

In short, a substantial part of Berengar's argument rested on an analysis of natural processes and, by extension, of how to recognize when divine or miraculous events intervened to alter them.[32]

But Berengar developed his argument in other important directions. As early as his letter to Adelmann, Berengar argued that Augustine, in taking *sacramentum* to mean *sacrum signum*, had recognized a difference between *res* and *signum*. Quoting Augustine that "a sign is a thing that inspires one image in the senses while making something else come into one's thought" [signum est res, praeter speciem quam ingerit sensibus, ex se faciens aliud in cogitationem venire], Berengar drew the implication: "he did not say [coming]: 'into the hand, into the mouth, into the teeth, into the belly,' but 'into one's thought'" [Non ait: 'In manum, in os, in dentem, in ventrem,' sed 'in cogitationem'].[33] Sacraments could not, therefore, be equated in a simple fashion in physical reality, and he invoked terms such as *similitudo, figura,* and *pignus*—language already used by the Fathers—to describe the relationship between Christ's body and the bread and wine of the altar.[34] If the bread and wine on the altar were sacraments, they could not have been the thing itself.

Finally, and most generally, Berengar insisted on the necessity of interpreting physical events and texts. Berengar did not deny Lanfranc's accusation that he preferred reason to the authority of the Fathers, but instead cited Augustine's own example in defending the use of dialectic.[35] "It is a mark of the greatest spirit in all things to have recourse to dialectic, because to have recourse to her is to have recourse to reason; and one who does not have recourse to that, inasmuch as he is made in accordance with reason in the image of God, has abandoned his honorable station and cannot be remade from day to day in the image of God. The blessed Augustine deems dialectic worthy of such

---

32. This aspect of Berengar's thought has recently received a careful analysis from Toivo J. Holopainen, *Dialectic and Theology in the Eleventh Century* [Studien und Texte zur Geistesgeschichte des Mittelalters, bd. 54] (Leiden/New York/Köln, 1996), ch. 4. Particularly interesting is Holopainen's discussion, pp. 80–95, of several passages in which Berengar directly tackles the question of how the external properties of an object depend on the material of which that object is made.

33. Montclos, p. 133.

34. Stock, pp. 275–78. See, for example, *Rescriptum*, pp. 164–67.

35. *Rescriptum*, pp. 85–86.

high definition that he says, 'Dialectic is the art of arts, the discipline of disciplines. She knows how to learn, she knows how to teach, and she not only wishes to make men wise, she actually makes them so'" [Maximi plane cordis est per omnia ad dialecticam confugere, quia confugere ad eam ad rationem est confugere, quo qui non confugit, cum secundum rationem sit factus ad imaginem dei, suum honorem reliquit nec potest renovari de die in diem ad imaginem dei. Dialecticam beatus Augustinus tanta diffinitione dignatur, ut dicat: dialectica ars est artium, disciplina disciplinarum, novit discere, novit docere, scientes facere non solum vult sed etiam facit].[36] As Stock observes, Berengar saw "Biblical and patristic writing on the Eucharist [as] a kind of figurative speech. . . . On 'mysteries' like the sacraments, Scripture cannot stand alone. It must be interpreted, preferably with the aid of reason."[37]

No simple summary can adequately convey the complexity of Berengar's reasoning. Even his adversaries respected his learning, adopting in places some of his most basic concepts. "And I do not intend to answer all your points," Lanfranc addressed Berengar, "because you weave roses in among the thorns, and you paint your fanciful creation with colors that are white as well as ones that are black" [Nec ad omnia responsurus sum, quia spinis rosas interseris, et albis atque nigris coloribus phantasma tuum depingis].[38] As Fr. Häring has noted, Berengar's conception of *sacramentum* came to be widely adopted in the twelfth century, despite the rejection of his specific position on the Eucharist;[39] and even in the context of the controversy many of Berengar's opponents found themselves forced to devise arguments of far greater philosophical sophistication than had previously been employed. In particular, most of them came to accept Berengar's argument that some interpretive criteria had to be applied to sacred texts. In this sense, too, the Eucharistic Controversy marked and was marked by the emerging scholastic culture of the later eleventh century.

---

36. *Rescriptum*, pp. 85–86, I.1795–1800; this passage is one of those discussed by Cantin in "Bérenger, lecteur du *De ordine*."

37. Stock, p. 279.

38. *Liber de corpore et sanguine domini*, PL 150: 409C.

39. N. M. Häring, "Berengar's Definitions of *Sacramentum* and Their Influence on Mediaeval Sacramentology," *Mediaeval Studies* 10 (1948): 109–46.

Berengar's Early Critics

Several works intended to refute Berengar survive from the first decade of the controversy, giving us more direct evidence for his critics than we have for Berengar himself. The earliest probably were the treatises of Hugh of Langres[40] and John of Fécamp,[41] both perhaps from 1049 or 1050. Possibly also from 1050, and certainly from before 1055, comes Adelmann of Liège's letter;[42] the treatise of Durand of Troarn is usually dated before 1054. Not all of these writers were particularly well informed as to Berengar's precise views or the reasons he gave for them, and not all of them need treatment here. But several themes recur consistently throughout these works:

1. The assertion that the Eucharist was the "true body of Christ" (*verum corpus Christi*). This was clearly meant to answer Berengar's claim that the matter of the bread remained after consecration, although it was not a formulation with which Berengar himself disagreed; for him the question was defining in what sense the "true" body of Christ was present. But Berengar's opponents saw the matter differently. Thus, Adelmann wrote Berengar that he had heard that Berengar maintained that the body and blood of the Lord daily sacrificed on the altar "was not the true body of Christ and his true blood, but a kind of figure and likeness" [non esse verum corpus Christi neque verum sanguinem, sed figuram quandam et similitudinem].[43]

2. The assertion that since God created the world, God's will was not in any way restricted by nature. As Hugh of Langres firmly reminded Berengar, "The will of God and his word are exalted above all nature." [Dei voluntas, et verbum omni naturae supereminet].[44] Much the same theme was taken up by Ascelin, who attacked more explicitly any idea that one could distinguish between nature and God: "For

---

40. Hugo Lingonensis, *De corpore et sanguine Christi contra Berengarium*, PL 142: 1325–31. For the date of this work, see O. Capitani, "Studi per Berengario di Tours," *Bulletino dell'Istituto Storico italiano e archivio muratoriano*, 69 (1957): 67–173 at 112n.

41. *Albini Confessio Fidei* (wrongly attributed), PL 101: 1027–98.

42. Capitani, "L'«affaire bérengarienne»," pp. 561–2, makes a strong case for an early date of at least the first of Adelmann's two drafts; Montclos prefers one closer to 1054.

43. *Serta Mediaevalia*, p.183, ll. 47–49.

44. PL 142: 1328D.

who that is truly wise would call nature the cause of things rather than confess that the will of God is the cause of all natures and of all things that are born after the nature of their kind? Further, the will of God is so efficacious and almighty that his will alone is creation" [Quis enim sane sapiens causam rerum naturam vocet ac non potius omnium naturarum et ex natura sui generis nascentium voluntatem dei esse fateatur? Porro voluntas dei tam efficax est et omnipotens, ut eius velle solum fieri sit].⁴⁵ Others of Berengar's earlier critics replied similarly, listing the miracles worked by God in the Bible, and the general point was taken up again by Berengar's later critics, Lanfranc and Guitmund.⁴⁶

3. Reliance on the authority of the church and the Fathers. The real question here, as Capitani observed, is how Pascasius's doctrine had become so firmly established by the mid-eleventh century;⁴⁷ but there is no doubting that this was a central point for all of Berengar's opponents; thus, as Hugh wrote, "For just as you do not comprehend how the word was made flesh, so you cannot comprehend how this bread is changed into flesh, and the wine transformed into blood, if faith in omnipotence shall not have instructed you" [Sicut enim non capis quomodo Verbum caro factum sit, sic non potes capere quomodo panis iste mutetur in carnem, et vinum in sanguinem transformetur, nisi te docuerit omnipotentiae fides].⁴⁸ But none addressed the issue more poignantly than Adelmann, Berengar's friend from the days they shared with Fulbert at Chartres, who reminded him of their master's injunction "that you [sing.] should love Catholic peace and not stir up trouble in the commonwealth of the Christian state so well settled earlier by our ancestors" [ut pacem catholicam diligas neque conturbes rem publicam christianae civitatis bene iam compositam a maioribus nostris].⁴⁹ Adelmann was typical in his conviction that Berengar was raising an issue that had long been settled; and he was typical as well in attempting to demonstrate this by citing abundantly from Scripture

---

45. *Serta Mediaevalia*, p. 152 ll. 52–56.
46. Durand, for example, took from Ambrose the argument that it was useless to speak of the *ordo naturae* in regard to Christ since his very birth from a virgin demonstrated that his body was exempt from that order. *Liber de corpore et sanguine Christi contra Berengarium et ejus sectatores*, PL 149: 1373–1424, at 1385B.
47. "L'«affaire bérengarienne»," p. 565.
48. *PL* 142: 1328C.
49. *Serta Mediaevalia*, p.184, ll. 72–75.

and the Fathers. Berengar himself, of course, knew and used the same sources, but for the most part his early opponents made little effort to refute his claim to the authority of, especially, Augustine and Ambrose. It appears to have been only Lanfranc who, in responding to Berengar's book instead of rumor, actually attempted to show that Berengar was using his sources incorrectly.

The Early Councils

Berengar was condemned twice in 1050, at Rome and Vercelli, but these decrees issued *in absentia* did little to silence him. A third council, in Tours in 1054, brought Berengar into contact with Hildebrand, who presided as papal legate. The council had many items of business demanding its attention, so the task of examining Berengar was assigned to the bishops of Orléans and Auxerre. According to Berengar's own, later account, which Montclos accepted as plausible, he rejected the views attributed to him that consecrated bread was no different from ordinary bread, asserting instead that he believed that the bread and wine on the altar after consecration were "truly" (*revera*) the body and blood of Christ;[50] subsequently he swore an oath he had written to that effect before the whole council.[51] Berengar's profession apparently satisfied no one, however, and a final judgment was supposed to be made at Rome. In fact, the death of Leo IX meant that a further four years would elapse before another council would take up Berengar's case.

Rather than the oath, which was meant to be superseded by a later council, the main importance of the Tours council may have been Berengar's encounter with Hildebrand. Berengar came away from their discussions persuaded that the legate was favorably inclined to his position, although unwilling to say so in public: a letter written by Berengar in the name of Geoffrey Martel of Anjou chastises Hildebrand for his Pilate-like timidity,[52] and the theme is also taken up in the *Rescrip-*

---

50. *Rescriptum* 1.627–29, p. 53.

51. *Rescriptum* 1.646–47, p. 54: "Therefore I wrote what I had myself sworn: The bread and wine on the altar after the consecration are the body and blood of Christ" [Scripsi ergo ego ipse quod iurarem: "Panis atque vinum altaris post consecrationem sunt corpus Christi et sanguis"].

52. The text of the letter is printed in *Briefsammlungen der Zeit Heinrichs IV.*, ed. C. Erdmann and N. Fickermann, *MGH Briefe* (Weimar, 1950), pp. 149–52. On this letter, see O. Capitani, "La lettera di Goffredo II Martello a Ildebrando (1059)," *Studi Gregoriani* 5 (1956): 19–31.

tum.[53] Because the Eucharistic Controversy reached its climax during Hildebrand's papacy, these claims have understandably attracted considerable scholarly attention; and scholars have differed in their assessment of Berengar's account. MacDonald accepted Berengar's assertions that Gregory sympathized with his position in the 1050s and in the 1070s, arguing that in letting Berengar be condemned Gregory VII had sacrificed his theological ideas for the sake of his political program; traces of this interpretation can perhaps be seen in Southern's suggestion that, as late as 1078, Berengar may have had the support of both the pope and a sizable portion of those attending the papal council.[54] Montclos, in contrast, concluded that "Hildebrand heard out the Touraine master with benevolence but never taking sides himself."[55] Capitani goes further, observing that the eucharistic question was just one of those that Hildebrand had had to deal with as legate to Tours in 1054, and it may not have seemed to him the most pressing.[56] Cowdrey also concludes that "there is nothing to suggest that the young Hildebrand shared or even sympathized with Berengar's eucharistic teachings,"[57] but he also noted the "orderliness and moderation" with which he proceeded. "Hildebrand had come prepared with a collection of marked passages about the Eucharist in books by ancient authorities, and he was at pains to determine fairly whether Berengar's teachings were compatible with them."[58]

Rendering all of this more difficult to judge is that the evidence about Gregory VII's attitudes comes overwhelmingly from Berengar himself, for nothing survives in which Gregory expresses an opinion on the Eucharist. Yet it seems to have been a tendency of Berengar to assume that intelligent men agreed with him. Southern noticed that in the *Rescriptum* Berengar expresses the opinion that even Lanfranc opposed him not out of sincere differences but from a desire to pander to

53. *Rescriptum*, I.590–615, I.651–66, I.1126–27, pp. 52–53, 54, 67.

54. MacDonald, *Berengar*, pp. 223–35; Southern, "Lanfranc and Berengar," p. 31. Southern, in turn, is followed by Somerville, p. 72.

55. *Lanfranc et Bérenger*, p. 153

56. O. Capitani, "Per la storia dei rapporti tra Gregorio VII e Berengario di Tours," *Studi Gregoriani*, 6 (1959–1961): 99–145; see also the earlier article by Carl Erdmann, "Gregor VII. und Berengar von Tours," *Quellen und Forschungen aus ital. Archiven und Bibliotheken* 28 (1937–38): 48–74. Now, see Capitani, "Status questionis dei falsi berengariani: note sulla prima fase della disputa," *Fälschungen im Mittelalter* [*MGH* Schriften 33.2] (Hannover, 1985).

57. Cowdrey, "The Papacy and the Berengarian Controversy," pp. 122–24.

58. Cowdrey, *Pope Gregory VII 1073–1085* (Oxford, 1998), p. 32.

vulgar opinion: "That which you write was quite at odds with the learning you possess" [quod scribis, multum erat contra eruditionem tuam].[59] He also claimed the agreement of Albert, abbot of Marmoutier; Eusebius Bruno, bishop of Angers; Peter Damian; and, as we shall see, Alberic of Monte Cassino.[60] This record means that Berengar's assertions about other men must always be read with a measure of caution.

The 1054 council eventually found its promised sequel at Rome in 1059. As at Tours, Berengar expected Hildebrand's support, and again he failed to receive it. Taking the lead against him in the debates was the formidable cardinal, Humbert of Silva Candida, who the previous year had completed his work *Adversus simoniacos*, which raised the issue of lay investiture of the clergy as a central issue for the reform movement. The discussions went completely against Berengar. In the end he was compelled to swear an oath, dictated by Humbert, which read:

> I, Berengar, unworthy deacon of the church of St. Maurice at Angers, acknowledging the true, catholic, and apostolic faith, abjure all heresy, especially that with which I have been hitherto slanderously charged, which strives to assert that the bread and the wine that are set upon the altar, after the consecration are sacrament alone and not the true body and blood of our Lord Jesus Christ, and cannot in a sensory fashion but only as a sacrament be handled or broken in the hands of the priests or ground between the teeth of the faithful. Moreover I am in agreement with the holy Roman and apostolic See and profess both with my lips and in my heart that I hold that faith which my lord and venerable pope Nicholas and this holy synod by their evangelical and apostolic authority have handed down for us to hold and have confirmed, namely that the bread and the wine that are set upon the altar, after consecration are not sacrament alone, but also are the true body and blood of our Lord Jesus Christ and in sensory fashion and not only as a sacrament but in truth are handled and broken by the hands of the priests, and ground between the teeth of the faithful; swearing by the Holy Trinity of one single being and by these all-holy Gospels of Christ. And I proclaim that those who shall have opposed this faith [doctrine], with their teachings and their followers, are deserving of

---

59. "Lanfranc and Berengar," p. 39, citing *Rescriptum*, folios 77, 100, 119, 135, 144, 219.

60. For Albert and Eusebius, see Montclos, p. 160, citing *Rescriptum* pp. 36–37. Berengar's claim regarding Peter Damian comes from the *Iuramentum*, to be discussed below, ch. 4.

eternal condemnation. But if I myself at any time shall presume to think and teach what is contrary to this, may I be subject to the severity of the canons. Having read and reread this, I of my own accord have signed it.

———

[Ego Beringerius, indignus diaconus aecclesiae sancti Mauricii Andegavensis, cognoscens veram, catholicam et apostolicam fidem, anathematizo omnem heresim, precipue eam de qua hactenus infamatus sum, quae astruere conatur panem et vinum, quae in altari ponuntur, post consecrationem solummodo sacramentum et non verum corpus et sanguinem domini nostri Iesu Christi esse nec posse sensualiter nisi in solo sacramento manibus sacerdotum tractari vel frangi aut fidelium dentibus atteri. Consentio autem sanctae Romanae et apostolicae sedi et ore et corde profiteor de sacramentis dominicae mensae eam fidem tenere, quam dominus et venerabilis papa Nicholaus et haec sancta synodus auctoritate evangelica et apostolica tenendam tradidit mihique firmavit, scilicet panem et vinum, quae in altari ponuntur, post consecrationem non solum sacramentum sed etiam verum corpus et sanguinem Domini nostri Iesu Christi esse et sensualiter non solum sacramento, sed in veritate manibus sacerdotum tractari, frangi, et fidelium dentibus atteri, iurans per sanctam et omousion Trinitatem et per haec sacrosancta Christi evangelia. Eos vero, qui contra hanc fidem venerint, cum dogmatibus et sectatoribus suis aeterno anathemate dignos esse pronuntio. Quod si ego ipse aliquando aliquid contra haec sentire ac predicare presumpsero, subiaceam canonum severitati. Lecto et perlecto sponte subscripsi.][61]

Overthrowing the doctrine expressed by this oath would be Berengar's principal objective for the next fifteen years, while his opponents would see in this same oath their first line of defense.

The Aftermath of the Council of 1059:
Lanfranc and Guitmund

Berengar was defeated but unpersuaded by his experience in Rome, and on returning to France he wrote an account of his experience including a defense of his beliefs. This *Opusculum* is lost, except for fragments quoted in Lanfranc's *De corpore et sanguine domini adversus Berengarium Turonensem*, and the few sentences transmitted in the later work by Lanfranc's student Guitmund. It is often said that twenty

———

61. From Lanfranc, as given by Huygens, *Serta Mediaevalia*, pp. 241–42.

or so fragments of Berengar's treatise contained in Lanfranc's book suffice to convey the contents of the lost work, but this is surely wrong; Lanfranc himself admits the value of parts of Berengar's work, which he specifically omitted to discuss. But Berengar's book did compel his opponents to answer his own words rather than rumor of what he had said, and this gave the debate a very different character from that which had occurred in the ninth century.

Lanfranc had opposed Berengar since the beginning of the controversy, and he did not hesitate to write a response when the Tours master published his attack on the council of 1059. Lanfranc's treatise is usually dated ca. 1063 to allow for the fact that Nicholas (1058–1061) had already died when it was written.[62] The salutation—for the treatise is cast as an epistle—sets the tone of the whole work: "Lanfranc, by the mercy of God a Catholic, to Berengar, opponent of the Catholic Church" [Lanfrancus, misericordia Dei catholicus, Berengario catholicae Ecclesiae adversario]. Lanfranc's strategy for the first part of the treatise was to quote excerpts from Berengar's *Opusculum* and then refute them, where necessary with an abundant application of the liberal arts. He makes a vigorous defense of Humbert, who had been the focus of Berengar's attack; and he also reinterprets some of the patristic quotations Berengar had offered to demonstrate his own links with tradition. For example, chapter 9 begins with the following quotation from Berengar's *Opusculum:*

> BERENG. Through the consecration of the altar the bread and the wine become a religious sacrament, not so as to cease to be what they were, but so as to be what they were and to be changed into something else, as the blessed Ambrose says in his book *On the Sacraments.*
>
> ———
>
> [BERENG. Per consecrationem altaris fiunt panis et vinum sacramentum religionis, non ut desinant esse quae erant, sed ut sint quae erant, et in aliud commutentur quod dicit beatus Ambrosius in libro *De sacramentis.*]

Lanfranc then responds by rejecting Berengar's reading of this passage, bringing in Ambrose's *De mysteriis.*

> Listen instead to what he says in the book *On the Mysteries* or the initiatory rites. For wishing to show the difference between the manna of the

———

62. Gibson, *Lanfranc,* p. 70 and, for the general context, pp. 63–71.

Jews and the sacrifice of the Christians, in this respect namely, that that was a shadow and a figure but this light and truth, [and] that that was from heaven but this the body of the lord of the Heavens, so that one's mind should not shrink from believing in such a great change of elements into such great things, he added the words (ch. 9): "Therefore with such great precedents as we cite, let us demonstrate that this is not what nature formed but what blessing consecrated, and that the power of blessing is greater than that of nature because even nature itself is changed by blessing." There is no one who doubts, no one who does not know that the bread and the wine are formed by nature. In regard to the true change of these into the true body of the Lord, he shows by obvious examples and asserts by suitable arguments based on likeness that one should have no doubt, relating first the example of Moses' staff turned into a serpent. . . . And that you might not set nature above divine power, as if God could not [*reading* potuit] change the nature of anything whatsoever, he continues by saying: "Why do you seek here the process of nature in Christ's body, when it was quite outside nature that the Lord Jesus Christ himself was born from a virgin?"

———

[Accipe potius quid in libro *de mysteriis* sive initiandis dicat. Volens enim discrepantiam ostendere inter manna Judaeorum et sacrificium Christianorum, per hoc videlicet quia illud umbra et figura erat, hoc vero lux et veritas; illud e coelo, hoc corpus Domini coelorum, ne tantam elementorum in tantarum rerum conversionem mens credere refugeret, subjunxit, dicens (cap. 9): "Quantis igitur utimur exemplis, probemus hoc non esse quod natura formavit, sed quod benedictio consecravit, majoremque vim esse benedictionis quam naturae quia benedictione etiam natura ipsa mutatur." Panem vinumque a natura formari nullus qui ambigat, nemo qui nesciat. De quorum vera in verum corpus Domini conversione non oportere dubitari manifestis ostendit exemplis congruis per similia asserit argumentis, narrans imprimis Moysi virgam in serpentem versam, . . . Et ne naturam potentiae divinae praeponeres, quasi non potuit Deus cujuslibet rei mutare naturam, occurrit dicens: "Quid hic quaeris naturae ordinem in Christi corpore, cum praeter naturam sit ipse Dominus Jesus partus ex Virgine?"][63]

This clash over the interpretation of specific passages is worth noting as a moment in the development of medieval intellectual method:

———

63. *PL* 150: 419D–420B. This chapter is also discussed from a different perspective by Stock, pp. 302–3.

until now the custom had usually been for each side in a debate to assemble its own quotations while ignoring those gathered by their opponents. Although the discussion here is often awkward and, to modern eyes, sometimes off the point, Lanfranc and Berengar were at least engaging on the same terrain. It is equally significant that, as in the passage just quoted, Lanfranc tries to anticipate, and answer, Berengar's possible responses to his own arguments.

But Lanfranc did not take the step of introducing the Aristotelian concept of accidents into the discussion of the Eucharist. Although this accomplishment is nearly universally attributed to Lanfranc, it is notable that scholars do not agree on where he does this,[64] and that the term "accidents" is in any case notably absent from his discussion. Indeed, it is unlikely that Lanfranc knew Aristotelian logic well enough for it to occur to him. Gibson notes that Aristotle's logical works are notably absent from the works that Lanfranc cites, so that "it is almost impossible to see him as a pioneer in the study of the *logica vetus.*"[65] Rather, he uses instead the much less technical and more generic term "qualities," and his discussion does little more than note the obvious fact that the eucharistic bread continues to look like bread even after being consecrated. Lanfranc's discussion does not, therefore, offer the advantages of a technical vocabulary that was to permit theologians of the twelfth and thirteenth centuries to build precise analogies between the events of the Eucharist and other events and philosophical problems, and he cannot really be said to have anticipated the discussions of the Eucharist that would occur later in the Middle Ages.[66]

At some time in the 1070s, Lanfranc's treatise was followed up by his student Guitmund.[67] After an early career as monk in Normandy,

64. For example, Rubin, *Corpus Christi,* pp. 17–18, cites *PL* 150: 416, while H. Chadwick cites the phrase (418B) mentioning the distinction between primary and secondary substances; "Ego Berengarius," *Journal of Theological Studies* n.s. 40 (1989): 414–45 at p. 426.

65. Gibson, *Lanfranc,* p. 49.

66. See the examples given by Rubin, p. 24, as well as Holopainen's detailed analysis of Lanfranc's position, pp. 67–76.

67. See M. Dell'Omo, "Guitmund v. Aversa," in *Lexikon des Mittelalters* 4 (Munich/Zurich, 1989), 1789; and the same author's extended, "Per la storia dei monaci-vescovi nell'Italia normanna del secolo XI: Ricerche biografiche su Guitmondo di La Croix-Saint-Leufroy, vescovo di Aversa," *Benedictina* 40 (1993), 1, 9–34. More recently, there have been the acts of the 1997 conference on Guitmund: *Guitmondo di Aversa. La Cultura europea e la riforma gregoriana nel Mezzogiorno,* 3 vols., ed. Luciano Orabona [Chiese del Mezzogiorno. Fonti e Studi, vols. 13–15] (Naples, 2000). In this collection, vol. 1, pp. 129–57 the late Norbert Kamp has discussed Guitmund's career in "Le fonti per una biografia di Guitmondo di Aversa." On the broader cultural background of

where he is said to have been offered a bishopric in England and perhaps the archbishopric of Rouen, Guitmund moved to Rome at some
time in the 1070s. He wrote his treatise on the Eucharist after the beginning of Gregory VII's pontificate in 1073, and apparently before the
debates began in Rome in 1078; whether he was in Normandy or Rome
is uncertain. Guitmund did become intimate with reform circles, par-
ticipating in a papal legation to Germany in 1077 and later, in 1088, being named bishop of Aversa by Urban II.[68]

Written as a dialogue between Guitmund and another monk, Guitmund's treatise *De Corporis et Sanguinis Christi veritate in Eucharistia*[69] resembles Lanfranc's in attempting directly to address Berengar
and his followers. Guitmund seems to have studied earlier Berengar's
treatise, which he occasionally quotes. He also reasserts many aspects
of the doctrine that had been developing to counter Berengar. Thus,
for example, he vigorously rejects Berengar's claim that, according to
nature, the survival of the appearance of bread after consecration must
mean that there was in fact still some bread; likening the transformation of bread and wine into flesh and blood to that achieved in the body
after the ingestion of food, Guitmund concludes that "There is no impossibility of things that can obstruct the will of God" [Nulla quippe
rerum impossibilitas potest impedire voluntatem Dei].[70] Further, and
clearly recalling the use of the verbs *tangere* and *frangere* in the oath of
1059, he argues that if Thomas could touch Christ's body with his
hands, why not the believer with his teeth? "For it is natural to flesh
that it can be touched" [Tangi namque naturale est carni].[71]

For our purposes, however, the most important aspect of Guitmund's treatise is his analysis of the variety within the broad group of
Berengariani:

> For all the Berengarians agree in this, that the bread and the wine are not
> changed in their essence; but as I have been able to force some ones of

---

Guitmund, see in the same volume the essays of Ovidio Capitani, "Problemi della cultura europea nel secolo XI—Prolusione," pp. 39–57, and Inos Biffi, "Guitmondo e Anselmo alla scuola di
Lanfranco e le arti liberali," pp. 59–78.

68. Somerville, pp. 70–71.
69. *PL* 149: 1427–94.
70. *PL* 149: 1432B.
71. *PL* 149: 1433B.

them to admit, they differ widely on this point: some say that nothing at all of the body and blood of the Lord resides in these sacraments, but they say that these are but shadows and figures. Others, in truth, ceding to the correct reasoning of the Church, but still not receding from their own folly, so that they may seem somehow or other to be with us, say that the body and blood of the Lord are truly contained therein, but in a concealed fashion, and, so that they can be consumed, are—so to speak—"breaded."[72] And this, they say, is the more refined position taken by Berengar himself. But others, no longer now Berengarians, but bitterly opposing Berengar, nevertheless—being led astray by his arguments and by certain words of the Lord (which we will discuss in greater detail in their proper place)[73]—at one time were accustomed to think that the bread and the wine are partly changed and partly remain. But for others, who shrank from the unreasoning interpretation of those latter ones, but did not themselves clearly understand the same words of the Lord that motivated them, it seemed that the bread and the wine were completely changed, but that when unworthy persons came forward to receive in communion the flesh and blood of the Lord, these once again returned to bread and wine.

———

[Nam Berengariani omnes quidem in hoc conveniunt quia panis et vinum essentialiter non mutantur, sed ut extorquere a quibusdam potui, multum in hoc differunt, quod alii nihil omnino de corpore et sanguine Domini sacramentis istis inesse, sed tantummodo umbras haec et figuras esse dicunt. Alii vero, rectis Ecclesiae rationibus cedentes, nec tamen a stultitia recedentes, ut quasi aliquo modo nobiscum esse videantur, dicunt ibi corpus et sanguinem Domini revera, sed latenter contineri, et ut sumi possint quodammodo, ut ita dixerim, impanari. Et hanc ipsius Berengarii subtiliorem esse sententiam aiunt. Alii vero non quidem jam Berengariani, sed acerrime Berengario repugnantes, argumentis tamen ejus, et quibusdam verbis Domini paulisper offensi (quod suo loco dicemus uberius) solebant olim putare quod panis et vinum ex parte mutentur et ex parte remaneant. Aliis vero irrationabilem istorum sensum longe horrentibus, eadem verba Domini, quibus isti moventur, non satis apte intelligentibus, videbatur

———

72. Guitmund's use of "quodammodo, ut ita dixerim" points to a play upon words in "impanari," breaded as a cooking term. For another example of satirical word-play introduced by a verbal marker in the Eucharistic Controversy, see below, at ch. 4, p. 115, n. 93.

73. In reference to Christ's words at Matt. 15:17, discussed by Guitmund at *PL* 149: 1450D and following.

panem et vinum ex toto quidem mutari, sed cum indigni accedunt ad communicandum carnem Domini et sanguinem, iterum in panem et vinum reverti. Quorum omnium erroribus, sicut Dominus dederit, obviare tentabimus.]⁷⁴

This last issue, of the taking Eucharist by an unworthy person, is discussed in more detail in Guitmund's third book: "Of these then one group affirms that part of the bread and wine is transmuted into the flesh and blood of the Lord, but that part, because of the unworthy, remains unchanged. Another group, however, asserts that all the bread and wine on the altar is transmuted into the flesh and blood of the Lord, but when unworthy persons come to communion, they revert once more to bread and wine" [Ex his ergo una, panis et vini partem in carnem et sanguinem Domini transmutari confirmat; partem vero propter indignos immutabilem retineri. Altera, vero, totum quidem panem et vinum altaris in carnem et sanguinem Domini asserit; sed cum indigni ad communionem veniunt, in panem et vinum iterum reverti].⁷⁵ This issue, as we shall see, is one of those that Alberic had to address in his own treatise.

The Movement Toward Rome

This scholarly debate operated in a kind of counterpoint with Berengar's relationship with the institutional church. No church council was going to take up these issues in all their complexity. In such a quasi-juridical context, discussion was certain to be focused on the need to arrive at agreement on an oath or confession to be sworn. Moreover, discussion of the Eucharist in church councils appears to have diminished even as the scholarly debate grew more intense. In the decade of the 1060s, Berengar's case is known to have been discussed at only two councils: Angers in 1062 and Lisieux in 1064. In 1075, however, discussion was intense to the point that Berengar was physically threatened at a council in Poitiers convened by Bishop Girald of Ostia, legate of Gregory VII.⁷⁶ Why the case came up at this time is far from clear;

---

74. 1430C.
75. 1491B.
76. For the Poitiers council, see Somerville, "Case," pp. 62–65.

the possibilities range from deliberate papal policy to more purely local concerns, perhaps a reaction to criticisms Berengar may have directed against the christology of St. Hilary of Poitiers—remarks that
Lanfranc was taking care to circulate in the mid-1070s to those most
likely to be offended by them.[77]

Robert Somerville has recently discovered the profession of faith
pronounced by this council, which shows some influence from the
scholarly debate of the previous decade:

> We believe in our hearts and profess with our lips that that bread and that
> wine which are set upon the altar for sacrifice, that that same bread and
> that same wine, after the consecration carried out there by the power of
> the Holy Spirit through the hand of the priest, is substantially transmuted
> into the true body and into the true blood of Christ—that is, into the very
> body that was born of the Virgin Mary, which suffered and was crucified
> for us, which rose from the dead, which sits at the right hand of God the
> Father, and into that same blood that flowed from his side as he hung on
> the cross, with no substance or nature of the bread and wine remaining
> beyond that likeness which we see there with our bodily eyes, that we
> might not abhor the sacrament by reason of the horror of the blood. For
> if I shall hereafter hold beliefs other than what is contained, inserted, and
> inscribed in this document, may I suffer the condemnation of the same
> Christ himself. And I condemn Berengar and all his followers who are in
> disagreement with the understanding of this sacrament, swearing by the
> holy Trinity of one nature and by these four holy Gospels that henceforth
> I shall so teach and so hold.

> [Credimus corde et ore confitemur panem illum et vinum illut que in al-
> tari ad sacrificandum ponuntur, ipsum eundem panem et ipsum idem
> vinum, post consecrationem que ibi fit virtute Spiritus sancti per manum
> sacerdotis, substantialiter transmutatum in verum corpus et in verum san-
> guinem Christi—in ipsum scilicet corpus quod natum est de Maria vir-
> gine, quod passum est et crucifixum pro nobis, quod surrexit a mortuis,
> quod sedet ad dexteram Dei patris, et in ipsum eundem sanguinem qui
> de latere illius pendentis in cruce emanavit, nulla ibi remanente panis et
> vini substancia vel natura preter ipsam similitudinem quam ibi corporeis

---

77. See the letter to Reginald, abbot of St. Cyprian's in Poitiers, *PL* 150: 543–46; for details, see
Somerville, "Case," p. 63 and n. 37.

oculis videmus, ne aborreamus sacramentum propter horrorem cruoris. Si enim deinceps aliter credidero quam his habeatur insertum et inscriptum, ipsius eiusdem Christi patiar maledictam. Et dampno Berengarium et omnes sequaces eius qui discordant ab huius sacramenti sententia, iurans per sanctam et homousyon trinitatem et per hec sancta quatuor evangelia me deinceps sic docere et sic tenere.][78]

Somerville called special attention to the use of the word *substantialiter* to describe the conversion of the bread and wine into the body and blood of Christ. This term, which Somerville observes "truly troubled the scholar from Tours," had been used most notably by Guitmund of Aversa, and was to play a key role in the discussions of 1078–1079.[79] It has not, however, been noticed that the invocation of terminology from the Arian controversy (*homousyon*) may also be due to Guitmund, who in his third book applied to the Eucharist the discussion of the substance of God in the literature of the Arian controversy and, especially, the work on the Trinity of Hilary of Poitiers;[80] it may, indeed, have been Guitmund's use of this material that prompted Berengar's remarks that were taken to be critical of St. Hilary. If this supposition is correct, one must date Guitmund's treatise to 1073 or 1074. One can further observe that, although the term *substantia* is usually assumed to have been borrowed from Aristotelian logic, the fact that it seems to have been first used by Guitmund suggests that it was really borrowed from the patristic sources, especially St. Hilary, that he himself uses: it is a remnant of the Arian debates rather than a harbinger of scholastic philosophy.

If the papal court had not previously taken an interest in Berengar's case, it may have been the council of Poitiers and the continued agitation of Lanfranc and his student Guitmund that forced it to act.[81] Berengar's only surviving letter to Gregory thanks the pope for intervening on his behalf with the papal legate Hugh of Die, one of the

---

78. Somerville, "Case," pp. 68–69.
79. See Somerville's summary, "Case," pp. 60–71; the quotation is from p. 75. Somerville notes Guitmund's use of the term *substantialiter* at PL 149: 1440B, 1467C, 1472B, 1474C, 1476A,B,C, 1477C,D, 1478A,B,D, 1481A, 1488B, and 1494D. Lanfranc, in contrast, had used rather the different terminology of *essentia*.
80. PL 149: 1469–78.
81. Somerville, p. 64.

pope's closest associates in the reform movement. It is not known precisely what Hugh had been doing in regard to Berengar—one interpretation has been that Hugh had been attempting to remove Berengar from his position as a clerk of Angers—nor the extent to which he acted independently of Gregory's instructions, although Hugh had been trained by Gregory himself, who in 1075 remarked of him that "there is no one in whom we may more fully trust, for we have found that he has faithfully performed all the duties that we have laid upon him" [nemini potius credere debemus quem in omnibus a nobis sibi iniunctis fideliter egisse comperimus].[82] Berengar's letter, however, reveals with certainty that the pope had instructed him to remain silent on the subject of the Eucharist, an order that, as Erdmann suggested, may explain why Berengar's answer to Lanfranc never went into circulation.[83] Berengar wrote: "Feeling, however, surprise that those who come to me in your name are so very unaware that your will in the matter has long been that you bade me through Durandus the clerk of Angers to set a guard upon my lips and to refrain even from good words, if a sinner stood up against me" [miratus tamen quam maxime ignorare eos, qui ab auctoritate tua ad nos deveniunt, voluntatem tuam in eo fuisse multo ante tempore, ut iuberes me per Durandum clericum Andegavensem ponere custodiam ori meo et silere etiam a bonis, si consisteret peccator adversum me].[84] Berengar therefore looked forward to presenting his case personally before the pope.

The date of Berengar's letter to Gregory must fall between Hugh's appointment as legate in 1075 and Berengar's departure for Rome in 1078, but Capitani has also suggested a later, more specific date. He noted that in councils of September 1077 and January 1078 Hugh of Die had conducted campaigns against suspected simoniacs, suspending and deposing abbots and bishops among whom was Berengar's metropolitan, Rudolf of Tours. This event, Capitani hypothesized, may have

---

82. H. E. J. Cowdrey, ed. and trans., *The Epistolae Vagantes of Pope Gregory VII* (Oxford, 1972), pp. 28–29; on Hugh, see also I. S. Robinson, "The Friendship Network of Gregory VII," *History* 63 (1978): 1–22, at pp. 3–4.

83. Erdmann, "Gregor VII.," p. 70.

84. The full text is published in Erdmann and Fickermann, *Briefsammlungen*, pp. 154–55. We accept Erdmann's emendation of perdurandum to per Durandum (see "Gregor VII." pp. 68–69), as does Cowdrey, "The papacy," p. 125; but see Capitani, "Rapporti," pp. 103–7; "L'«affaire bérengarienne,»" pp. 369–71.

made Berengar feel more exposed than ever, leading him to seek judgment outside France. Since Rudolf was reinstated in March 1078, Capitani proposed that Berengar's letter must be dated to the moment of Berengar's greatest insecurity, the first three months of 1078.[85]

But the pope's motives for summoning Berengar to Rome may have been very different from Berengar's reasons for asking him to do so. Gregory was under pressure to do something about Berengar: he wrote Hugh of Cluny on 7 May 1078 that he had summoned Berengar to Rome, *unde nobis scripsistis*.[86] Capitani detects a certain reluctance in Gregory's remarks, and certainly Gregory does not seem to have intervened until events forced his hand. But much of the reform movement was directed toward affirming the primacy of papal judgments over the actions of local authorities, and despite his other, pressing concerns in 1078, the pope could hardly refuse to preside over a final judgment.

In response to this summons, Berengar arrived in Rome at some time in the summer of 1078. Although his case was discussed in a council held in November on All Saints, it was not until early February, during a Lenten council packed with many items of business, that a final decision was pronounced. But evidence attesting to what occurred at these councils or the intervening period has been, as Meyvaert noted, "rather meager,"[87] and this circumstance has lent importance to the somewhat later remarks of the *Chronicle* of Monte Cassino that Alberic of Monte Cassino, the abbey's most famous scholar of the late eleventh century, wrote a treatise against Berengar of Tours at the time of the Rome synod "in which he destroyed all his assertions and consigned them to eternal oblivion."[88] The *Chronicle* is not an entirely trustworthy source, especially where the honor of Monte Cassino is concerned, but in this case its account is confirmed by a fragment preserved in a Subiaco manuscript in which Berengar expresses great bitterness toward Alberic for Alberic's role at this council.

85. "Rapporti," pp. 110–12; the date is accepted by Somerville, "Case," pp. 62–63. Montclos preferred a somewhat earlier date for both letter and Berengar's arrival in Rome, placing the latter in late 1077 on the basis of Berengar's remark in the *Iuramentum* that he had been in Rome nearly a year by All Saints 1078; *Serta Mediaevalia*, pp. 257.

86. *Das Register Gregors VII*, ed. Erich Caspar, *MGH Epp. sel.*, vol. 2 (Berlin, 1955), V.21, pp. 384–85; see the comments of Capitani, "Rapporti," pp. 120–21.

87. "Bérenger," p. 326.

88. *Chronica Monasterii Casinensis*, ed. H. Hoffmann, *MGH, SS* 34, 3.35, p. 41.

Alberic's treatise itself has been regarded as lost, a circumstance that has led to some speculation over what it may have contained. In the next two chapters, however, we shall show that his text can be identified, although it has a different character from what has previously been supposed. Moreover, once that identification has been made we shall be in a position to reconsider the evidence surrounding the events of Berengar's condemnation and the synod of 1079.

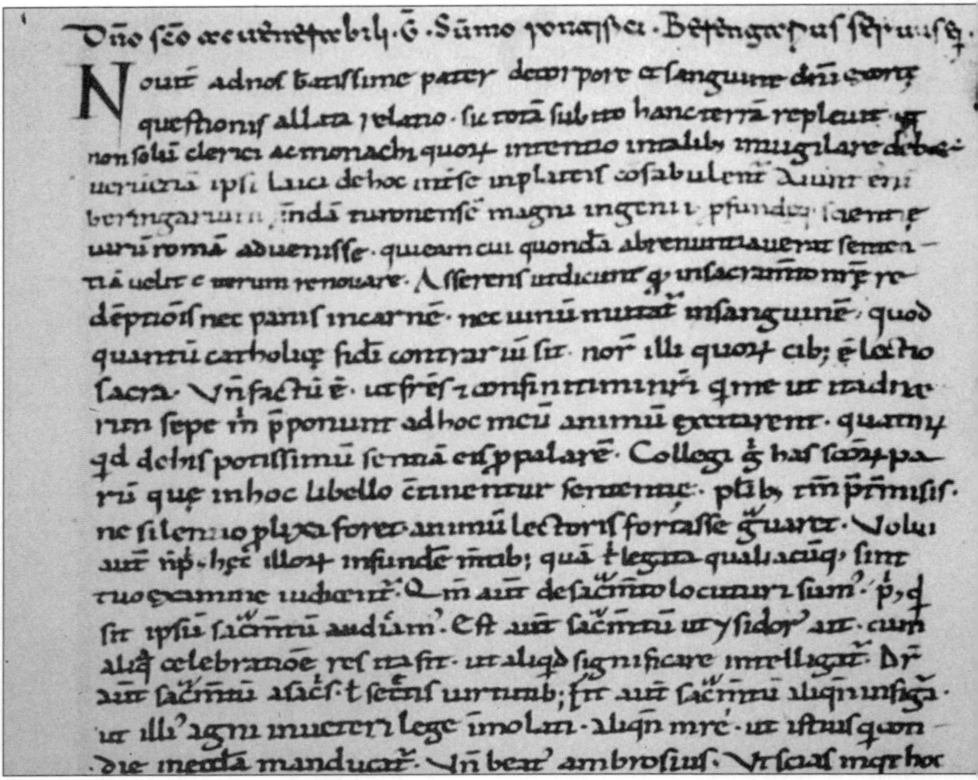

FIGURE 1

Aberdeen, University Library, MS 106, Augustine, De Doctrina Christiana, etc.; here is shown fol. 55v, the beginning of the libellus against Berengar.

The text is in an Italian minuscule hand of the first half of the twelfth century. The heading, however, is in Beneventan of the same period; it shows the New Angle characteristic of books copied after the development of the canonical form of the Monte Cassino script under Abbot Desiderius (1058–1087). The heading reads, with expansion of all but one abbreviation: "Domino sancto ac venerabili. G. Summo pontifici, Berengarius servus eius."

TWO

The Aberdeen Libellus
Against Berengar of Tours

The Manuscript

Manuscript 106 in the University Library, Aberdeen, is a codex written in the first half of the twelfth century, partly in ordinary Italian minuscule and partly in contemporary Beneventan script.[1] (See Fig. 1.) Although it possesses some gold paint and elaboration in its initials,[2] the book is an unpretentious *livre d'étude* containing principally Augustine, *De doctrina Christiana* (1r–55r) and the commentary *In Cantica Canticorum* (beginning on 65r) that is ascribed now to Haimo of Auxerre.[3] Nevertheless, between the two major works it preserves what, so far as we know, is a unique text. It is a libellus on the Eucharistic Controversy, against the doctrines of Berengar of Tours. The opening paragraph of this libellus has occasionally been quoted, for a phrase asserting that Berengar's doctrines were winning a hearing

---

1. This is F. Newton's suggested date. It was dated in the eleventh century by M. R. James, *A Catalogue of the Medieval Manuscripts in the University Library, Aberdeen* (Cambridge, 1932), pp. 35–38, esp. p. 35, and plates facing p. 65. (James's plates are only rather more than one-half size.) E. A. Lowe assigns it to "saec. xii in." in *Beneventan Script,* 2nd ed. by Virginia Brown, vol. 2, p. 11.

2. For example, the *Q* on 11r and the *H* on 25v.

3. James gives an account of the contents that was necessarily rough, since some elements of the manuscript have never been published. James was uncertain how the manuscript got to Aberdeen from Italy except to suggest that, like manuscript 242, it may have come from S. Maria de Caritate of either Milan or Venice. For the Song of Songs commentary, previously ascribed to Ps.-Haimo of Halberstadt, see Dominique Iogna-Prat, "L'oeuvre d'Haymon d'Auxerre. État de la question," in *L'école carolingienne d'Auxerre de Murethach à Rémi 830–908,* ed. Dominique Iogna-Prat, Colette Jeudy, Guy Lobrichon (Paris, 1991), pp. 157–79.

33

among laymen as well as ecclesiastics;[4] but the contents of the treatise have gained almost no attention or discussion. Even J. de Montclos, in his detailed monograph on the Berengarian controversy, passes over this libellus with the most minimal discussion.[5]

The indifference among scholars occasioned by the little treatise is understandable. It discredits Berengar's position without addressing his arguments directly, proposing interpretations that were neither new in the context of the eleventh-century debate nor important in the subsequent development of sacramental theology. Moreover, the author's identity has never been pinned down, in spite of some sporadic discussion of the problem, with the only candidate mentioned being a South Italian bishop for whom no other writings are known. It is our view that there is ample evidence to identify the author, and that the treatise itself is in fact a key piece, hitherto considered missing, in the Berengarian puzzle.

The Rubric and Morin's Attribution
to Berengar of Venosa

The contents of Aberdeen 106 were made known to the scholarly world in 1932 by Montague James's catalogue. That same year also saw the publication of two articles treating the libellus: one by G. Morin took the form of a critical edition of the work prefaced by a suggestion as to its author;[6] the other article, really little more than a note, by A. J. MacDonald briefly analyzed the contents of the treatise and its bearing on the eucharistic question.[7] Already in these two articles, however, the problems that surround the libellus are made clear by the sharp difference between Morin and MacDonald in their handling of the heading of the work in the Aberdeen manuscript. The heading reads: *Domino sancto ac venerabili . G. summo pontifici. Berengarius servus*

---

4. R. W. Southern, *Making of the Middle Ages* (New Haven, 1953), p. 199, and Colin Morris, *The Papal Monarchy. The Western Church from 1050 to 1250* (Oxford, 1989), p. 358, both quoting from James's catalogue entry.

5. J. de Montclos, *Lanfranc et Bérenger,* p. 217. The Aberdeen treatise is also mentioned by O. Capitani, "Rapporti," p. 129, n. 62; Capitani explicitly reserved judgment on Morin's attribution.

6. G. Morin, "Bérenger contre Bérenger. Un document inédit des luttes théologiques du XIe siècle," *Recherches de Théologie ancienne et médiévale* 4 (1932): 109–33.

7. A. J. MacDonald, "Berengariana," *Journal of Theological Studies* 33 (1932): 181–86, of which pp. 181–83 concern this text.

eius. It stands above the opening of our text on 55v, and, whereas the text is in ordinary minuscule in black ink, the heading is in Beneventan script and in red ink, in a hand using the Monte Cassino style. Since this Beneventan hand is not found at the beginning of the Augustine text with which the volume opens (the incipit there, like the text, is in ordinary minuscule), nor at the beginning of the Commentary on *Cantica Canticorum* (whose heading, like its text, is in the "Bari type" of Beneventan), it is fair to conclude that the heading was not the work of an official rubricator for the book but rather a less official and less authoritative intervention.[8]

This heading, attributing the treatise that follows to one Berengarius, appears at first glance to offer a choice of ironies. Anyone who reads the opening three sentences with any care would realize that the treatise is directed *against* the eucharistic doctrines of Berengar of Tours, named in the second.[9] If we accept the data of the heading, two courses are open to us. We may imagine, as MacDonald seems to in a single paragraph, a kind of "anti-Bérenger chez Bérenger," an impulse that prompted Berengar to write this treatise against his own teaching; but MacDonald himself refuted this possibility in a brief and trenchant discussion.[10] Or we may posit the existence of a second Berengarius as the author of the treatise, which is what Morin did: this strange situation is summed up in his thought-provoking title, "Bérenger contre Bérenger." This other paradox presents a picture of two men named Berengarius pitted against each other—a seemingly Italian Berengarius writing to refute the teaching of the French Beren-

---

8. That the *Cantica Canticorum* commentary is in "Bari type" (or "Puglia type") was first noted in print by Virginia Brown, "A New Commentary on Matthew in Beneventan Script at Venosa," *Mediaeval Studies* 49 (1987): 443–65, esp. p. 463 n. 44. As we shall see, this fact cannot really be used to support the authorship of Berengar of Venosa for our text, since the rubric over the eucharistic text is in the Cassinese stye of Beneventan. The South Italian elements, however, are notable. Even the Caroline parts of the manuscript have Beneventan features, such as the Beneventan suprascript 2-shaped tonal sign over *Quomodo* on fol. 2r and *Quis* on 57v (Quîs sermo Christi?, in our treatise l. 227; this letter occurs in the work of the hand that shows no other Beneventan influence, so that we may take it as reasonably certain that the text descends from an ancestor in Beneventan script), and the *ri* ligature as in *fieri* on 3r and *inveniri* on 12 r. All this gives a strong South Italian connection for the entire manuscript. It should be noted, at the same time, that the 2-shaped tonal sign and the *ri* ligature are frequently found in manuscripts of the region of Rome; see the fundamental survey of P. Supino Martini, *Roma e l'area grafica romanesca (secoli x–xii)* [Biblioteca di Scrittura e Civiltà I] (Alessandria, 1987), passim, and for example, tav. 45 (*ri* ligature) and 18 (2-shaped tonal sign).

9. In Morin's text, 117.6, in our text, l. 5.

10. MacDonald, pp. 181–82.

garius. Morin goes on to propose a candidate. Confining his search, as the manuscript evidence strongly suggested, to Southern Italy, he found a single figure who might conceivably be identified as the author: a Berengarius originally of Saint-Evroul in Normandy who followed Abbot Robert of Grentemesnil to Southern Italy during the pontificate of Nicholas II (1059–1061), subsequently becoming abbot of the monastery of the Holy Trinity in Venosa and, in the time of Urban II, bishop of Venosa. Morin's source for all of this was Orderic Vitalis.[11]

Venosa in the eleventh century was endowed with interesting scholarly texts, as an illuminating article of Virginia Brown's has recently revealed.[12] Nevertheless, the reasons for doubting Morin's attribution are many. To begin with, it rests entirely on the rubric's attribution of the text to a Berengar and the scarcity of that name in Southern Italy. There is no contemporary evidence that Berengar of Venosa wrote against Berengar of Tours; or that he was interested in the controversy; or even that he wrote on any subject at all. In regard to Berengar of Venosa's cultural achievements, Orderic's description in the passage in 2.90 seems especially important: "He, born of noble stock, from early childhood served as a warrior for Christ at St. Evroul under Abbot Theodoric and excelled by reason of his skill in reading and chanting and fine writing." [Hic nobile parentela exortus, ab infantia sub Teoderico abbate apud Uticum Christo militavit, peritiaque legendi et canendi optimeque scribendi floruit.] Orderic's use of the term *scribendi* in the context of reading and chanting clearly refers to Berengar's skill as a scribe, rather than literary composition; this is not a skill that Orderic would have despised, as he was himself a fine penman.[13]

The absence of information about Berengar of Venosa's career as an author, moreover, is especially significant given the very excellence of the prose in which the treatise was written. Morin himself commented

11. Morin, pp. 113–16; Ordericus Vitalis, *The Ecclesiastical History of Orderic Vitalis*, 2.90 and 3.188, ed. M. Chibnall, 2: 100–102 and 4: 38 (Oxford, 1969 and 1973).

12. "New Commentary on Matthew." In addition to Brown's discussion of the Matthew commentary, we now have a fundamental new study of Santissima Trinità with a broad-based introduction concerning Venusine history in our period in H. Houben, *Il "libro del capitolo" del monastero della SS. Trinità di Venosa (cod. Cas. 334: una testimonianza del Mezzogiorno normanno* (Galatina [Lecce], 1984), esp. the historical survey, pp. 21–52.

13. See, for example, Paris, B.N. Lat. 6503, depicted in the collection of plates from France, *Catalogue des manuscrits en écriture latine portant des indications de date, de lieu, ou de copiste*, vol. 2, ed. M.-Th. d'Alverny, M.-C. Garand, M. Mabille, and J. Metman (Paris, 1962), pl. XVIIa.

on the high quality of the Latin, which was well above the standard for the time,[14] and we shall see below that the presentation and argument are skillfully contrived. It is unlikely that the man who wrote this treatise wrote nothing else, or that he could have remained otherwise unnoticed in Southern Italy. But such literary obscurity is in fact a distinguishing characteristic of Berengar of Venosa, whose career is known to us chiefly because his activities were marked by a confrère in his former monastery in Normandy. The most recent discussions of Berengar of Venosa question Morin's attribution, or mention it with great caution.[15]

Two additional difficulties can be mentioned. The first is that, although Berengar of Venosa was abbot of SS. Trinità from 1066,[16] the language of the treatise does not accord with an abbot writing for his monks; instead, it is consistent with a monk writing, one who submits his work to his abbot before showing it to his fellow-monks.[17] There is also a second consideration that may be partly psychological, and perhaps partly dependent on the ear of the individual reader of Latin prose. In the second sentence of the treatise, the name of Berengarius is introduced in a cool manner: *Berengarium quendam Turonensem*, which might be rendered, "one [*cough*] Berengarius of Tours." This impression that the reader receives, of a deliberately used distancing technique, is not erased by the subsequent tribute to the opponent's talent and knowledge. It seems rather improbable to us that our treatise writer, if his name had also been Berengarius, would have adopted this particular form of language in introducing the name of Berengarius from Tours.

All these considerations lead us to conclude that, rather than basing an attribution of authorship on the rubric, one must instead reject its authenticity altogether. In fact, this had been MacDonald's position at the beginning of scholarly discussion in 1932 when he wrote: "The rubric, or introductory ascription, written in a different script (Beneventan) was inserted by another scribe, who made a hasty examination of the contents of the tract, and assumed it was a copy of a letter

---

14. Morin, p. 117 n. 21.
15. *Dizionario biografico degli italiani* 9 (1967), pp. 35–36 and Houben, pp. 30–31, fn. 57.
16. Houben, *Il "libro del capitolo."*
17. See below, pp. 42–43 of this chapter and p. 71 of ch. 3.

sent by Berengar [of Tours] to Gregory VII."[18] At that time, Mac-
Donald offered as evidence mainly the fact that the form of heading
was not appropriate for a treatise, but for a letter, and that our text is
not epistolary in nature.[19] It is certainly true that our text is not a letter, and strictly speaking MacDonald's general observation is correct;
but in the eleventh century the line between treatise and letter was not
so definitively drawn as it was to be later, as one can see in such manuscripts as Monte Cassino 358 and 359, containing the works of Peter
Damian and copied by Monte Cassino scribes in the decade after the
saint's death in 1072.[20]

Yet there are other reasons for concluding that the heading is not to
be trusted. What is seriously wrong with it, apart from its look as an
afterthought added to the text by a different scribe, is the information
it furnishes. The pope of the heading, *G.*, in the context of the Berengarian Controversy, must be Gregory VII. Yet the treatise cannot be
addressed to him. Its addressee is an unnamed churchman, referred to
at the very opening in the vocative case, *beatissime pater* (l. 1).[21] Later
in the Middle Ages it would be the pope who generally was addressed
in this form, but matters were still fluid in the eleventh century; thus
DuCange cites Hugh of Cluny addressing an unknown count as
"beatissime pater."[22] In any case, we can be certain the recipient of this
treatise was not Gregory VII because halfway through the treatise (ll.
362–85) he is referred to, in a handsome tribute linking him to Gregory
the Great, *in the third person*. The heading is simply wrong, due to an
ignorant reader who scanned the text hastily and, finding the name of
Gregory, rashly concluded that he was the *beatissimus pater* of the
opening sentence.[23] This finding reinforces our deep suspicion of
the heading's other "fact," that the writer was a Berengarius.

18. MacDonald, p. 183.

19. Ibid., p. 181.

20. M. Inguanez, *Codicum Casinensium Manuscriptorum Catalogus*, vol. 2 (Monte Cassino, 1928), pp.
    201–207. For the date, see the study by Francis Newton, *The Monte Cassino Scriptorium and Li-
    brary (1058–1105)* (Cambridge, 1999), pp. 76–77 and 376–83 and plates 167–68.

21. Here and throughout, citations to the Aberdeen treatise are made, by line numbers where ap-
    propriate, to the new edition by F. Newton printed as part of this study.

22. *Glossarium Mediae et Infimae Latinitatis* (1883–87, rep. 1954). Similarly, *Mittellateinisches Wörter-
    buch bis zum ausgehenden 13. Jahrhundert* (Munich, 1967), reports a number of usages of "beatis-
    simus" from the ninth and tenth centuries.

23. This was MacDonald's firm conclusion, pp. 181–83, with summary on p. 183, quoted below, al-
    though he did not notice that Gregory was referred to in the body of the text, in the third person.

At first glance, this conclusion on a manuscript rubric may seem unparalleled. Not so. In the case of South Italian texts, there are many that were left without a heading in the oldest surviving manuscript, and for a large number of these the omission was never made good. Poems of Alfanus of Salerno in Monte Cassino 453 and Vat. lat. 1202 are not identified in those books, and it is only because of the existence of other evidence that we know of Alfanus's authorship.[24] In fact, that is the case with wide areas of eleventh-century literary production in South Italy. Important works by Lawrence of Amalfi, by Alberic of Monte Cassino, by John of Gaeta (Pope Gelasius II), by Constantine the African, and by Abbot Desiderius himself, as well as the poems by Alfanus, have had to be identified in modern times, often by painstaking stylistic analysis.[25] There were even two Lawrences in modern scholarship before Holtzmann in a brilliant article proved that Lawrence of Amalfi/Monte Cassino was identical with the Lawrence who in Florence wrote the life of St. Zenobius.[26] In the case of other works, the author's name was inserted in manuscripts by a subsequent hand: this occurred in the text of the *Vita S. Dominici,* which a later Beneventan scribe has identified in Monte Cassino 101, p. 491.[27] Here

24. A. Lentini and F. Avagliano, *I carmi di Alfano I arcivescovo di Salerno* (Monte Cassino, 1974), pp. 17, 32–35.

25. For Lawrence of Amalfi, see W. Holtzmann, "Laurentius von Amalfi. Ein Lehrer Hildebrands," *Studi Gregoriani* 1 (1947): 207–37, repr. in Holtzmann's *Beiträge zur Reichs- und Papstgeschichte des hohen Mittelalters* [Bonner historische Forschungen 8] (1957), pp. 9–33, and Francis Newton in *Benedictina* 20,1 (1973): 91–107. For Alberic, see Francis Newton, "A Third and Older Cassinese Lectionary for the Feasts of Saints Benedict, Maur, and Scholastica," in *Miscellanea Cassinese 47,* p. 59 and n. 32 with extensive discussion of the evidence in manuscripts, as well as works cited below. For John of Gaeta, see the Engels article cited below, ch. 3 fn. 5, and F. Dolbeau, "Recherches sur les oeuvres littéraires du Pape Gelase II," *Analecta Bollandiana* 107 (1989): 65–127. For an example of a work by Constantine the African, see Monica H. Green, "The *De genecia* Attributed to Constantine the African," *Speculum* 62 (1987): 299–324, and for a fundamental survey of this important figure, H. Bloch, *Monte Cassino in the Middle Ages* (Cambridge, Mass., 1986), 1.98–110 and the important edition of Peter the Deacon's account on pp. 127–34. For Abbot Desiderius, see P. Meyvaert's convincing argument regarding the epanaleptic verses addressed to St. Maur in Vat. lat. 1202, in the introduction to the facsimile of that manuscript, *Codex Benedictus: an eleventh-century lectionary from Monte Cassino* (New York, 1982), pp. 18–19. It is interesting to note, in connection with the problem of authorship in the Aberdeen treatise, how many of these studies on previously unidentified works begin with the information furnished by Peter the Deacon.

26. Holtzmann, art. cit.

27. The whole Dominic dossier has been examined by François Dolbeau, "Le dossier de saint Dominique de Sora d'Albéric du Mont-Cassin à Jacques de Voragine," *Mélanges de l'École française de Rome: Moyen âge-Temps modernes,* 102 (1990): 7–78 and by Carmela Franklin, "The Restored *Life and Miracles of St. Dominic of Sora* by Alberic of Monte Cassino," *Mediaeval Studies* 55 (1993): 285–345 in her wide-ranging and sensitive survey of the problems presented by this hagiographical complex. For Dominic himself in the South Italian context, see John Howe, *Church*

the heading hand has entered correct information, but in many works of the Fathers in South Italian manuscripts these added ascriptions are false; perhaps the best-known instance is the text of the *Anticimenon* in Monte Cassino 187, which modern scholarship attributes to Julian of Toledo, but which an eleventh-century entry in verse, on the first page of the manuscript, led readers to assign to the Cassinese abbot Bertharius.[28] Other examples could easily be found. In short, the student of any South Italian text or South Italian manuscript must look with a critical eye, at least initially, at the information furnished by added headings.

The Treatise and Its Author

The case of the Aberdeen rubric is clear. It is spurious, and the information it gives has no historical basis. The time has therefore come for a reexamination of the fundamental questions that MacDonald raised: who wrote the libellus, and when, and where, and to whom was it addressed? In facing these questions, the manuscript and the text provide some useful clues. The presence of two different scribes using Beneventan script in different parts of the book and the occurrence of Beneventan features, even in the Caroline, connects the Aberdeen manuscript closely with Southern Italy. Furthermore, the passage already mentioned in which the author makes a graceful allusion to a reigning Pope Gregory establishes the date closely. It reads:[29]

> Perchance these words of Augustine would suffice; but according to Cicero it is better for *some remnants* to be left over, *than* for us *to allow* anyone to go away *from here unfilled.* Come then, let others now speak; and yet let us mix in among them passages that bear witness from the same Augustine. Let then blessed Gregory, the Roman pope, speak—let the *present* one pass judgment, who now, endowed with the same name and the same spirit, himself a Gregory, holds the place of Gregory; to the present Gregory, as we believe, it was reserved by divine providence that

---

Reform and Social Change in Eleventh-Century Italy: Dominic of Sora and His Patrons (Philadelphia, 1997); the dossier is discussed in his appendix A.

28. For the verses, see *Bibliotheca Casinensis* (Monte Cassino, 1874–94), vol. 4, p. 72, and the manuscript, Inguanez, vol. 1, pp. 270–71.

29. Here and throughout, the edition of the Latin text and the English translation are by Francis Newton. For the purposes of discussion, throughout the remainder of this chapter the English translation is given first, with the Latin text following.

he should carry out what the former one had said; moreover, these words of the blessed Gregory, which I am about to rehearse, are so deeply implanted in the heart of the present one who now gives light to the world, that he does not fail to carry out daily what the former one said should be done daily—*we ought*, says Gregory, *with all our minds to despise the world that is present now, precisely because we see that already it has slipped away, and to yield up to God the daily sacrifice of tears, the daily offering of his flesh and blood.*

[Fortasse ista Augustini verba sufficerent: sed melius est secundum Tullium *aliquid* superesse *reliquiarum, quam non saciatum* aliquem *hinc* abire *patiamur.* Age ergo, nunc alii loquantur, inter quos eiusdem tamen testimonia misceamus. Dicat igitur beatus Gregorius papa Romanus— diiudicet iste, qui nunc eiusdem nominis eiusdemque spiritus Gregorii et ipse Gregorius possidet locum; cui, ut credimus, divinitus reservatum est ut, quod ille dixerat, iste confirmet; haec autem, quae dicturi sumus, beati Gregorii verba sic istius, qui nunc mundum illustrat, pectori insita sunt, ut, quod ille cotidie fieri debere dixit, iste cotidie agere non praetermittat —*debemus*, inquit Gregorius, *praesens saeculum, vel quia iam conspicimus defluxisse, tota mente contempnere, cotidiana deo lacrimarum sacrificia, cotidianas carnis eius et sanguinis hostias immolare.*] (ll. 359–72)

MacDonald overlooked this passage when he suggested that the treatise might have been composed ca. 1059. The opening paragraph speaks of Berengar's coming to Italy and renewing his teaching on the Eucharist, which would indeed fit 1059; but that date is categorically ruled out because the presence of a Pope Gregory requires a date no earlier than 1073, the year in which Hildebrand ascended the papal throne. Furthermore, the treatise must be no later than the Lenten synod of 1079, which settled the eucharistic issue. In fact, it would be most natural for the date to fall in 1078–1079, during the final working-out of the Controversy, and this same passage points to precisely that period, since Pope Gregory is adjured to render a decisive judgment in the case (*diiudicet*). This is what he did, in fact, at the synod. Our treatise therefore has strong connections, in the book in which it has come down to us, with Southern Italy, and on internal evidence it was composed between Berengar's arrival in Italy during the summer of 1078 and the decision of the synod in Lent 1079.

But what of the author? The opening of the treatise sets the work in context:

The report recently brought to us, O most blessed Father, of the questioning that has arisen in regard to the body and blood of the Lord, has suddenly filled all this land to such an extent that not only clerics and monks, whose watchful attention should be devoted to such matters, but even laymen themselves are chattering about it among themselves in the town squares. What they say is that a certain Berengar of Tours, a man of great talent and profound knowledge, has come to Rome and wishes to revive anew the interpretation which he had once renounced: asserting, as they say, that in the sacrament of our redemption neither is the bread turned into flesh nor the wine into blood. How contrary this is to the Catholic Faith is well known to those whose food consists of the reading of sacred texts. The result of this has been that my brothers and neighbors, who (so to speak) often set me above myself, have stirred up my spirit to this undertaking, that I should lay out for them my own particular views on these matters. Therefore I have gathered together these sentences of the holy Fathers that are contained in this little tract, yet with the omission of many, so that the reading might not be burdensome to the spirit of my reader, as it would perchance be if it were too long. Moreover, I have chosen not to pour these teachings into *their* minds until they might, such as they are, be presented to *you* and be weighed and judged on your own balance-scales.

———

[Noviter ad nos, beatissime pater, de corpore et sanguine domini exortae quaestionis allata relatio sic totam subito hanc terram replevit, ut non solum clerici ac monachi, quorum intentio in talibus vigilare debet, verum etiam ipsi laici de hoc inter se in plateis confabulentur. Aiunt enim Beringarium quendam Turonensem magni ingenii profundaeque scientiae virum Romam advenisse, qui eam cui quondam abrenuntiaverat sententiam velit iterum renovare: asserens, ut dicunt, quod in sacramento nostrae redemptionis nec panis in carnem nec vinum mutatur in sanguinem. Quod quantum catholicae fidei contrarium sit, norunt illi quorum cibus est lectio sacra. Unde factum est ut fratres et confinitimi nostri, qui me ut ita dixerim saepe mihi praeponunt, ad hoc meum animum excitarent, quatinus quid de his potissimum sentiam eis propalarem. Collegi igitur has sanctorum patrum, quae in hoc libello continentur sententiae, pluribus tamen praetermissis: ne, si lectio prolixa foret, animum lectoris fortasse gravaret. Volui autem non prius haec illorum infundere mentibus, quam tibi legata qualiacunque sint tuo examine iudicentur.] (ll. 1–18)

The author's reference to his brothers identifies him as a monk or a regular canon, although in the context of Southern Italy a monk is far

more probable.[30] He must also have had a reputation for learning sufficient for them to urge him to write in defense of orthodox doctrine.

This same passage illustrates the author's style as well. At first
glance, it would be easy to underestimate the achievement of the
writer. The style is so simple that it could seem negligible. In fact, the
original editor was initially deceived by it. When Morin came to examine the treatise more closely, however, he revised his earlier impression, and being a conscientious scholar he acknowledged his change of
opinion.[31] These opening sentences of the libellus are graceful and
well paced in their movement, moderate but authoritative in tone, and
lucid in expression. They are not the work of a novice; such simplicity
is the achievement of a master, an expert prose stylist at the height of
his powers.

The passage on Gregory VII, already cited, from the middle of the
treatise, also provides a valuable clue to the education of the author in
the reference it makes to Cicero (*secundum Tullium*). Morin did not
identify the specific source. In fact, it is a paraphase from the section
in the *Topica*, in which, having given an overview of his subject, Cicero addresses his young friend, Gaius Trebatius, to whom the work is
dedicated, in these words (*Topica*, 25):

> Well then, is this enough, what has been said to this point? I think so, for
> one so keen-witted and busy as you are. But since I admitted a greedy man
> to this feast of learning, I shall take you with the understanding that it is
> better that there be *leftovers than that I should permit you* to go away *from
> here unfilled.*

———

> [Utrum igitur hactenus satis est? Tibi quidem tam acuto et tam occupato
> puto. Sed quoniam avidum hominem ad has discendi epulas recepi, sic ac-
> cipiam, ut *reliquiarum* sit potius *aliquid quam te hinc patiar non satiatum*
> discedere.][32]

———

30. We are indebted to C. Stephen Jaeger for this suggestion, which is indirectly confirmed by Peter Damian's regular practice of addressing his fellow cardinals as "frater." Examples include
Briefe des Petri Damiani, ed. Kurt Reindel, [*MGH Briefe*], vol. 4 (1983), 2.57.4, 2.221, 2.309.17;
but Damian was also free with the term, for example 2.366.23/367.18, in a letter to an unknown
bishop Albertus, and 2.447.1/448.7 in a letter to Abbot Desiderius of Montecassino.

31. See the footnote, apparently added as his article was on the way to publication, p. 117, n. 21.

32. *Topica* 25–26, Loeb Classical Library (Cambridge, Mass., 1949), p. 398.

The *Topica* was a standard text in the eleventh-century Italian liberal arts curriculum,[33] but it is not likely that monks without special expertise would have recalled such a turn of phrase as easily and as appositely as did the author of the Aberdeen treatise. This quotation points directly toward a master of the arts.

Expertise in the arts is also shown by a passage midway through the treatise in which the author employs the dialectical terminology of *res* and *species* in discussing the transformation of bread and wine.

> For substance is changed into substance either in seeming and in reality, or in seeming and not in reality, or in reality and not in seeming. It is changed in seeming and in reality, to be sure, as earth is [changed] into mankind and the other animate creatures; similarly also water into salt, and ice into crystal; and you will be able to find many examples of this kind. Moreover, change takes place in seeming and not in reality, as the very angel of Satan transforms himself into an angel of light; and often many things are changed by craftsmen in such a way that, although they have not lost their own nature, yet they are believed to be something else altogether. Further, substance changes in reality and not in seeming, as wine changes into vinegar.

> [Mutatur enim substantia in substantiam aut specie et re, aut specie et non re, aut re et non specie. Specie quidem mutatur et re, ut terra in hominem et caetera animalia; similiter et aqua in sal, et glacies in cristallum, et multa quidem huius generis repperire poteris. Specie autem et non re mutatio fit, ut ipse angelus satanae transfigurat se in angelum lucis; necnon et ab artificibus ita quaedam saepe mutantur, ut, quamvis propriam naturam non amiserint; omnino tamen aliud esse credatur. Re autem et non specie mutatur substantia, ut vinum in acetum. . . .] (ll. 505–14)

The dialectical analysis is not at an especially technical level, at least compared to what was being taught in northern France by the 1070s; the distinction between *res* and *species* is neither especially clear nor grounded in philosophical concepts.[34] But the introduction of cate-

---

33. See the discussion in Radding, "Geography," which shows that the *Topica* was a text used for training in literary composition as early as the first decades of the eleventh century.
34. See, for example, the passage in Garlandus Compotista's *Dialectica*, a work from about 1080, where the author first introduces *substantia* into his discussion. "Equivoca plane volumus ex-

gories into which phenomena must be fitted is a familiar rhetorical strategy (e.g., *Topica* 14), and its use here suggests an author accustomed to teaching the arts.

These specific details pointing to a master of the arts are lent force by the author's whole style of argument, which focused on the meaning of key words in the dispute. The opening passage will serve to illustrate this method. Following immediately upon the introductory address to the recipient, the author broaches his topic as follows:

> Now since we are to speak of the sacrament, let us first hear what a sacrament is in itself. *A sacrament is,* as Isidore says [*Etymologies* 6.19.39,40], *when a thing is done with some celebration in such a way that it is understood to signify something; and a* sacramentum *is called after* sacred *or* hidden *forces.* Now a sacrament takes place at times figuratively, as the sacrament of the well-known lamb sacrificed under the Old Law; and at times in reality, as the sacrament of him who is daily eaten in the Church. Whence Blessed Ambrose says [*On the Sacraments* 4.5.25], *That you may know that this is a sacrament, the figure of it preceded it and came before.* Therefore it is called a sacrament in this way, not because it points to something, but because it is pointed to by something; just as on the other hand the former thing was called a sacrament not because it was pointed to by something, but because it carried the prefiguring of this present one. These things have been said to this end, that no one should choose to understand the sacrament of the Church typologically. And it is just the same to say, *That you may know that this is a sacrament, the figure of it preceded it and came before,* as if one said, "that you may know that this is true in reality, another thing has preceded it in seeming." For this which Blessed Gregory prays for [*Gregorian Sacramentary*], saying, *that that which we do in outward seeming, we should take in real truth,* ought to have such force with us that we should believe that it is in reality the flesh and blood of him in commemoration of whom we do these things. It is done in seeming indeed, because what is, is not seen. Now so much for these matters down to this point; now let us come to the orderly laying out of the subject itself.

> [Quoniam autem de sacramento locuturi sumus, prius quid sit ipsum sacramentum audiamus. *Est autem sacramentum,* ut Ysidorus ait, *cum ali-*

---

cludere a predicamentis, quia neque subiecta sunt neque existentia in subiectis; subiecta non sunt, quia neque prima neque secunda substantia sunt. utrum. omnis substantia, sive prima sive secunda, sufficiens subiectum est alicui accidenti." L. M. de Rijk, ed. (Assen, 1959), 12.6–9.

qua celebratione res ita fit, ut aliquid significare intelligatur; dicitur autem sacramentum a sacris vel secretis virtutibus. Fit autem sacramentum aliquando in figura, ut illius agni in veteri lege immolati; aliquando in re, ut istius qui cotidie in ecclesia manducatur. Unde beatus Ambrosius: *Ut scias,* inquit, *hoc esse sacramentum, huius figura ante praecessit.* Hoc igitur modo dicitur sacramentum, non quod aliquid significet, sed quod ab aliquo significatum sit: sicut e contra illud vetus, non quod ab aliquo significatum fuerit, sed, quoniam huius figuram gerebat, sacramentum dicebatur. Haec autem ideo dicta sunt, ne quis ecclesiae sacramentum tipice intelligere velit. Nichil est autem aliud dicere: *Ut scias hoc esse sacramentum, huius figura ante praecessit,* quam si diceret: Ut scias autem hoc esse in re, iam aliud praecessit in specie. Illud enim, quod beatus Gregorius deprecatur dicens *ut quod specie gerimus, rerum veritate capiamus,* ad hoc nobis valere debet, ut in cuius commemoratione haec agimus, eius revera carnem et sanguinem esse credamus. In specie quidem agitur, quia quod est non videtur. De his autem hactenus; nunc vero ad ipsius rei seriem veniamus.] (ll. 19–38)

The quotation from Isidore is itself significant. Although this definition of *sacramentum* had been widely discussed in the ninth century, Häring believed it was unknown in the eleventh;[35] this passage constitutes the sole exception. Again we get the impression of an author immersed in the liberal arts and the books used to teach them, such as the *Etymologies,* who was taking a fresh look at the issues. This beginning sets a pattern followed in the rest of the treatise, moreover, in presenting the question, What is a sacrament? as one of verbal definition, to be answered out of explicit patristic statements on the subject. Subsequent sections continue the focus on words: discussion of the word "sacrament" leads to consideration of the visible *sacramentum,* specifically wine and blood, bread and flesh; flesh and blood lead in turn to a treatment of what it means to eat (*manducare*); and this leads to a discussion of whether one can be said to eat with one's heart and not with one's mouth (*corde et non ore manducare,* l. 270). With great consistency the question is posed in the form: What are we to understand "from these words" (*in his verbis,* l. 317)?

---

35. Häring, "Berengar's Definitions of *Sacramentum*," pp. 115–16.

Alberic of Monte Cassino and His
"Lost" Treatise

The evidence thus far considered gives us a date of composition for the treatise in 1078–1079 and an author who was a monk, very likely in Southern Italy, and who was close to Gregory VII, and certainly a master of the arts. In that period and region there is only one plausible candidate for the authorship. It is Alberic of Monte Cassino. Alberic was a monk and the most eminent scholar in the arts of his day in central or Southern Italy. A native, like his abbot Desiderius, of the ancient duchy of Benevento, he tells us in a recently discovered preface to his life of St. Cesarius that he was writing at the age of thirteen, when he had already been engaged in liberal studies for six years. As a deacon at Monte Cassino, he went on to become a friend of the famous writer Peter Damian,[36] with whom he exchanged letters, and a pioneer in the nascent *ars dictaminis*. We possess his works on rhetoric, a series of saints' lines that he composed, and grammatical treatises; in addition he composed libelli on contemporary affairs.[37]

Alberic's monastery was intimately aware of the questions that came before the papal court through abbot Desiderius's close relationship with Gregory VII.[38] Indeed, Alberic is also known to have been involved in refuting Berengar, and specifically to have written a treatise as part of this effort—the only treatise written against Berengar at this period of which we have reports. Alberic's work is mentioned in the continuation of the *Chronicle* of Monte Cassino, probably written by Leo Marsicanus's successor Guido; the form in which the *Chronicle* comes down to us also possibly incorporates some revisions by Peter the Deacon. The relevant passage reads:

---

36. See the appendix, for an excerpt in the Aberdeen dossier from Peter's work.

37. For a survey of Alberic, see the articles by the late A. Lentini in *Dizionario biografico degli italiani* 1 (1960), pp. 643–45, and by C. Lanham in *Medieval Italy: An Encyclopedia* (New York/London, 2003, with recent bibliography). The most important study of his literary works is H. Bloch, "Monte Cassino's Teachers and Library in the High Middle Ages," *Settimane di studio del Centro italiano di studi sull'alto Medioevo* 19 (1978), pp. 563–613, esp. 587–99. New information on Alberic's early life was discovered and published by Jean Mallet and André Thibaut, in their *Les manuscrits en écriture bénéventaine de la Bibliothèque Capitulaire de Bénévent* I (Paris, 1984), esp. pp. 246–47.

38. Cowdrey, *The Age of Abbot Desiderius*, pp. 94–95, and A. Lentini, "Alberico di Montecassino nel quadro della Riforma Gregoriana," *Studi Gregoriani* 4 (1952): 55–109, esp. pp. 89–109 where Lentini discusses the style and gives the text of Alberic's life of St. Aspren.

In Alberic's time was held a synod in Rome against Berengar deacon of the church of Angers, who among many other statements that he strove to establish said that the sacrifice of the body and blood of the Lord was a figure. And since no one was able to resist him, the same Alberic was called to the synod; and when he went, after various kinds of conflicts in which neither side yielded to the other, Alberic having received a leave of one week wrote against the same deacon a book on the body of Christ, supported by the testimony of the holy Fathers, in which he destroyed all of his assertions and consigned them to eternal oblivion.

[Temporibus vero eius facta est sinodus in urbe Roma adversus Berengarium diaconem ecclesie Andecavensis, qui inter multa, que astruere nitebatur, dicebat sacrificium corporis et sanguinis Domini figuram esse. Cumque nullus ei resistere valeret, idem Albericus evocatur ad sinodum; quo dum venisset, post varia conflictationum genera, cum pars parti non cederet, idem Albericus ebdomade unius accepta licentia librum adversus eundem diaconem de corpore Domini edidit sanctorum patrum testimoniis roboratum, in quo omnes assertiones eius dextruxit eterneque oblivioni tradidit.][39]

In its nature this description corresponds admirably to the Aberdeen treatise, which one could call precisely a "librum adversus eundem diaconum de corpore Domini . . . sanctorum patrum testimoniis roboratum." The author of this passage seems to have had the opening of this very treatise before him, as his language echoes the "de corpore et sanguine Domini," the "asserens" (in the Chronicler's "assertiones"), and the "sanctorum patrum, quae in hoc libello continentur sententiae" of its first paragraph.

It is possible that the treatise in the Aberdeen manuscript was completed in one week. Given that the extracts from the Fathers would already have been gathered in the course of study and debate that led up to this point, a master stylist could have composed the treatise as it stands in such a brief period, although not during the council itself. What must be kept in mind is that the treatise is the work of a master; its stylistic finish—to be discussed in extenso in the next section—is skilled and polished. The treatise possesses an inner consistency of structure. The body of the text (after the proem and the definition of

39. *Chronica Monasterii Casinensis*, 3.35, p. 41.

sacramentum quoted above) begins at line 39 with a passage from John 6:53, and the "brevis quasi epilogus" which begins at l. 667 takes this same Johannine passage in reprise after the argument is completed; the whole is therefore characterized by a deliberate ring-composition. Discussion of a passage from Augustine is promised at ll. 493–94, and the promise is fulfilled at ll. 574–81. The "brief epilogue" takes up a quotation from Pope Leo, given in full at ll. 465–69, and uses it as a closing exhortation to faithful believers at ll. 680–83. These and many other details reveal the author's care and skill.

In fact, in this connection it should be noted that the actual treatise is a bit shorter than the text printed by Morin. The author as self-conscious artist marks the final paragraph, as follows:

And now as a brief epilogue, as it were, let us repeat the words of the Gospel itself, and let us put an end to those objections that can be objected. VERILY VERILY I SAY TO YOU, UNLESS YOU WILL HAVE EATEN THE FLESH OF THE SON OF MAN, AND DRUNK HIS BLOOD, YOU SHALL NOT HAVE LIFE IN YOU [John 6:53]: that is, either with your heart, or with your lips and heart. FOR MY FLESH IS TRULY FOOD, AND MY BLOOD IS TRULY DRINK [John 6:55]: since it makes those immortal and incorruptible who consume it, either with their heart, or with their lips and heart. WHOSO EATS MY FLESH, AND DRINKS MY BLOOD, HAS ETERNAL LIFE [John 6:54]: that is, either with his heart, or with his lips and heart. JUST AS THE LIVING FATHER HAS SENT ME, I ALSO LIVE BECAUSE OF THE FATHER; AND WHOSO EATS ME, ALSO LIVES BECAUSE OF ME [John 6:57]: that is, either with the heart, or with the lips and the heart. It is therefore good to eat with the heart, but better with lips and heart. For he who eats and drinks only with the lips, eats and drinks judgment upon himself. Therefore let us, being mindful of the words of blessed Pope Leo, "so make our communion at the holy table that we have no doubt at all of the verity of Christ's body and blood." [Sermon 91]

———

[Nunc autem ipsius evangelii verba brevi quasi epilogo repetamus, et solas quae obici possunt obiectiones determinemus. AMEN AMEN DICO VOBIS, NISI MANDVCAVERITIS CARNEM FILII HOMINIS, ET BIBERITIS EIUS SANGUINEM, NON HABEBITIS VITAM IN VOBIS: videlicet vel corde, vel ore et corde. CARO ENIM MEA VERE EST CIBVS, ET SANGUIS MEVS VERE EST POTUS: quoniam immortales et incorruptibiles eos facit, qui eum sumunt, vel corde, vel ore et corde. QUI MANDVCAT MEAM CARNEM, ET BIBIT MEVM SANGVINEM, HABET VITAM AETERNAM:

videlicet vel corde, vel ore et corde. SICVT MISIT ME VIVENS PATER, ET
EGO VIVO PROPTER PATREM; ET QVI MANDVCAT ME, ET IPSE VIVIT
PROPTER ME: videlicet vel corde, vel ore et corde. Bonum est igitur manducare corde, sed melius ore et corde. Qui enim solo ore manducat et
bibit, iudicium sibi manducat et bibit. Nos igitur beati papae Leonis sententiae memores *sic sacrae mensae communicemus ut nichil prorsus de veri-*
tate Christi corporis et sanguinis ambigamus.] (ll. 667–83)

The text in the Aberdeen manuscript has no explicit at all, here or elsewhere. Nor is any space left to mark the close. The writing continues
on the last line of folio 6ɪv, and Morin printed what follows on the next
two pages, down to 63r l. 4, as part of the treatise. It is our conclusion,
however, that the text proper ends at this point. Rhetorically, the ending as indicated above is satisfying. In recursive style, the first sentence
of the epilogue with its play on *obiectiones/obici* parallels the first sentence of the prologue with its play upon *allata relatio*.[40] In the same
way, the last sentence echoes ("de veritate Christi corporis et sanguinis") the first sentence of the treatise ("de corpore et sanguine domini").
It has also announced as the subject of the "brief epilogue" a reexamination of the words from John's Gospel, and this is what it has carried
out. It also possesses a rhetorical pattern: returning to these Gospel
words, it quotes them sentence by sentence, with the author's repeated
and echoing comment on each, "vel corde, vel ore et corde." Then it
rounds off the epilogue with the exhortation based on Pope Leo's
words.[41] That the ending is drawn from this pope's writings is not an
accident. As has been noted, the middle of the treatise, just after the
second start, cited Gregory I and rhetorically aligned with him the
figure of the present pope Gregory VII. The ending cites Leo I. The
teaching and practice of these two leaders of the church in late antiq-
uity are given a privileged position within the libellus because the present crisis is to be resolved with careful judgment (*diiudicare*) by their
successor in the chair of St. Peter.

What follows in the manuscript is a series of extracts without any
clearly discernible structure, and for the most part without surrounding text to integrate them into an argument; throughout Morin's chapter 19, his last, the added words are reduced to tags such as "Dicitur

---

40. On this, see also p. 56.
41. On the importance of Leo, see our table p. 73.

autem et in sinodo Efesina," and "Unde Augustinus," and "Audi etiam quid Eusebius Emisenus dicat."[42] These tags are, however, typical of the author of the treatise. We shall return to this point in a moment.

Another indication of a change at this same point is the presence of a serious textual error, of a type not found in the body of the text that preceded. The sentence immediately after the adaptation from Pope Leo begins: "Cui et Hieronimus in libro ad Edibiam concordans ait . . ." As Morin points out, the extract that follows is not from this or any work of Jerome's. Morin did not identify the passage, but it is a brief passage from Peter Damian.[43] Nowhere else does the Aberdeen manuscript present such a drastic textual error. It would be reasonable to conclude that at this point in the text some aspect of the exemplar from which the Aberdonensis was copied (or of a more distant ancestor) was confusing to the scribe; this would fit with our suggestion that in fact the text proper ended just before the words "Cui et Hieronimus in libro ad Edibiam concordans ait." The copyist had before him at this moment perhaps a relatively disordered jumble of extracts, and it was easy for him to become disoriented and lose the thread of what he was to copy.

This conclusion is not to be construed as grounds for dismissing as unimportant the extracts that follow. It is clear that they were part of the material gathered by the author of the treatise as part of the preparations for its production. In fact, they are specifically alluded to in the opening of the treatise as it stands; in the proem, which was cited in full above, the author stated: "Therefore I have gathered together these sentences of the holy Fathers that are contained in this little tract, *yet with the omission of many*, so that the reading might not be burdensome to the spirit of my reader, as it would perchance be it were too long" [Collegi igitur has sanctorum patrum, quae in hoc libello continentur sententiae, *pluribus tamen praetermissis:* ne, si lectio prolixa foret, animum lectoris fortasse gravaret]. The libellus, in other words, was deliberately kept short for the greater convenience of the reader. Yet, by

---

42. The citation of Ambrose, "in sexto sacramentorum" (App. l. 9) is unprecedented in our treatise proper, in giving book references. The passage on Ambrose's list of physical miracles (beginning "deinde a virga Moysi" Appendix l. 43) has already been treated (libellus ll. 385–91). Most telling of all, the first sentence in the added material raises a new subject, the role of the Virgin Mary in human redemption; this takes the argument into new and unexplored themes, beyond the scope of the treatise.

43. Sermo XLV. II. In nativitate beatissimae virginis Mariae. (VIII Sept.) [PL 144: 743A].

a fortunate accident of transmission, the rest of the "dossier," as we propose to call it, was preserved. The result is that modern students have it both ways; on the one hand they can read the libellus in the form in which the writer wished to give it to the world, and on the other hand they can study at least some of the writer's excised or rejected materials (*sententiae praetermissae*) as they once lay on his writing-table. We shall come back to these rejected materials a little later. In fact, to return to the *Chronicle* of Monte Cassino, it seems impossible to take its account of the council and of Alberic's part in it completely literally. If the "sinodus" that the *Chronicle* refers to is the Lenten council of 1079, there was, it seems, no pause of a week during which our treatise could have been composed. The Register of Gregory VII (discussed in detail in chapter 4) is explicit in placing Berengar's capitulation on the third day of the council.

Although the account in the Chronicle of Monte Cassino cannot be squared with this in its details,[44] one can accept, first, that Alberic did compose a treatise against Berengar and, second, that the treatise of Alberic was composed in urgency. In general, that Alberic played an important role in the synod and its decision is corroborated by other evidence, to be discussed in chapter four.

These are matters that must be investigated in the light of the sequence of events that stretched from the synod of November 1078 to the Lenten synod of February 1079. Before opening these questions, however, our next step must be, first, to consider whether the style of the treatise in Aberdeen 106 is consistent with Alberic's authorship and, second, to provide an overview of its contents.

---

44. In fact, if this account is the work of Peter the Deacon, it shares a pattern of discrepancies that are common when Peter the Deacon's accounts can be tested against other evidence. Marie-Thérèse d'Alverny comments, for example, that Peter's description of Alberic's contemporary, Constantine the African, "arouses some suspicion" with its tales of his journeys to "Babilonia" (probably Old Cairo) where he was instructed in "gramatica, dialectica, geometria, arithmetica, mathematica, astronomia nec non et phisica Chaldeorum, Arabum, Persarum, Saracenorum, Egiptiorum ac Indorum." She accepts only " the main points—that Constantine came from Africa, was a monk in Monte Cassino in the time of Abbot Desiderius, and wrote many books there." "Translations and Translators," in *Renaissance and Renewal in the Twelfth Century*, ed. Robert L. Benson and Giles Constable (Cambridge, Mass., 1982), p. 422 and n. 4; the citation is to *Chronica Monasterii Casinensis* 3.35, pp. 411–12. Reading Peter's account of the Eucharistic Controversy in a similarly cautious spirit would lead to the unelaborated conclusion that Alberic wrote a treatise against Berengar of Tours of the type found in the Aberdonensis.

THREE

Style and Content
of the Libellus

Alberic's Literary Work

Alberic is best known today for his pioneering manuals on *Ars Dicta-minis*, the *Breviarium de dictamine* and *Dictaminum Radii*.[1] Some re-cent scholars have expressed doubt that these works qualify Alberic as the originator of *ars dictaminis*, arguing that there was an earlier tradi-tion of instruction in letter writing,[2] but these objections to some ex-tent miss the point. Not only were Alberic's treatises certainly the first to expound the elements of letter writing in a systematic way, but the very act of writing them provided a conceptual framework that the dis-cipline previously had lacked. Subsequent dictatores did not repeat all

1. Of Alberic's technical works, the *Breviarium de dictamine* is edited only in excerpts by L. Rockinger, *Briefsteller und Formelbücher des elften bis vierzehnten Jahrhunderts. Quellen und Erörterungen zur bayerischen und deutschen Geschichte* 9,1 (Munich, 1863), pp. 3–46. The *Flores Rhetorici*, referred to more correctly as *Dictaminum Radii*, was published by Don Mauro In-guanez and H. M. Willard in *Miscellanea Cassinese* 14 (Monte Cassino, 1938); see also H. Ha-gendahl, "Le manuel de rhétorique d'Albericus Casinensis," *Classica et Mediaevalia* 17 (1956): 56–70. A new edition of these two of Alberic's works, together with his *De barbarismo et soloe-cismo*, is being prepared by Thomas J. Coffey of Creighton University. Our thanks to Prof. Cof-fey for allowing F. Newton to see his working text, notes, and translations, which reached us af-ter the stylistic analysis included in this chapter was completed but provides a framework that confirms these conclusions. Coffey has shown the interesting and valuable results that can be obtained by comparing Alberic's theoretical works with a sample of his composition in his article, "The Homily of Alberic the Deacon on Saint Scholastica," in *Diakonia. Studies in Honor of Robert T. Meyer* (Washington, D.C., 1986), pp. 289–301.
2. V. Licitra, "Il mito di Alberico di Montecassino iniziatore dell'Ars dictaminis," *Studi Medievali* 3rd ser., 18,2 (1977): 609–28; and William D. Patt, "The Early 'Ars Dictaminis' as Response to a Changing Society," *Viator* 9 (1978): 133–55.

of Alberic's precepts, but where they differed from him they felt the need to explain why.[3]

Alberic's writing manuals reveal him as a systematic expositor of Latin prose. It is therefore especially significant that the author of the Aberdeen libellus is also keenly aware of the style of others. When he first introduces Augustine and a quotation from the *Tractatus in Iohannem*, he says that he (ll. 42–43)," quasi aquila post aquilam volans, divina et spirituali utitur locutione" [like an eagle following an eagle, uses divine and spiritual language]. A striking simile of the same Father's is noted (ll. 322–23), "In cuius assertione sententiae eleganti panis et vini utitur similitudine" [in the assertion of this position he uses the elegant simile of bread and wine]; and shortly before that his choice of words (ll. 292–93): "Idipsum autem et alibi exponens prope eisdem utitur verbis" [And, expounding this very thing elsewhere, he uses virtually the same words]. Our author is a critic of patristic style and usage (*utitur locutione, utitur similitudine, utitur verbis*) as well as of patristic doctrine.

It follows that such a writer is himself a master of rhetorical tropes and figures. Naturally, they are more evident in later passages than in the opening paragraph, whose style in this dialectical genre would not be conducive to elaboration. In chapter 15, when the author has imagined Christ speaking to his disciples, a greater intensity is seen: "Scandalizati estis, quia dixi: NISI QUIS MANDUCAVERIT CARNEM MEAM, ET BIBERIT SANGUINEM MEUM, NON HABEBIT VITAM IN SE. HOC, inquit, VOS SCANDALIZAT. Non fiet ut putatis; non dilaniabitur, non coincidetur, non in frusta diminuetur caro mea. Nolite aestimare, quod more ferarum meam carnem devoretis, vel crudelitate bestiae meum sanguinem bibatis. Nolite hoc putare" [You are offended that I have said: UNLESS ONE SHALL EAT MY FLESH, AND DRINK MY BLOOD, HE SHALL HAVE NO LIFE IN HIM. THIS, he says, OFFENDS YOU. It will not be as you suppose; my flesh will not be torn, will not be cut up, will not be divided into bits. Do not imagine that you devour my flesh in the manner of wild animals or drink my blood with the cruelty of a beast. Do not suppose this]. Or the author exclaims (ll. 194–95): "Quid

---

3. Ronald Witt, "Medieval Italian Culture and the Origins of Humanism," in *Renaissance Humanism. Foundations, Forms, and Legacy*, ed. Albert Rabil, Jr. (Philadelphia, 1988), vol. 1, pp. 28–71, at 40–44, esp. pp. 41–42; and also "Medieval 'Ars Dictaminis' and the Beginnings of Humanism: A New Construction of the Problem," *Renaissance Quarterly* 35 (1982): 1–35.

autem planius, quid apertius, quid evidentius dici potest?" [Now what can be said more plainly, what more openly, what more evidently?] A particularly striking rhetorical color pervades the passage (ll. 359–85), quoted above, that marks the turn from principally Augustinian passages on the Eucharist to a quotation from Gregory the Great, a passage that gives the opportunity for the tribute to the current Pope Gregory. The metaphor of the quotation from Cicero, "it is better for some remants to be left over, than for us to allow anyone to go away hungry," echoes the major theme of the *cena*. The discussion of patristic views on the *cena Domini* is itself a meal, and this has been a latent metaphor from the third sentence of the treatise (ll. 9–11), in the opening passage quoted above: "How contrary this [the Berengarian doctrine] is to the Catholic Faith, is well known to those whose food consists of the reading of sacred texts."[4] At the same time, the quotation from Gregory the Great enjoining daily offering of the flesh and blood of Christ, an injunction that the present Gregory observes in his daily life, looks back to the discussion of *sacramentum in re* at the opening (*cotidie in ecclesia manducatur*) cited above. The little work is marked by an inner artistic unity that has never been commented upon.

It is not, of course, enough to note that the author of the Aberdeen treatise had the sensitivity to style one would expect from the author of Alberic's manuals of *dictamen*. It is therefore fortunate that the list of Alberic's other known works has grown markedly in recent decades, thanks to the efforts of scholars who have identified a whole series of other Alberician works, mainly saints' lives, many of which come down to us without attribution.[5] These works are noteworthy as literary

---

4. For the use of such metaphors, see Klaus Lange, "Geistliche Speise. Untersuchungen zur Metaphorik der Bibelhermeneutik," *Zeitschrift für deutsches Altertum und deutsche Literatur* 95 (1966): 81–123.

5. The hagiographical works are cited under the following abbreviations and from the following editions:

Aspren = Vita S. Aspren [A. Lentini, "Alberico di Montecassino nel quadro della Riforma Gregoriana," *Studi Gregoriani* 4 (1952): 89–109, with text on pp. 100–109.]

Ces = Passio S. Cesari [Text in *Bibliotheca Casinensis* 3 (1877), *Florilegium*, pp. 150–58; proof of authorship in O. Engels, "Alberich von Monte Cassino und sein Schüler Johannes von Gaeta," *Studien und Mitteilungen zur Geschichte des Benediktiner-Ordens* 66 (1955), pp. 35–80; and prologue, apologia, and fivefold acrostic verses for Ces, J. Mallet and A. Thibaut, *Les manuscrits en écriture bénéventaine*, pp. 246–47.]

Dom. = Vita S. Dominici [The fundamental studies are: Dolbeau, "Le dossier de saint Dominique de Sora"; and Franklin, "The Restored Life and Miracles of St. Dominic of Sora." Dolbeau's edition replaces the edition of A. Lentini, "La 'Vita S. Dominici' di Alberico Cassinese," *Benedictina* 5 (1951): 57–77, an article which remains, however, most useful for questions of

compositions. But Alberic's book refuting Berengar cannot have been exactly like either his manuals of *dictamen* or his works of hagiography, because it can have followed neither an expository nor a narrative strategy. We therefore must bear in mind that there is no precise *comparandum* among Alberic's works as we turn to a consideration of the literary qualities and specifically the stylistic qualities of the little treatise. What is needed to test the possibility of Alberic's authorship is a more detailed analysis of the style of the Aberdeen manuscript's treatise. The present stylistic analysis is intended to show that the style of the treatise is consistent with Alberic's authorship.

The Literary Style of the Aberdeen Libellus

Let us consider first the specific rhetorical character of our libellus.[6] It is striking. The opening sentence presents the reader with a familiar type of wordplay in *allata relatio* (l. 2); cf. the somewhat different *obici possunt obiectiones* at the conclusion (l. 668). Alberic is fond of this device, as of all the related forms of it, for example in *Aspren* 100 *oppetat appetere*. Other *passiones* contain even more flamboyant variations in compounding, such as *Mod.* 372, *ferre . . . conferre . . . superferre*, and *Mod.* 371, *magnanimis . . . unanimis . . . longanimis*. Antithesis in the treatise may be combined with wordplay, or at least homoeoteleuton, in a sentence like (ll. 505–7), *Mutatur enim substantia in substantiam, aut specie et re, aut specie et non re, aut re et non specie.* Alberic's *Modestus* again shows a close parallel at 372, *quod spe temerant ipsa experiuntur in re.*

The author of the little treatise sums up the mystery of the Eucharist in these words (l. 645): *Bibis igitur, et non bibis.* Paradox of this sort delighted Alberic; especially vivid examples are seen in his *Aspren* (101): *infantem fari et perorare mutum,* and again (101): *verba non verba et litteras illitteratas,* and particularly (103): *pateretur non patiens, moreretur non moriens.* The friends and colleagues of the treatise's author

---

style. For a survey of the textual questions involved, see especially J. Howe, *Church Reform and Social Change,* esp. his Appendix A, pp. 163–78. For the stylistic questions with which this section is concerned, see above all Franklin, pp. 310–17; the aspect of cursus in the text that we are discussing is not treated because our text is a somewhat technical one.]

Mod. = *Passio S. Modesti* [Ed. A. Poncelet in *Anal. Bolland.* 51 (1933): 369–74.]

Scol. = *Vita S. Scolasticae* [A. Lentini, "L'omilia e la vita di S. Scolastica di Alberico Cassniese," *Benedictina* 3 (1949): 217–38.]

6. In this section, with its many short quotations from the libellus and from Alberic's demonstrated works, we have generally not given translations.

value his gifts beyond his deserts (ll. 11–12): *qui me ut ita dixerim saepe mihi praeponunt;* and so does Archbishop Peter who expects Alberic to try (*Aspren* 101.16): *ipsum me ipse longe exuperare.* The artful arrangement of words known as *climax* is seen in our treatise's injunction (ll. 99–100): *Intellegendo crede, credendo manduca, manducando imitare.* Again, Alberic's *Aspren* provides close parallels (104): *qualiter per devia in devia, per mala in peiora, per peiora in pessima;* and (107): *de bonis ad potiora, de potioribus diatim conscensum facere ad potissimum.* The synonymy that Alberic speaks of at the beginning of the *Aspren* (101–02) as suitable to the panegyric is a mark of the style of our treatise, as at ll. 592–94 (paraphrase of Christ's words): *Quid est, commendavi? Insinuavi, intimavi, indidi, laudavi, et ut post me in mei memoriam omni tempore fieret praecepi.* It is common in Alberic's works, as when St. Peter rebukes the illness of a woman (*Aspren* 105.48): *effuge, evanesce, dissolvere et evacuare in nihilum;* or when Scholastica makes her plea to Benedict (*Scol.* 235.20): *ecce modo non postulo, non flagito, non exoro ut maneas, ut moreris.* As in Scholastica's words, at times, synonymy may be used with anaphora in our text (ll. 421–22): *Vide refugium, vide probationem, vide argumentum, vide sillogismum insuperabilia.* Cesarius's prayer to God when he sees the human scapegoat sacrificed by the citizens of Terracina furnishes a precise parallel (*Ces.* 153, col. 2): *Vide facinus. Vide scelus. Vide et ulciscere.* In fact, anaphora is a consistent feature of Alberic's style.[7] The insistence on key words, often pronouns or pronominal adjectives, is seen both in our treatise, as in (ll. 363–65): *iste, qui nunc eiusdem nominis eiusdemque spiritus eiusdem Gregorii et ipse Gregorius possidet locum;* and in Alberic, as in (*Scol.* 236.31–32): *quos eadem generatio, et regeneratio eadem, et eadem in Christi servitute voluntas.* All this is not a matter of mere ornament. It reflects a deeply ingrained rhetorical habit of thought and expression, shared by our author and Alberic.

It is the same with grammatical constructions. One who reads Alberic's works attentively will observe his predilection for the future active participle. The first sentence of the *De Dictamine* ends with the words (29): *generis arbiter creditur futurus inani;* and the sentences that follow show *donaturum, ediscituros, collecturos,* and *addisciturum* in the introduction alone. This manner of looking forward in the opening of

---

7. See the remarks of Coffey, p. 291 n. 6.

a work, with this participle, is seen in the second paragraph of our treatise, which begins (l. 19): *Quoniam autem de sacramento locuturi sumus:* cf. also (l. 366): *dicturi sumus.* It is very closely paralleled by the beginning of the narrative in *Aspren* (102, ch. 20): *De primo neapolitane civitatis antistite locuturi.* The great frequency of the grammatical form may be related in part to Alberic's rhythmical preferences, e.g., the nominative form in the sentence ending (*Scol.* 72.19–20): *cum nostri generis hoste vetere congressurus;* and the clause ending (*Scol.* 233, ch. 28): *veni ad te esuriem intimam depulsura.* The ablative of the gerund is a favorite construction of Alberic's as well, and again the *Aspren* illustrates his most lavish deployment of it, five in a single period; for example, the words (*Aspren* 103, ch. 25): *librando aera, fundendo maria, tendendo caelos, fundando terram,* and *ambulando per terram.* Such a cluster is seen in the expression already cited from the treatise (ll. 99–100): *Intellegendo crede, credendo manduca, manducando imitare.*

The ablative absolute is among the constructions treated by Alberic near the beginning of his *De Dictamine,* and sometimes the construction and even the vocabulary of our treatise is strikingly similar to Alberic's own, as (l. 528): *domino iubente;* and (*Ces.* 150): *quasi diis immortalibus iubentibus.* [The somewhat rare use of the infinitive as a noun occurs in the Dossier (App. l. 63): *pro esse ponitur,* in *Mod.* (370): *in id esse,* in the preface to *Ces.* (Mallet-Thibaut, p. 246): *iuxta posse,* and in *Aspren* (101.16): *ultra posse.*]

The formation of the noun *bibitio* (ll. 272) from the verbal stem *bibere* is in keeping with similar formations in Alberic's works: not only *exhibitio* (*Scol.* 232 and 235; cf. also the common *expositio* at l. 615 in our treatise), but also the unusual *redditio* (*Aspren* 108 and *Ces.* 158). The treatise evinces a strong liking for adverbs ending in *-ter,* as the rare opening word shows (l. 1): *Noviter;* in addition, its sixteen pages show *subsequenter, breviter, multipliciter, similiter* (three times), *pariter, spiritualiter* (four times), *consequenter, carnaliter, corporaliter* (three times), *visibiliter* (twice), and *invisibiliter;* the first two chapters of Albericus's *Modestus* attest to his partiality to the same forms (369–71, chs. 1–2): *concorditer ac unanimiter; instanter invigilanterque; nimisque terribiliter nimisque horribiliter; fideliter, festive ac sollemniter;* and *insolubiliter inseparabiliterque.*

The heaping up of comparatives as well as positives is another feature of the style of the treatise, as in (ll. 194–95): *Quid autem planius, quid apertius, quid evidentius dici potest?* Alberic uses the same device, as in chapter 2 of *Mod.*, just cited (371, ch. 2): *citius agiliusque,* or (*Mod.* 373, ch. 6): *melius et verius;* in any case, *plane* is a favorite adverb of Alberic's (*Ces.* 156: *planissime,* and *Dom.* 72.16: *plane*).

The unusual prepositional phrase in *per omnia infelix* (l. 473) is exactly paralleled in *Ces.* 150: *per omnia vincti.* A mode of introducing a subordinate clause that is shared by the treatise and the works of Alberic is the formula *ad hoc . . . ut* (l. 35) or *ad hoc . . . quatinus* (ll. 12–13) found in *Ces.* 151 as *ad id ut.*

The vocabulary of the treatise also reveals striking correspondences with that of the saints' lives by Alberic. The works of the latter are marked by frequent compounding with the prefix *prae,* as in *praesignare* (*Dom.* 12), *praetendere* (*Dom.* 205), and *praedivinare* (*Mod.* 371, ch. 3); our treatise has *praecedere* (l. 155) and *praefigurare* (l. 244). The proem to the treatise contains in its sixteen lines several favorite Alberician words: in the first sentence, *confabulentur,* here used of the chattering of laymen, derives from a root that Alberic is particularly devoted to, since *confabulari* occurs in *Scol.* (232.10, in the eighth full sentence from the beginning), and *confabulatio* in *Mod.* (369, ch. 1, in the second full sentence, and 370, ch. 1, in the third full sentence), *Dom.* (210, in the sixth sentence from the end), and *Scol.* (232.26, in the thirteenth full sentence from the beginning). As in the treatise, the word is found at the beginning usually, and once at the end of the works. In the same first sentence the expression (ll. 3–4) *quorum intentio in talibus vigilare debet,* is closely parallel to *Aspren* 107.77, *doctrinae verbo invigilare.* The word *abrenuntiare* (treatise l. 7, of Berengarius's recantation of his own earlier teaching) is seen in Alberic's *Ces.* (152) and *Dom.* (39).[8] The term *confinitimi* (treatise l. 11), used of the author's neighbors, is similar to *confinior* (*Aspren* 101, 15—part of the prologue) used of the lesser of two evils that Alberic might embrace, in obedience to Archbishop Peter's stringent request. The author of the treatise, furthermore, in explaining that he seeks to avoid wearying his readers, refers to *lectio prolixa* (ll. 15–16); the adjective ("long") is another favorite of Alberic's, as in *Aspren* 103.28 *prolixioris tristitiae; Aspren* 103.33 *prolixi itineris;* and *Mod.* 369 *nimis nimisque prolixam* (sc. *aegritudinem*), in the second full

---

8. The word *abrenuntiare* would have been especially well known from its occurrence at the beginning of *Reg. S. Ben.*

sentence of the *passio,* and 370, chapter 1 also, *in prolixum,* in the third full sentence. In other words, the prologue to the treatise shows a significant group of words that are distinctly Alberician, and they are used as they are in the *passiones,* for a passage worked out with particular care. It is striking and may be significant that the *Modestus* shows in its prologue two of the same favorite words—each of them being used twice—found in the prologue to our treatise.

It is the same with the vocabulary of the rest of the treatise, though not in such a concentrated cluster as in the prologue. Some of the favorite words, usual and unusual, that our author shares with Alberic include: *determinare* (l. 134 and *Mod.* 373, ch. 6); *liquido* (l. 166) and *liquet* (l. 627), and *luce liquidius* (*Aspren* 108.79) and *erit liquidum* (*Scol.* 232.6); *subdere* (l. 241, and *Mod.* 369, ch. 1); *sequestrari* (l. 324, and *Ces.* 156); and *innotescere* (l. 325, and *Ces.* "apologia" in Mallet-Thibaut p. 247, and *Ces.* 151); *refugium* (l. 421) and *refugere* (*Dom.* 10); *nec illud silentio praetereundum* (l. 533) and *non sunt obvelanda silentio* (*Dom.* 51), *minime reticendam* (*Dom.* 53), *insinuare* (treatise l. 593 and *Ces.* 152 [bis]); and *intimare* (treatise l. 593 and *Dom.* 38)

The *topos* of the inner man and the outer man (*homo interior/exterior,* or adverb *intrinsecus/extrinsecus*) is familiar enough in medieval literature, but it is worth noting that it occurs in our brief treatise (ll. 137–38): *interiori homine et exteriore apostoli manducaverunt,* and is also very frequent in the Alberician *passiones,* often in the same context of food and eating as in the treatise (*Mod.* 369, ch. 1; 370, ch. 1; 371, ch. 3; 372, ch. 4 [here *lumine orbati utroque*]; 373–74, ch. 6 [of the palate]; *Scol.* 232.13–18 [several versions of the food/hunger theme], 235.22 [hunger], and 236.8).

In the matter of his fondness for Greek words, our author shows his resemblance to Alberic as well. The treatise's *fantastice* (l. 536) corresponds to *Ces.* 156 *phantasticos.* The treatise introduces its final section as a *brevis epilogus,* a technical word that is not surprising in so polished and rhetorical a writer as our author.[9] Alberic, of course, makes free use of Greek terms, such as *phrenesis* (*Aspren* 100.2 and *Ces.* 153) and *atomus* (*Scol.* 104.42 and *Mod.* 373, ch. 5).

---

9. "conclusiones, quae apud Graecos epilogi nominantur," *Rhetorica Ad Herennium* 2.47, ed. F. Marx (Leipzig, 1923).

A striking feature of the treatise's style is the strong marking of stages in the argument. At l. 270 a new section begins, *His igitur ita dispositis,* and at l. 539 a paragraph opens with the words, *His igitur sic expeditis.* At l. 125 *His et enim similibus* is a similar striking linking phrase within a section; Morin rightly concluded that *enim* was an error, and he proposed reading *His et horum similibus.* An examination of Alberic's texts, however, leads to the correct emendation: *Scol.* 235.38 *in his et in his similibus ceteris* (cf. also *Mod.* 372 *In his igitur et in ceteris huius modi*) show that our treatise should be emended to the form that *Scol.* has, *His et his similibus,* meaning, "For these persons and for ones similar to these."

The most striking phrase that the treatise writer uses, however, is *Sed de his hactenus* (ll. 502 and 665–66) and *De his autem hactenus* (l. 38); this too marks a stage in the argument. As Engels saw, this is an Alberician expression.[10] It is seen in *Ces.* 157; *Sed de his hactenus,* and *Dom.* 9: *Verum de his hactenus. Hactenus* (our author likes compounds with *–tenus;* cf. *quatenus* at ll. 13 and 320) is, in general, a word that Alberic was fond of; it is found in his *Dictamen* in the introduction (p. 30); the remainder of the phrase is seen also in the *Dictamen* (p. 32): *Set de his [pauculis]. Hactenus* also stands at the opening of the *Flores Rhetorici (Dictaminum Radii)* in the form in which we have that work, and because of this one word, as Herbert Bloch has justly pointed out, we know that, "this cannot be the beginning of an independent work, least of all a work on rhetoric!"[11] The full expression, *Sed (Verum) de his hactenus* is idiosyncratic. We would venture to assert that, occurring as it does twice in our brief treatise, and once more in a variant form (*De his autem hactenus*), it is as good as a Cassinese or even Alberician signature.[12] The expression itself is unusual, but what is equally important is the stylistic and mental habit that lies behind it: it stands each time at the end of sections of argument or narrative and sums them up ("But so far now on these subjects"). Like the linguistic markers for the beginning of sections, this distinctive marker points to a personality trait. The reader can verify this habit of neat and tidy categorizing

10. Engels, pp. 41–42.

11. Bloch, "Monte Cassino's Teachers," p. 591.

12. Other Cassinese authors use it as well; see Leo Marsicanus in *Chronica Monasterii Casinensis,* 3.25 (p. 393) and Hoffmann's note 18.

throughout the treatise, and in the works that have been assigned to Alberic in past times as well.

To conclude the comparative analysis, let us examine further distinctive elements of style in this broader sense. The first concerns the author's fondness for playing with numbers. In the beginning of the summing-up, which ends with the last *Sed de his hactenus,* the author says (ll. 640–41): "Behold, these four doctors as though with one voice, confirm that we drink that blood which was shed by the spear of the soldier." Alberic especially loves to ring the changes on numbers in this manner.[13] After all, it is he who tells us in the "apologia auctoris" that accompanies his *Cesarius* that he composed the saint's life when he was thirteen years old, only six years after he had begun the pursuit of liberal studies. A quite elaborate play on numbers is found in the *Modestus* (p. 373, ch. 6): "Such then were the glories that distinguished Modestus as he was passing through the fifth year of his seventh *lustrum* [that is, in his thirty-third year], when behold! they strove to drag him, all unwilling, refusing, and resisting long and vigorously, to the summit of the sixth level and to the heights of the diaconate. He was therefore one of the seven deacons of the Holy and Apostolic Roman Church, the son of seven women, protected by seven horns, before whom seven candelabra gave light, which is the spirit of sevenfold glory sent into all the earth." In the treatise on the Eucharist, the fascination with numbers is not given the free rein that it has in the *Modestus.* It appears, however, in a restrained and paradoxical manner.

Second, it should be recalled that Alberic at times thinks of his craft of writing as parallel to the painter's. The most striking passage is his simile in the introduction to the *De Dictamine* (30): there he says that his method will be "in imitation of the painter first to sketch out a design somehow or other with (as it were) ugly charcoal, and then afterwards (as it were) to spread a suitable variety of colors over the sketched-out lines." The simile is not surprising, since Alberic's writing is characterized by vivid description: his sharply etched account of the last meeting of St. Scholastica with her brother Benedict is well known. The same is true of the treatise. Its first sentence ends with the concrete picture of the excitement created in Italy by the doctrines of

---

13. Coffey, "The Homily of Alberic the Deacon," p. 291, demonstrates this clearly, as an Alberician trait, in the translation of a passage from the Homily on St. Scholastica and in his note 7.

Berengarius, which has stirred so much interest that (ll. 4–5) "even the very laymen are 'confabulating' about it among themselves in the town squares." One thinks also of the author's tribute to Augustine the commentator on John in the beautiful simile (ll. 42–43), "like an eagle flying after an eagle." Ambrose, with Alberician paronomasia, is (ll. 59–61) "the fountain of knowledge, the key to unlock secrets, whose flowers give forth their scent, as they say, in the Church."[14] And the author of the treatise presents it to the recipient (ll. 16–18): "I have chosen not to pour these teachings into the minds of those [his *fratres* and *confinitimi*] until they might, such as they are, be presented to you and be weighed and judged (*iudicentur*) on your own balance-scales." The picture of the *beatissimus pater* sitting in judgment and weighing the treatise in his balances, which stands at the end of the proem, is echoed by the later picture of the pope (ll. 362–68): "let him [Gregory] pass judgment (*diiudicet*). . . . These words of the blessed Gregory [the Great] . . . are so implanted in the heart of the present Gregory, who now gives light to the world." The treatise's effects are often accompanied by the slightest and simplest verbal means, but unmistakably the end of the proem and the center of the treatise are marked by the image of the *beatissimus pater* and the pope, each as *iudex*.

In the third place, in a passage already cited, the author of the treatise depicts Christ in a kind of *prosopopoeia* (ll. 583–94), in which he explains his own words (John 6:53) by expansion, paraphrase, and synonymy: These words are as if he were saying, "You are offended that I have said, UNLESS ONE SHALL EAT MY FLESH, AND DRINK MY BLOOD, HE SHALL HAVE NO LIFE IN HIM. THIS (he says) OFFENDS YOU. It will not be as you suppose; my flesh will not be torn, will not be cut up, will not be divided into bits. Do not imagine that you devour my flesh in the manner of wild animals or drink my blood with the cruelty of a beast. Do not suppose this. There is another thing that I say: THE WORDS THAT I HAVE SPOKEN TO YOU ARE SPIRIT AND LIFE. Understand them spiritually, if you wish to have life. For I have commended a sacrament to you. What is this, I have 'commended'? I have instilled it, I have impressed it, I have inserted it, I have praised it, and I have bidden it to be observed throughout all time after me, in remembrance of me." Now it is known that Alberic paraphrased an

---

14. On Alberic's use of antonomasia, see Coffey, p. 300 n. 4 and references there.

author, a classical one, in a passage to which Bloch has called attention: "In one instance Alberic could not resist the temptation of competing with Horace."[15] Bloch then quotes the lines from the *De Dictamine* (Rockinger, p. 45):

> In silvam ne ligna feras, nec in equora pisces:
> fornaci ne flare velis, iubar aut dare soli.

> prior versus est Oracii, secundus meus. id est *ne velis docere doctissimum virum, nec ditare ditatissimum virum muneribus.*

As Bloch shows, Alberic conflated two half-lines from Horace (*Serm.* 1.10.34 and *Serm.* 2.3.235), and then, as he openly boasts, adds a line of his own invention with the same sense. What has not been sufficiently observed is that Alberic elsewhere makes a practice of this type of composition, but in prose. When Cesarius (*Ces.* 153) sees the human scapegoat cast himself from the cliff at Terracina, he cries, "What madness? What insanity [is] this, o my fellow citizens? What great frenzy, so unheard of in all the ages before, has corrupted your mind, has poisoned your spirit, has stolen away feeling, and covered up your understanding, that you regard night as day, cloud as clear sky, and as light shadows? that you find in crime virtue, in death life, and salvation in destruction?" As in the case of Alberic's contamination of the two Horatian lines and invention of his own, so here the opening phrases (*Quis furor? quae tanta insania ista, o cives? quae tanta . . . frenesis . . .*) are taken from two passages in Virgil's *Aeneid;* they are 5.670–71 (Ascanius's rebuke to the matrons who have set fire to the Trojan ships): quis furor iste *novus? quo nunc, quo tenditis, inquit, heu miserae* cives? and 2.42 (Laocoon to his fellow Trojans who wish to receive the Trojan Horse): O *miseri* quae tanta insania, cives? Alberic has reshaped the poetry as prose and out of two separate questions has created three interrogative expressions. The elements are broken up and redistributed, and after the second *quae tanta* the rest is Alberic's own invention.

The process of conflation of quotations and texts, combined with their "deconstruction" and reshaping anew through paraphrase and synonymy is seen in other vivid passages in Alberic's work, for example in a passage on Fama in the *Dominicus,* 23, with elements from Horace, *C.* 1.4, and in Scholastica's speech to Benedict (*Scol.* 233.35–38),

---

15. "Monte Cassino's Teachers," pp. 592–93. On Alberic's use of paraphrase, P. Gehl, "Vat. Ottobonianus lat. 1354," is also fundamental.

with elements from Virgil, *Buc.* 1 and *Cant. Cant.* 2. In the light of this practice, it is possible to understand more clearly the treatise's expansion of Christ's words from John 6. In turn, this becomes one further pointer still in the direction of Alberic's authorship.

There is general agreement that Alberic practiced a variety of styles. In fact, in the opening of the *Dictaminum Radii* this is what he taught also. We cannot expect that Alberic's more striking rhetorical devices would be as frequently and overwhelmingly deployed in a treatise that forms part of a theological debate as they are in the grand panegyrical style of the *Aspren*, for example. It is precisely the process that Alberic announced at the end of the prologue to that work (101–2): "Et quia synonima laudibus praeconiis ve alludunt, quam maxime Ioannem illum ore aureum aemulans, ad calcem historiae per synonima laudes decrevi sancti praesulis texere, et per exornationem illam, quam expolitionem rhetores nuncupant, quae pauca admodum sunt, plures extendere [And because *synonima* imaginatively embroider praise or panegyric, imitating most particularly the famed John Chrysostom, I have decided upon the foundation of the history to weave the praises of the holy bishops with *synonima,* and through that type of adornment which the rhetoricians call *expolitio* to extend and multiply the facts, which are very few]."[16] As a rule, a soberer tone prevails in our libellus than in the *passiones* generally, just as in turn the *passiones* vary among themselves in the intensity of their rhetorical level. In spite of the differences that are inevitable and traceable to the rules of distinct genres, the treatise shows ample indications of Alberic's style. This is true in the broadest ways, such as the manner treatment of biblical quotations, the marking of the stages of the discourse, and the rhetorical figures, and also in tiny details of vocabulary and sentence structure. Some of these aspects are more characteristically Alberician than others. The cluster in the libellus of so many parallels to the hagiographical works speaks for itself. From a stylistic point of view, Alberic's fingerprints are found throughout the entire treatise.

It is not so hard to discover a major influence in the creation of this style. In the passage quoted earlier from the opening of chapter 11 the

---

16. As Lentini saw, the reference to *expolitio* (and *exornatio*) is based on *Ad Herennium* 4.54. The Monte Cassino manuscript of this classical work, Flor. laur. [No]51.10, a product of the Cassinese scriptorium, as F. Newton would date it, of the time of Oderisius I (1087–1105) contains at this point (80v) the very noticeable heading "Expolitio" in red Beneventan.

author of our libellus "restarted" his discussion with a classical reference: "it is better for *some remnants* to be left over, *than* for us *to allow* anyone *to go away from here unfilled.*" (ll. 359–61) These are Cicero's words to his friend Trebatius in the *Topica*. The student who has the opportunity to study a Monte Cassino manuscript of the *Topica* now in the Vatican Library, Vaticanus Ottobonianus Lat. 1406, will find himself facing what is probably the most splendid classical manuscript of the eleventh century. From the opening the manuscript proclaims itself a book of dialectic. (See Fig. 2.) It is a product of the scriptorium of Desiderius, and in fact was penned by one of the abbey's master scribes, an artist whose work is found in other books.[17] Our passage from Cicero's *Topica* is found on fol. 47v. Looking at this passage in its context, the student is struck by other familiar elements in addition to the quotation itself. Here is the context, as Cicero addresses his young friend Trebatius: "His igitur locis qui sunt expositi ad omne argumentum reperiendum tamquam elementis quibusdam significatio et demonstratio datur. Utrum igitur hactenus satis est? Tibi quidem tam acuto et tam occupato puto. Sed quoniam avidum hominem ad has discendi epulas recepi, sic accipiam ut reliquiarum sit potius aliquid quam te hinc patiar non satiatum discedere." The marking of the stages of an argument by the word *hactenus* is a favorite device of Cicero's.[18] It afterward influences the dialectical style of Boethius; for example, in the Ottobonianus on fol. 66r, Book 1 of his *De Topicis Differentiis* ends with the words, "Sed de his actenus, nunc de reliquis explicemus."[19] In our libellus chapter 2 ends, "De his autem hactenus; nunc vero ad ipsius rei seriem veniamus." Similarly, at the end of chapter 13 and again at the end of chapter 17 of the libellus we find the expression, "Sed de his hactenus." Other organizing markers are found frequently, such as in Boethius, *De Syllogismis Categoricis* on fol. 132r of the Ottoboni manuscript: "His igitur expeditis," and in *De Hypotheticis Categoricis* on fol. 143r, "Expeditis igitur his syllogismis"; compare the "His igitur" in the

---

17. For its date and home, see F. Newton, *Scriptorium and Library*, pp. 114–18, and plate 210, with plate description on p. 390. The same discussion emphasizes the superb quality of the book; it is a display manuscript, and in this way set apart from and above all the fine manuscripts of the classics produced at the abbey in this time. See also pp. 109–13 and Fig. 3.

18. As Carol Lanham has pointed out in a letter, "sed/verum haec hactenus" is Cicero's signature (cf., for example, *Tusc.* 3.84).

19. The same text of Boethius is found in a manuscript still at Monte Cassino; it is MC 191, and the concluding clause for bk. 1, "Sed de his hactenus; nunc de reliquis" is found on p. 191.

FIGURE 2

Vatican City, Biblioteca Apostolica Vaticana, MS Ottobonianus latinus 1406, Porphyry, Isagoge; Aristotle, Categoriae; Cicero, Topica; Boethius, etc.

Produced at Monte Cassino in the time of Abbot Desiderius (1058–1087), the manuscript is the work of a single scribe who created other masterpieces at Monte Cassino, such as the fine Exultet Roll now at Pisa (Museo Nazionale di S. Matteo).

The frontispiece (1r) marks the character of the volume as a collection of logic texts with the figure of Lady Dialectica, one of the Liberal Arts. She is depicted with her traditional symbol, the serpent, and before her stand three of her students. Berengar, defending the use of dialectic in the great controversy, quoted Augustine's tribute to this branch of learning, "Dialectic is the art of arts, the discipline of disciplines. She knows how to learn, she knows how to teach, and she not only wishes to make men wise, she actually makes them so." (See above, pp. 13–14.) It is Berengar who cites the noble defense of Dialectic, but it is Monte Cassino that produces this fine volume in tribute to her. It was from the texts found in this volume that the author of the Aberdeen libellus—if he did not learn the techniques of logical argument—certainly learned the techniques of organizing a prose treatise. (See pp. 65–68, 109–13.)

In a solemn gesture, Dialectica is here depicted bestowing a chaplet on one of her pupils. It is argued on p. 112 that this figure represents the author of our treatise, the Monte Cassino monk who gained the victory over Berengar.

Trebatius passage from Cicero's *Topica*, just cited. The libellus shows the following at opening of sections:

Ch. 9 beg.: His igitur ita dispositis;[20]

Ch. 12 beg.: His autem ita dispositis;

Ch. 15 beg.: His igitur sic expeditis.

The same Boethian work just cited shows on fol. 142r of the Ottobonianus: "Ex his igitur constat"; and the libellus begins chapter 14: "Constat igitur," and chapter 16: "Ex his ergo manifestum est."[21]

It is clear that the author of the Libellus learned the art of organizing stages of an argument verbally from studying the treatises of Aristotle, Porphyry, Cicero, and Boethius as preserved in a collection like that of the Ottobonianus. This careful study of style fits well with what is known about the *grammaticus* (as his contemporaries called him) to whom we propose to ascribe the treatise. It is of great interest that Alberic chose to quote from Cicero's *Topica* in this work. Cicero's treatise opens with Cicero and Trebatius turning over books in the library at the great orator's Tusculan villa. As has recently been argued, the monks of Monte Cassino in its Golden Age saw themselves as heirs of the illustrious Romans who had preceded them in their region.[22] The Desiderian monks and writers Alfanus of Salerno and his fellow-countryman Guaiferius noted the parallels between ancient Romans and themselves, and Guaiferius specifically, through his borrowings from Cicero's *De Oratore*, glorified the abbey of Monte Cassino as the home of literary and philosophical study and writing and so a continuation of the activities pursued in the villas of Cicero and Varro in the last generation of the Roman Republic. It would appear that Alberic's study of these influential texts, as preparation for his composition directed against Berengar, took place against the background of his close friend Guaiferius's conception of a revival of the philosophical activities of those times in the new monastic setting.

---

20. The identical phrase is seen in Boethius, *Peri hermeneias comm.* 5.10: "his igitur ita dispositis," and in his *In Porphyrii Isagogen comm.* 1.14: "His igitur expeditis."
21. The same words "Constat igitur," in the same order are seen in Boethius, *Peri Hermeneias comm.* 5.12: "constat igitur"; and in this passage the verb "diiudicandi" is the verb that the libellus employs at the beginning of ch. 11 for the judgment that Pope Gregory VII is to make: "diiudicet." The expression "manifestum est" is found in Boethius, *Peri hermeneias comm.* 3.9.
22. Newton, *Scriptorium and Library,* pp. 276–91, on "Triumphs, villas, convents."

Finally, we should note the overall tone of the whole treatise. Berengar is treated gently. The only time that he is named, in the second sentence, the author introduces him with marked coolness but pays tribute to his ability and his learning. One might have expected, in an age that produced the *Libelli de Lite,* that Berengar would have been repeatedly attacked or derided with epithets in this refutation of his views; this is precisely what Berengar's other opponents, such as Lanfranc, had done. But not this treatise. After the second sentence, Berengar simply passes out of consideration, and the focus rests upon his teaching. In fact, even this is treated at a further remove; what the author addresses is what people are saying about Berengar's views, rather than the views themselves (observe *Aiunt* and *ut dicunt* in the second sentence). It is the *relatio* or *report* of the matter that is the subject of the opening sentence, being said to have spread through "all this land," and this same sentence ends with the *conversation* (*confabulentur*) of the laity in the town-squares. Everything removes the debate from the person of Berengar, and the affair is handled with great tact and diplomacy. If Alberic's personal discussions with Berengar were similarly gentle, then it becomes easy to see how Berengar misread Alberic's position on the Eucharist.

Such a tone is wholly in keeping with the Monte Cassino of Desiderius, who was famous for his diplomatic skills. At the climax of the poem in Desiderius's honor which stands, with the abbot's portrait, at the beginning of the fine lectionary Vat. lat. 1202, Alfanus of Salerno says of his close friend:[23]

> Amor et sacra copula pacis
> facit hunc genus esse Tonantis . . .
>
> [Love and the sacred bond of peace
> stamp him as the offspring of the Thunderer.]

The classicizing reference to God under the epithet of Jupiter *Tonans* should not hide from us the biblical reference here. Desiderius deserves his name as a child of God according to the seventh of the Beatitudes (Matt. 5:9): "Blessed are the peacemakers: for they shall be called the children of God." The pacific tone of this treatise is in keeping with the spirit of Desiderius that Alfanus admired.

---

23. Poem 54 in the Lentini-Avagliano edition, p. 219.

The Desiderian themes of charity and unity find expression in chapter 10 of our libellus. After citing Augustine on the elements of the Eucharist (*Tract. 26 in Ioh.*), Alberic sets forth in an only partially veiled manner the danger of separation from the body of Christ, the Church.

> Now what else does the blessed Augustine advise us to understand in these words, nay rather compel us to feel with, as it were, a kind of force? That in taking the body and blood of Christ we should hold unity and charity; so that we may love him, whose blood we drink, with all our heart, with all our soul, with all our strength, and our neighbors as ourselves. In the assertion of this opinion he uses the elegant simile of bread and wine, which are brought together out of many things in such a way that the individual elements can by no means be separated or taken apart.
>
> ———
>
> [Quid autem nos aliud beatus Augustinus in his verbis intelligere ammonet, immo quasi vi quadam id sentire cogit? Ut Christi corpus et sanguinem sumendo unitatem et caritatem teneamus; quatenus et ipsum, cuius sanguinem bibimus, toto corde, tota anima omnibusque viribus, et proximos nostros tamquam nos ipsos diligamus. In cuius assertione sententiae eleganti panis et vini utitur similitudine, quae sic ex pluribus unita sunt, ut iam nullo modo singula a se vel discerni vel sequestrari possint.]
> (ll. 317–24)

These Desiderian themes assist in the solution of the last of the questions with which we began: the addressee.

Even without the themes, Alberic's address to his *beatissimus pater*, to whom he submits the libellus for approval before sharing it with his monastic brothers, points directly to Alberic's abbot, Desiderius. Born ca. 1027 into the ruling house of Benevento, Desiderius entered religious life in around or about 1048–49; he eventually transferred to Monte Cassino in 1055, becoming its abbot in 1058. Under his leadership, the monastery reached the highest point of its cultural achievement, with extensive building projects, an important group of scholars within the monastic community, and a scriptorium that was one of the most important centers of book production in eleventh-century Europe. These cultural achievements, however, depended on Desiderius's ability to gain donations and protection from possible rivals and enemies. As abbot, he skillfully protected the monastery's interests by forming alliances both with the reforming papacy, whose circles he had entered even before his move to Monte Cassino, and with the Norman

conquerors of South Italy, who became the monastery's more generous patrons. This achievement was particularly notable since the papacy and the Normans were frequently at odds with one another.[24]

In dedicating his treatise to Desiderius, Alberic is following proper
monastic procedure. Furthermore, the treatise's hierarchical approach,
which grows out of monastic obedience, in reality gives Alberic an opportunity to address a wider audience: he submits his conclusions to
Desiderius to be *judged* upon the abbot's balance-scales (*tuo examine
iudicentur,* at the end of the opening paragraph, l. 18), and later urges
that the pope should form a *definitive judgment* upon the Berengarian
question (*diiudicet iste,* in the middle of the treatise, in the paragraph
following the discussion of church unity, l. 363). The clear implication
of this echo is that Alberic's treatise, submitted vertically to the abbot,
then after receiving Desiderius's judgment, was to be transmitted
horizontally to Alberic's fellow monks, but also beyond this was to be
submitted vertically for Gregory's judgment as well, and afterward
transmitted horizontally to Desiderius's fellow abbots and other ecclesiastics in the Synod.

The Content of the Libellus

The Aberdeen manuscript therefore preserves what can only be Alberic's influential *liber,* for which we can furnish a title out of Peter the
Deacon's description: *Adversus Berengarium Diaconum de Corpore et
Sanguine Domini.* As already noted, Alberic's treatise begins with the
address to the *beatissimus pater*—Desiderius—and continues in the
often-quoted passage describing how even laymen stood in public
squares to debate Berengar's ideas on the Eucharist. Although historians have often quoted this passage as evidence for the turmoil Berengar was causing, in fact it may be less simply a representation of reality than an expression of rhetorical art. In his study of the Investiture
Contest, I. S. Robinson noticed that both Manegold and Sigebert of
Gembloux invoked very similar images "of unwholesome publicity . . .
using a time-honoured rhetorical device to discredit their opponents:
to claim [as Manegold did] that an author's opinions had reached an

---

24. For the political career of Desiderius, see Cowdrey, *Age of Abbot Desiderius,* pp. 1–45; Desiderius's
personal history is sketched on pp. 115–17.

audience of working-class women was equivalent of accusing him of 'giving that which is holy to the dogs (Matt. 7:16).'"[25] The author of our libellus was simply invoking the same trope for the purpose of discrediting Berengar's teaching.

The other achievement of the opening is subtly to misstate Berengar's position, as other opponents of his had done, attributing to him the view "that in the sacrament of our redemption neither is the bread turned into flesh nor the wine into blood." (ll. 8–9) This cannot be merely an error, for Alberic later gives Berengar's position correctly, although without attributing it to him (ch. 14: "But lest anyone should perhaps suppose that after this change the substance of the bread and the wine still remained, let us . . . "). In the misstatement, Alberic is preparing the way to refute Berengar by disproving the commonly formulated position that he believed the sacrament to be a figure rather than reality.[26] The contrast between figure and reality, indeed, is one of the principal themes of the treatise, especially in its first half, but there are several others that are woven through the work. The opposition between figure and reality is echoed by other pairings: between the visible and the invisible sacrament, and between receiving with the lips and with the heart, taking the Eucharist carnally and spiritually. This last theme is of particular importance, as Alberic transforms the argument that the Eucharist must be taken spiritually into a refutation of Berengar. Doubting or even questioning—as Berengar certainly was doing—will be seen, in light of I Corinthians 11:29, as "drinking judgment upon oneself," and even linked to heresy and the participation of Judas at the last supper. The following table shows how the interplay of these different themes gives structure to the treatise. (Here and in the edition we retain Morin's useful chapter divisions, while reminding the reader that these are not found in the manuscript.)

---

25. *Authority and Reason in the Investiture Contest* (New York, 1973), p. 8, citing *MGH Libelli de Lite* 1: 420 and 2: 438.

26. See p. 15; but that formulation continued throughout the controversy. Guitmund, for example, describes Berengar's views in these terms: "Berengar and those who follow him assert that the Eucharist of the Lord is not truly and in substance the body and blood of the Lord, but is called that in name only, in that it is, as it were, a shadow and a figure signifying the body and blood of the Lord" [Berengarius et qui eum sequuntur, asseverant Eucharistiam Domini non esse vere substantialiterque corpus et sanguinem Domini, sed sola voce sic appellari, pro eo quod tanquam umbra et figura significativa sit corporis et sanguinis Domini] (*PL* 149: 1430A).

The Structure of the Libellus

1 **Preface** to the blessed father Berengar of Tours's teaching on Eucharist The blessed father to judge	10 **Conclusion to first part:** Augustine on unity and charity Spiritual food Unity in the Lord's body
2 **Definition** of sacrament (Isidore) Figure and reality Greg. M. in the Mass: appearance and truth	11 **Restart:** hungry readers/leftovers (Cicero) Two Gregories: Greg. M. and Greg. VII Choirs of angels at Mass Ambrose on miracles of God His logic on words of consecration
3 **Argument** begins John 6:53: eating for salvation or destruction Tribute to Augustine Eating with heart or with teeth	12 Unity of Christ's body Figure and truth Unity of Christ's body
4 Tribute to Ambrose Visible and invisible sacrament (horror of blood) Eating for salvation or destruction	13 Leo I: taking communion in faith Doubting and heresy Augustine agrees with other doctors? But enough for now
5 I Cor. 11:29 Heretics and Eucharist Eating unworthily	14 So it is clear: so many authorities agree Substance changed into substance Reality and appearance (horror of blood) Miracles of God
6 With lips and with heart Figure and truth Eating unworthily I Cor. 11:29	15 John 6:53: spiritual/corporeal Jesus: "it will not be as you suppose" Consecration by the speech of God Dispositions of nature
7 Judas at the Last Supper (Chrysostom) Figure and reality Words of consecration Heretics and Eucharist	16 Unity of Christ's body Words of consecration Unity of Christ's body Greg. M: learning by drinking Judas at the Last Supper (Chrysostom)
8 Greg. M.: blood of the lamb on both doorposts signifies: With lips and with heart	17 Four doctors agree But Jerome and Augustine a little different Both views are true Humility in the face of insoluble mystery: *catena* of texts
9 Augustine: With heart and not with lips Spiritual food	18 **Epilogue:** with lips and with heart (John 6:53) Truth of Christ's body and blood Leo I: taking communion in faith

Following upon the opening address, Alberic introduces his subject (ch. 2) by citing Isidore, Ambrose, and Gregory on *sacramentum* in the already-quoted passage.[27] Alberic shows the advantage of this starting point by using it immediately to refute some of the claims ascribed to Berengar: thus, he observes, while the sacramental lamb sacrificed in the Old Testament was a *figura,* sacraments might equally be a *res* "as the sacrament of him who is daily eaten in the Church. . . . Therefore it is called a sacrament in this way, not because it points to something, but because it has been pointed to by something; just as on the other hand the former thing was called a sacrament not because it was pointed to by something, but because it carried the prefiguring of this present one. These things have been said to this end, that no one should choose to understand the sacrament of the Church typologically." What Alberic has done is deprive Berengar of the advantage of a definition that saw a sacrament as opposed to and distinct from the thing of which it was a sign; and he follows by immediately quoting Ambrose, *That you may know that this is a sacrament, the figure of it preceded it and came before,* a statement that he interprets to mean "that you may know that this is true in reality, another thing has preceded it in seeming." At this point, as elsewhere in the treatise, it is a quotation from Gregory I, namesake of the present pope, that marks a critical transition, in this case to the distinction between appearance (*species*) and truth (*rerum veritas*): the central issue in the Eucharistic Controversy. Gregory's words alone, Alberic concludes, "ought to have such force with us that we should believe that it is in reality the flesh and blood of him in whose commemoration we do these things. It is done in seeming indeed, because what is, is not seen. So much, then, for these matters for the moment; now let us come to the orderly laying out of the subject itself."

Alberic's own exposition begins (ch. 3) with John 6:53—a text he will return to at the very end—and Augustine's comment on it. In quick order he introduces some of his main themes: the importance of the correct, spiritual attitude toward the sacrament; the distinction be-

---

27. In this section, in order to focus upon our analysis of the argument more closely, all the quotations are given in English alone. The reader is reminded that in our text the Latin is presented facing the English.

tween visible and invisible sacraments; the danger to those who, taking the Eucharist, doubt its reality.

VERILY, VERILY I SAY UNTO YOU, UNLESS YOU SHALL EAT THE FLESH OF THE SON OF MAN, AND DRINK HIS BLOOD, YOU WILL NOT HAVE LIFE IN YOU (John 6:53). These are the words of him who could not lie. He wrote these words whose testimony is true. In his exposition of them, the blessed Augustine, like an eagle following an eagle, uses divine and spiritual language. Therefore he says [*Treatise 26 on John*, c. 15] ... *The sacrament of this, that is, of the unity of the body and blood of Christ, is prepared on the Lord's Table in some places every day, and in some places at a fixed interval of days, and taken from the Lord's Table, by some people for life and by others for destruction; but the thing itself, of which this is the sacrament, is taken by every man who participates in it for life and by no-one for destruction.* (ll. 39–51)

Alberic paraphrases this thought, "the sacrament is one thing, and the force of the sacrament is another" [Aliud igitur est sacramentum, aliud virtus sacramenti (ll. 51–52)], then returns to Augustine [*Treatise 26 on John*, c. 13] for the distinction between visible and invisible sacraments: *what pertains to the force of the sacrament, not what pertains to the visible sacrament; he who eats it within, not without; who eats it in his heart, not who grinds it with his tooth.* (ll. 56–58)

Pivoting again on the precise phrases of his sources (ch. 4), Alberic then subtly shifts the direction of the discussion: "But what is the visible sacrament?" (l. 59) Quoting Ambrose, Alberic agrees that it must be the bread and wine on the altar, and then confronts the sensory evidence that underlay much of Berengar's challenge: "But you say, 'Why then do I who see the wine, not see the blood?'" (l. 68) Alberic does not, however, linger on this issue. Instead he passes quickly over it with a citation of Ambrose [*On the sacraments*, 4.4.20] (*That there may not be the revulsion of [seeing] blood*, l. 71–72), his own paraphrase of Ambrose's thought ("If it were not for the revulsion caused by seeing [it], you would see both the flesh that you eat and the blood that you drink," ll. 72–74) to return to Augustine and his discussion in *Tract. 26 in Ioh.* of the difference between what one eats carnally and spiritually. The passage quoted recalls the theme of figure and truth by its comparison of manna with the eucharistic bread, and proceeds directly to the other themes of the treatise, the distinction between visible and invisible, and between taking the Eucharist carnally or spiritually. What does this expositor tell us, Alberic concludes, "if not that we not believe those things that we see, and that we understand those things that we do not see? You see bread: understand flesh; you see wine: understand blood. Understanding, believe; believing, eat; eating, imitate . . . Whence also the same Augustine says, *This is then eating that food and drinking that drink: to remain in Christ, and to have Christ remaining in one. And because of this, one who does not remain in Christ, and in whom Christ does not remain, without a doubt does not eat his flesh or drink his blood, even if he eats and drinks the sacrament of this mighty thing for judgment upon himself."* [*Treatise 26 on John*] (ll. 96–106)

Having argued that only those who believe eat the body and blood of Christ, Alberic arrives (ch. 5) at the darker arguments that he wishes to make. His point of departure is Paul's first letter to the Corinthians: "[W]hy is it that the Apostle says, HE WHO EATS AND DRINKS UN- WORTHILY, EATS AND DRINKS JUDGMENT UPON HIMSELF? (I Cor. 11: 29) For either no one eats unworthily, or, eating unworthily, he re- mains in Christ. But if, eating unworthily, he remains in Christ, then he eats not to judgment, but to life." (ll. 108–13) This was a troubling issue in the eleventh century; Guitmund, for example, had been driven to the conclusion that he who eats unworthily "eats corporeally, but does not eat spiritually, not with such feeling, not with such character, not with such charity that he eats worthily" [manducat corporaliter, sed non manducat spiritualiter, non eo sensu, non eis moribus, non ea charitate, ut digne manducet].[28] In Alberic's hands, however, the rhet- oric is considerably more pointed. "Well then, are heretics to come running? Are murderers to come running? Are criminals of every kind to come running? Are they to eat the flesh of Christ, that they may re- main in Christ, and Christ in them?" (ll. 120–22) Alberic does not name Berengar here, but his image of heretics taking the Eucharist was surely intended to call him to mind.

"And so [ch. 6] we must determine what the saying means: HE WHO EATS MY FLESH AND DRINKS MY BLOOD, REMAINS IN ME, AND I IN HIM." (ll. 134–36) Alberic's answer is to distinguish different modes of receiving the Eucharist: "For some eat with lips and with heart; others with heart and not with lips; others with lips and not with heart. The apostles ate with lips and with heart, that is, with the inner and outer man, and the rest of the faithful after them, those faithful who were

---

28. *PL* 149: 1492B.

and are and are to be, so ate, eat, and will eat." (ll. 136–40) Working out
the implications of these three possibilities, indeed, will carry Alberic
to the midpoint of his exposition. Alberic begins by quoting Matthew
on the Last Supper, moving immediately to Jerome's exposition of the
passage that revived the distinction made at the beginning of the treatise between figure and truth; Alberic then emphasizes that point by
quoting Augustine in a passage of his own that concludes by invoking
I Cor. 11:39. "Therefore it can be clearly understood in these words that
the sacrament of the church is not a figure, not a promise, not a signifying; it is the truth." (ll. 166–68)

It is not the promise Alberic seizes on, however, but the warning.
"But we must ponder how he says, FOR HE THAT EATS AND DRINKS
UNWORTHILY, EATS AND DRINKS JUDGMENT UPON HIMSELF. For
earlier he had said, *One who does not remain in Christ, and in whom
Christ does not remain,—have no doubt—does not eat his flesh, nor drink
his blood, and even eats and drinks the sacrament of this mighty thing as a
judgment upon himself.*" (ll. 168–73) And (ch. 7) in a passage echoing the
earlier image of heretics and murderers running to take the Eucharist,
he quotes John Chrysostom's exposition of the same passage of
Matthew that focused on the idea of Judas at the Last Supper, faith-
lessly drinking the blood of Christ whom he had already betrayed.
Quotations from Augustine, Ambrose, and Pascasius then turn the
discussion back to the miracle of the Eucharist and the power of
Christ's words of consecration. An extended discussion (chs. 8–10)
drawing on Gregory the Great and Augustine develops the theme of
consuming the Eucharist spiritually, with the lips of the heart as well
as the lips of the body. He concludes: "This we must ponder deeply, as
the blessed Augustine says, that we should not eat the flesh and blood
of Christ only in a sacrament: for in this he indicates that the true flesh
and blood of Christ is in this sacrament, and he shows that one should
not receive it only with the bodily lips." (ll. 354–58)

It might seem that, although asserting that Berengar was wrong, Alberic has done little up to this point to refute him. In fact, he has
shifted the discussion in two ways: explicitly, by opposing the reality
of the Eucharist, not to the physical bread, but to a variety of Jewish
rituals—blood on the doorposts when the angel of God passed over,
manna in the desert, and the lamb of the Passover at the Last Supper;
and, implicitly, by contrasting the proper, spiritual attitude toward the

Eucharist with heresy, murder, and even Judas. Now, roughly halfway through the treatise (ch. 11), Alberic reopens his discussion with the paraphrase of Cicero's *Topica:* "Perchance these words of Augustine would suffice; but according to Cicero it is better for *some remnants* to be left over, *than* for us *to allow* anyone *to go away from here unfilled.*" (ll. 359–61) What follows, however, is not just more of the same. It is faster paced, as the work done in the first part of the treatise makes it possible for Alberic to invoke themes in a few phrases and to direct them more specifically against Berengar's ideas.

The second part begins, as we have already seen, with the reference to the two Gregories—the current pope who must judge Berengar's case, and his great predecessor, whose authority is invoked in a highly colored passage that concludes by describing how the heavens open and choirs of angels are present when the priest completes the consecration of Christ's flesh and blood. The words of consecration are then linked by a passage from Ambrose (partially paraphrased, as Alberic accelerates the pace of his discourse) to the miracles of the Old Testament and the words of creation, which Alberic claims as decisive proof. ("Observe the recourse, observe the proof, observe the argument, observe the syllogism—all elements that are quite unassailable.") (ll. 421–22).

In this passage alone, Alberic brings in technical and quasi-technical terms of logic, but not in relation to an argument that he has framed. It is instead his comment upon the logic of Ambrose's words: the recourse ("refugium") is the fallback or escape-hatch argument at the end (ll. 419–21), the testimony of Christ himself that we receive his body and blood; the proof ("probatio") which precedes (ll. 394–410) is the demonstration that the word was a heavenly word; the argument ("argumentum") is Ambrose's inference (ll. 410–19) on the great effectiveness of the heavenly word; and the syllogism or quasi-syllogism ("syllogismus") is found in the sentence (ll. 392–94) "If the heavenly word produced its effect upon an earthly spring, if it produced its effect upon other things, does it not produce its effect upon heavenly sacraments?"

The next paragraph (ch. 12) relies on Remigius (really Haimo of Auxerre)[29] to reassert that the sacrament was truth, not a figure, and

---

29. For the correct attribution, see Iogna-Prat, "L'oeuvre d'Haymon d'Auxerre," pp. 157–79.

then to attest the unity of Christ's body. The two following paragraphs are perhaps the most complicated in the treatise, as Alberic first attacks doubters, admits ambiguity in the patristic tradition, then attacks again. First (ch. 13) he quotes Leo the Great: *You ought* (Leo said) *to share in the holy table in such a way that you have no doubt at all regarding the verity of Christ's body and blood. For that is taken in by the lips which is believed by faith; and it is vain for those to respond "Amen" who are disputing against what they receive.* (ll. 465–69) Following this passage with a similar one from Ambrose, Alberic then points, by implication, directly at Berengar: "O wretched the man and unfortunate every way, who receiving Christ's body doubts, who eating is of two minds, and who unbelievingly disputes that which he receives; one who says with his tongue, 'It is true,' and with his heart, 'How can that be so?'" (ll. 473–76) The last phrase would have reminded readers of Berengar's offer in 1054 and again in the autumn of 1078 to swear that the bread and wine became the "verum corpus Christi"; and Alberic continues by comparing such an attitude to those disciples who were scandalized by Christ's teaching.

Moving rapidly, Alberic then develops the theme of belief in a series of brief passages from Augustine that seem to say belief is enough even without consuming the consecrated bread: *Why do you ready your teeth and your belly? Believe and you have eaten; To believe in him is to eat the bread of life.* (ll. 487–88) *You will not eat this body which you see; nor drink that blood which they who shall crucify me will shed.* (ll. 492–93) At first glance it is hard to see why these passages are here, since they appear to undercut Alberic's argument rather than support it. But they (and, indeed, the passage from Leo) were cited by Berengar himself in the third book of his *Rescriptum*,[30] and even if that work did not circulate we may reasonably suppose that Berengar was invoking them in support of his own views. Rather than enter a debate, Alberic concedes the ambiguity only to assert that it does not matter.

> But if perchance this present chapter could not be reconciled with the former one according to our understanding, is it not rather this one that should be rejected instead of the other? For just as the former one, which is confirmed by many statements of the holy Fathers, is the more to be

---

30. *Rescriptum*, book 3.197–201, 30–31; the passage from Leo, evidently a favorite of Berengar's, is cited multiple times: 3.410–11, 416, 448, 459–60.

embraced, so also that which is in disagreement with them—if perchance there is any disagreement—is not to be retained. Far be it from us to believe that the blessed Augustine's position was different from that of the holy Fathers who are cited in this little treatise. For indeed even the Evangelists themselves, though they said the same things, have nevertheless been supposed by some to have said things that conflicted. (ll. 494–502)

And he closes the subject. "But enough on this subject for now." (l. 502)

The next passage (ch. 14) marks a profound shift in the libellus. The tone hardens, as Alberic takes off the gloves. The shift is seen here in four different respects. First, Alberic, who has just said at the end of the preceding chapter that there is a discrepancy between what Augustine says in one passage and the words of the other Fathers (a discrepancy that Alberic has said he will explain later), now says repressively, "Therefore it is established by the authority of so many holy Fathers, both that the bread is changed into flesh and the wine changed into blood." Second, he then changes the subject. After he has wrenched attention away from the fascinating question of the potential disagreement among the Fathers, the new topic is the *quomodo?*—the how?—of the change that takes place in the Eucharist, a topic that introduces the key term *substantia* for the first time in the libellus, in the words: "mutatur enim substantia in substantiam." In the third place, Alberic changes tactics, dramatically shifting from, essentially, an argument based solely on patristic *sententiae*—the method promised in the prologue (ch. 1) and followed faithfully down to this point—to an argument constructed by Alberic himself. The new method is announced in the sentence, "nunc autem de ipsa mutatione aliquid dicamus"; Alberic, who before has emphasized hearing the words of the Fathers with markers like *audiamus* (chs. 2, 12) and *audi* (chs. 4 [bis], 7, and 8), now speaks himself *(dicamus)* and later in the chapter does so again *(introducamus)*. The new method is also visible in the very look of the page of our text: here is a chapter with hardly any words quoted from the Fathers; the exceptions are a brief phrase from Ambrose (in this way the unusually tight structure of the treatise is seen, as the whole Ambrosian passage has already been given and discussed earlier, in ch. 4) and a Psalm verse. The rest is Alberic's.

The passage, dealing with the change of substance into substance in regard to *res* and *species,* already quoted, is deceptive, for it seems to invoke the methods of logical analysis without really doing so, relying instead on the speed and power of the language rather than on demonstration.

> Now then, let us say something about the change itself. For substance is changed into substance either in seeming [*species*] and in reality [*res*], or in seeming and not in reality, or in reality and not in seeming. It is changed in seeming and in reality, to be sure, as earth is [changed] into mankind and the other animate creatures; similarly also water into salt, and ice into crystal; and you will be able to find many examples of this kind. Moreover, change takes place in seeming and not in reality, as the very angel of Satan transforms himself into an angel of light; and often many things are changed by craftsmen in such a way that, although they have not lost their own nature, yet they are believed to be something else altogether. Further, substance changes in reality and not in seeming as wine changes into vinegar; for even if it were to be another thing, nevertheless the seeming cannot easily be distinguished except by smelling or tasting; yet the thing is so far removed from it that the one has a warm nature and the other a cold. Therefore, of these three changes, which do the bread and the wine, when transformed in the sacrifice, undergo? Why, it is the one that we said takes place in seeming and in reality. For if there were not a horror of blood, as the blessed Ambrose said, the true form of flesh and blood would be obvious. (ll. 504–20)

Unlike the dialectical terms used regarding a patristic argument at the conclusion of chapter 11, the dialectical terms here are Alberic's own application of traditional terminology found in the Aristotelian/Ciceronian/Boethian material with which he was familiar.[31] The absence of true proof and logical rigor is, however, in keeping with the tenor of, especially, the quotations from Gregory the Great in chapters 7 and 17: the nature of the Eucharist is a *mysterium*. Asserting without proof that the transformation of the bread and the wine is one of both reality and appearance, he implicitly acknowledges the obvious question raised in chapter 4—Why do we not perceive the changed appearance?—and answers it with Ambrose's phrase about the horror of blood from the same chapter. Furthermore, the present chapter is privileged in a fourth way: At this point Alberic refers in passing to Berengar's actual position ("lest anyone should perhaps suppose that after this change the substance of the bread and the wine still remained");

---

31. See pp. 65–68.

the readers or hearers would certainly have recognized this covert reference to the adversary. Alberic replies to this position by bringing in "other changes that have been done as proof of divine power" (ll. 522–23), by which he means the usual catalog of divine miracles— Lot's wife, Moses' rod, rivers of blood, the marriage feast at Cana.

Then (ch. 15), without further discussion, he sets the subject aside as settled. "Therefore, having so explained these matters, let us look at the passage in the Gospels." (l. 539) The passage he takes up is, again, John 6:53 ("Unless one eats my flesh and drinks my blood, he shall not have life in him") and John 6:60 ("This saying is harsh, and who can comply with it?"). By quoting Augustine in a passage ringing with the adverbs *spiritualiter, carnaliter*—evocative of the *substantialiter* that Berengar would be made to swear—Alberic arrives at the passage in which he imagines Christ warning us not to be too literal in our understanding:

> Do not imagine that you devour my flesh in the manner of wild animals or drink my blood with the cruelty of a beast. Do not suppose this. There is another thing that I say: THE WORDS THAT I HAVE SPOKEN TO YOU ARE SPIRIT AND LIFE. Understand them spiritually, if you wish to have life. For I have commended a sacrament to you. . . . What is this "sacrament"? Why, that which now is both visibly carried out in the holy Church and invisibly understood. Visibly, precisely because we see both the priests and the altar, and the bread and wine from which it is made. But invisibly, because we can see neither how it is changed nor by whom it is changed. NONE HAS EVER SEEN GOD. (ll. 587–99)

The paragraph as a whole combines all the main themes of the treatise: the need for spiritual understanding, the opposition between visible and invisible truths, the power of God's words of consecration.

Moving now toward the end, Alberic (ch. 16) reasserts his conclusion: "[I]t is clear that Christ's flesh would never be eaten corporeally, unless the substance of the bread were changed into it spiritually, that is, by the working of the Spirit." (ll. 606–8) The key adverbs continue. Rather than rush on, however, he unexpectedly concedes that some may still be unpersuaded. For them, he quotes Jerome on the twofold fashion in which the body and blood of Christ must be understood, remarking of this quotation: "Observe this as well, how he made a distinction between that flesh of Christ which is eaten, and that which hung on the cross. For such a statement is as if he were to say, 'This one is eaten, that one is not eaten.' That is, that one is eaten which is spiritual and divine, that is, which is daily sacrificed, which is spiritually consecrated, which by divine blessing is changed into Christ's true flesh." (ll. 616–21) Even after citing Ambrose, Gregory, Remigius/ Haimo, and John Chrysostom on the unity of Christ's body, Alberic cannot but concede (ch. 17, returning to the question banished from the discussion in ch. 13) that Jerome and Augustine "seem to utter something that sounds different." (ll. 642–43) We must, he concludes, simply accept the limits of our understanding.

> What then shall we say? Surely there could not be discord, could there, among those who are taught by one Spirit? For those say that you drink it; these say, "You do not drink it." Therefore you drink it, and you do not drink it. Both of these are true. For that one is drunk through this one, which would never be drunk corporeally according to itself. This is changed into that; that is drunk in this; and inasmuch as both are the same, it cannot fail to be true that he himself is drunk. (ll. 643–48)

The decisive word comes, significantly, from Gregory the Great's formulation of the "mystery of the sacred oblation," and the exposition concludes with a *catena* whose theme is a warning against trying to understand too much:

> Yet how it is changed, how he, living, is sacrificed, how he is eaten in this, do not ask, if you wish to avoid error.[32] Recall what that famous John said, than whom no greater has arisen among the sons of women: BEHOLD (he said), THERE COMES AFTER ME ONE THE FASTENING OF WHOSE SANDALS I AM NOT WORTHY TO LOOSEN.[33] And the Apostle: O THE DEPTH OF THE RICHES OF WISDOM AND KNOWLEDGE OF GOD; HOW UNSEARCHABLE ARE HIS JUDGMENTS, AND UNTRACEABLE ARE HIS WAYS. And the Psalmist: YOUR JUDGMENTS ARE A GREAT DEEP. For this cause also it was said by Moses: IF ANYTHING REMAINS, LET IT BE BURNED IN THE FIRE. For this indeed is CHANGE WROUGHT BY THE RIGHT HAND OF THE ONE ON HIGH. For he is changed as he will, he is sacrificed as he will, he is eaten and drunk as he will. But enough on this subject for this time. (ll. 654–66)

---

32. There is a play upon the words *interrogare* = (virtually) *errare*.

33. The underlying thought is that the humble worshiper is no more worthy to untie the knotty problems of the *how* of the Eucharist than John the Baptist was worthy to untie the knots of Christ's sandals. The problems of the *how* are only resolved *(solvuntur)* by Gregory's words acknowledging the mystery, and the language of John the Baptist *(solvere)* echoes them.

The first three quotations of the *catena* are images of humility—John the Baptist in comparison with Christ, Paul, and then the Psalms on the impossibility of knowing God's judgments. The passage from Exodus is at once a reference to the Passover feast—the figure for the Eucharist—and also a warning to let loose any remaining doubts. Again, the debate itself on the *Cena* is indirectly cast in terms of sacrifice and spiritual food. The last quotation, from Psalms, and Alberic's own conclusion (an answer to the *quomodo* question raised in ch. 14) stand as reminders of God's power.

The last section—the *brevis quasi epilogus* (ch. 18)—quickly reviews the main themes of the treatise. Now, drawing upon his mastery of Latin prose, Alberic confidently dismisses difficulties by using passages from John 6—quoting that passage directly from the gospel for the first time—punctuating the quotations with the phrase *vel corde, vel ore et corde* almost as a kind of refrain.

> VERILY, VERILY, I SAY UNTO YOU, UNLESS YOU SHALL EAT THE FLESH OF THE SON OF MAN, AND DRINK HIS BLOOD, YOU WILL NOT HAVE LIFE IN YOU (John 6:53), that is, either with your heart, or with your lips and your heart. FOR MY FLESH IS TRULY FOOD, AND MY BLOOD IS TRULY DRINK (John 6:55), since it makes immortal and incorruptible those who take it, either with their hearts, or with their lips and their hearts. HE WHO EATS MY FLESH, AND DRINKS MY BLOOD HAS ETERNAL LIFE, that is, either with heart, or with lips and heart. AS THE LIVING FATHER SENT ME, I ALSO LIVE BECAUSE OF THE FATHER; AND HE WHO EATS ME ALSO LIVES BECAUSE OF ME, that is, either with heart, or with lips and heart. It is therefore good to eat with the heart, but better with lips and heart. For he who eats and drinks with the lips alone, eats and drinks judgment upon himself. Let us therefore, being mindful of the words of the blessed Pope Leo, "so partake of the sacred table that we have no doubt at all of the truth of Christ's body and blood." (ll. 669–83)

This passage is in many ways typical of Alberic's strategy throughout his libellus, for he asserts the reality of the transformation, and its importance in the spiritual life of the believers who partake of the Eucharist, without permitting himself to be drawn into questions about the persistence of bread and wine that had enmeshed both Berengar and Berengar's opponents. Having earlier rejected the idea of asking *quomodo est?*, Alberic is not about to be drawn into this discussion himself. The passage then ends with the paraphrase of Leo I: a significant choice if we remember that it was another Leo who had both recalled the young Hildebrand to papal service and propelled the papacy to the forefront of the church reform movement. Again we are led to the conclusion that, although the treatise was addressed to Desiderius, its author also had in mind another eventual reader whose actions would directly affect Berengar's fate.

Conclusion

It is easy to see why this treatise has gotten little attention from students of the Eucharistic Controversy. Its approach to the issues is very unlike that of other contributions. To begin with, Alberic takes as his point of departure not the concept of a sacrament as a sign but Isidore's definition of a sacrament as that which occurs *cum aliqua celebratione res ita fit, ut aliquid significare intelligatur;* Alberic thus sets to one side the whole discussion of signs that has led many modern scholars to take an interest in the Eucharistic Controversy. Alberic also turned decisively against the focus on the material bread and wine that is so apparent in other treatises. For Berengar, the appearance of the bread and wine is a key to understanding what occurs during the ceremony; Guitmund and Lanfranc, answering Berengar, are just as adamant that appearances can be deceiving. But for Alberic, the question of matter and appearances is simply secondary. Alberic's conception of substance is far less precise and philosophical than Berengar's or Guitmund's, but he does a much better job than they do of insisting on the spiritual component of the Eucharist and of placing the bread and wine in the context of an entire ceremony and the ceremony in the context of a Christian life and daily practice. Asking how, or by what, the bread and wine are transformed into the body and blood of Christ misses the point. What matters is not what one sees; it is what one understands. Consuming the bread and wine without belief or faith is meaningless, or worse.

Although disappointing to historians of theology, Alberic's approach certainly would have found resonance with the daily experience of many of the priests and monks in Alberic's intended audience—a resonance that may have contributed to its effectiveness as a piece of controversial writing. Before taking up this question, however, we must return to probe more carefully the historical situation that led Alberic to intervene so strongly in this question.

FOUR

Berengar of Tours
and the Roman Councils
of 1078 and 1079

The Sources

The final phase of the Eucharistic Controversy may be taken to run from Berengar's arrival in Rome at some time in 1078 to the Lenten council of early February 1079.[1] Apart from the uncertainty about the date of Berengar's arrival in Rome, the chronological framework in which he, Alberic, and Desiderius worked is reasonably clear: it took two councils, at All Saints and in Lent, before the case of Berengar of Tours was finally resolved. But for understanding the events that led to the Lenten council, five sources have provided nearly all we know:

1. An apologia by Berengar known as the *Iuramentum*, published by Martène and Durand and reedited by Huygens, that gives his version of how he came to take his oath. This is a difficult text to work with, in part because Berengar does not recount his events chronologically but rather inserts telling anecdotes as asides. There are also the usual difficulties of how well Berengar understood the motives of other actors in the events he describes.[2]

---

1. The papal safe-conduct under which Berengar traveled is given by Huygens, "Bérenger, Lanfranc, Bernold," now in *Serta Mediaevalia*, p. 257 n. to l. 31, with references to the historiography. The text is also given by Cowdrey, *Epistolae Vagantes*, no. 73, p. 157. Cowdrey accepts Erdmann's argument that it was drafted by Berengar in 1079; "Gregor VII.," pp. 54–55, but see the remarks of Capitani, "Rapporti," pp. 130–37.
2. See above, pp. 18–19.

2. A text preserved in the late twelfth-century Monte Cassino manuscript 276 and published in the 1930s by the late M. Matronola.[3] After initial sections extensively bolstered by patristic quotations and setting forth what we know was Berengar's position on the Eucharist, the writer continues by summarizing the response of his opponents Alberic and Bonifiglio. The principal crux of this text has been whether it was written by Berengar himself or one of his supporters. Being written in the first person, it presents itself as the voice of Berengar, and Matronola believed that he was the author; this attribution has not won universal acceptance,[4] but there is no strong reason for doubting the text's authenticity. The style is consistent with other writings of Berengar. If this is not an authentic Berengarian text it is a deliberate forgery, and it is difficult to conceive what motives a forger could have had for composing a plausible defense of Berengar's views.

3. A fragment, also by Berengar, first published by Mabillon and recently rediscovered in Subiaco MS LXII and reedited by Rudolf Maurer,[5] in which Berengar attacks Alberic. Specifically, Berengar charges that Alberic once had supported Berengar's own position against using the word *substantialiter* in discussing the conversion of the bread and wine of the Eucharist, but then threw his weight behind Berengar's opponents.

4. The official account of the Lenten synod in the Register of Gregory VII, especially VI.17a.[6] This text poses no problems of authenticity, but it provides relatively few details. Nor does the register mention the council of All Saints 1078, at which Berengar made his first formal defense of his views. The late addition to Lanfranc's *De corpore et san-*

---

3. *Un testo inedito di Berengario di Tours e il Concilio Romano del 1079* [*Orbis Romanus* 6] (Milan, 1936).

4. The authenticity of this text as a work of Berengar himself was criticized by J. Geiselmann, "Ein neuentdecktes Werk von Berengar von Tours über das Abendmahl?" *Theologische Quartalschrift* 118 (1937): 1–31, 133–72, and M. Cappuyns, review of Matronola, *Bulletin de Théologie Ancienne et Médiévale* 3 (1937–1940): 241–42 nn. 552–53; their doubts are accepted by Cowdrey, *Desiderius*, p. 92 n. 159. The attribution to Berengar has been supported by Lentini, "Alberico . . . nel quadro della Riforma Gregoriana," and, cautiously, by Meyvaert, "Bérenger . . . contre Albéric du Mont-Cassin," who also provides a survey of the previous discussion. Capitani, "Rapporti," p. 127 n. 57, accepts the authenticity of the Monte Cassino text.

5. "Berengarii ut videtur"; see also the discussion of this text by Meyvaert, "Bérenger contre Albéric."

6. Cited above, p. 30, n. 86.

guine domini, and the report of the council given in the chronicle of
Hugh of Flavigny both derive from the account in the papal register.[7]

5. The treatise *De veritate corporis et sanguinis domini,* an eyewitness
account of Berengar's condemnation written by Bernold, canon of
Constance and later monk of St. Blasien, who became a convinced supporter of Gregory VII and the papal party after the bishop of Constance proved unwilling to pursue reforms on his own. Even apart from
the information it contains, his account is of interest because it makes
clear that for him, and probably for many other supporters of the Gregorian movement, the crucial point about the Eucharistic Controversy
was that the decision was rendered by the papal court rather than some
other body. Bernold carefully lists the papal condemnations of Berengar, from Leo IX to 1079, concluding by comparing the council that
condemned Berengar with early church councils that likewise had condemned heresies.[8] Any doubts about the reasons for Bernold's interest
are removed by consulting his other works. The *Micrologus de ecclesias-
ticis observationibus* "is a polemic in favor of the general adoption of the
Romana consuetudo in liturgical matters, since, thanks to the diligent
research of Gregory VII, the Roman liturgy conformed to 'all the apostolic traditions.'"[9] Telling in a different way is the detailed account of
the Lent 1079 council in Bernold's *Chronicon,* where the condemnation
of Berengar is passed over in one sentence.[10]

Bernold's treatment of Berengar also serves to remind us that the
eucharistic issue was just one of many confronting the pope and his
advisers in 1078–1079. In the summer of 1078, war broke out between
Henry IV and Rudolf of Swabia, the pretender to the royal title who
had substantial support in the papal party. The resulting crisis engaged
the attention of the councils where Berengar's case was discussed, and
the individuals who played key roles in the theological discussions were

7. The addition to Lanfranc is edited in Huygens, "Bérenger, Lanfranc et Bernold;" now in *Serta Mediaevalia* pp. 239–46; the relevant passage from Hugh of Flavigny may be found at *PL* 154: 316.

8. *Serta Mediaevalia,* pp. 252–53.

9. Robinson, *Authority and Resistance,* p. 165; the *Micrologus* was published by S. Bäumer, "Der Micrologus ein Werk Bernolds von Konstanz," *Neues Archiv der Gesellschaft für ältere deutsche Geschichte* 18 (1893): 431–46.

10. Of Berengar Bernold says only: "Beringarius Turonensis heresim suam illic abiuravit, catholicam fidem professus." *MGH SS* 5: 435.

often those with political roles as well.[11] Indeed, most of the participants other than Berengar may have regarded his case as distinctly secondary in importance.

This assessment may have been shared at Monte Cassino.[12] The
collaboration between monastery and papacy, which led Klewitz to describe Monte Cassino as "the spiritual armory of the reform papacy,"[13]
went back to the 1050s. Abbot Frederick of Lorraine was made a
cardinal-priest by Victor II and elected pope as Stephen IX in 1057;
Desiderius's career was to follow the same path. But these are not the
only ties that go back to the 1050s and 1060s. Peter Damian in particular had enjoyed a special relationship with the monastery, to the extent that Borino observed that he was "like a second abbot to Monte
Cassino."[14] Damian's approach to *ars dictaminis* survived at Monte
Cassino, perhaps through Alberic himself. Alberic himself certainly
was close to Damian, having apparently studied with him and received
letters from him in the 1060s; Alberic's *Breviarium de Dictamine* includes excerpts from Damian's writings.

Although Hildebrand himself had studied under Lawrence of
Amalfi,[15] Cowdrey believes that the early years of Gregory VII's pontificate marked a cooling in papal relations with Monte Cassino, principally over papal relations with southern Italy.[16] But the extent of the
break should not be overstated. Desiderius and Monte Cassino played
a key role in the implementation of reform in southern Italy,[17] Monte

---

11. This period of the Investiture Contest has been studied in detail by Jörgen Vogel, *Gregor VII.
und Heinrich IV. nach Canossa* [Arbeiten zur Frühmittelalterforschung, 9] (Berlin/New York,
1983).

12. A complete review of the evidence is in Cowdrey, *Age of Abbot Desiderius*, pp. 46–106; see also
his remarks in *Pope Gregory VII*, pp. 667–68.

13. *Reformpapsttum und Kardinalkolleg* (Darmstadt, 1957), p. 103, quoted by I. S. Robinson, *The Papacy 1073–1198* (Cambridge, 1990), p. 213.

14. "Per la storia della riforma della Chiesa nel secolo XI," *Archivio della società romana di storia patria* 38 (1915): 60, quoted by Robinson, *Authority and Resistance*, pp. 28–29. For an overview of
Damian's contacts with Monte Cassino, see the recent article by J. Howe, "Peter Damian and
Monte Cassino," *Revue Bénédictine* 107 (1997): 330–51. The dossier in our Aberdeen manuscript
contains an excerpt from Peter Damian.

15. Robinson, *Authority and Resistance*, p. 31. See also the sketch of Lawrence's life in the edition by
F. Newton, *Laurentius Monachus Casinensis Archiepiscopus Amalfitanus Opera*, MGH, *Quellen zur
Geistesgeschichte des Mittelalters*, vol. 7 (Weimar, 1973). All modern studies of Lawrence rest upon
the fundamental article of W. Holtzmann, "Laurentius von Amalfi, ein Lehrer Hildebrands,"
Studi Gregoriani 1 (1947): 207–37.

16. *Age of Desiderius*, p. 66.

17. Nicola Cilento, "La riforma gregoriana, Bisanzio e l'Italia meridionale," *Studi gregoriani* 13
(1989): 353–72.

Cassino's dependent house of Santa Maria in Pallara continued to operate like a "branch of the papal archive," with the result that the monastery's literary style can be noticed in some of Gregory VII's letters,[18] and by the mid-1070s relations appear to be back to normal. Desiderius's *Dialogi* from these years contains one of the earliest retellings of a miracle in the presence of Hildebrand in the 1050s.[19] The activities of Alberic and Desiderius toward Berengar belonged, therefore, to a longstanding pattern of cooperation with the reform.

The list of sources also makes apparent the problem scholars have faced: too much of our information comes from Berengar, and it comes in isolated bits and pieces rather than as a coherent narrative. It is this scarcity of evidence that made the *Chronicle*'s account of Alberic's role, confirmed as it is by the Subiaco fragment, such an appealing basis for speculation. Possessing Alberic's text, however, does more than permit us to correct errors about his own role. As the only direct evidence of what actually was said against Berengar in 1078–1079, it is a valuable addition to our knowledge of the whole period.

The Council of All Saints, 1078

The least documented aspect of this period concerns the council of All Saints 1078.[20] Berengar is repeatedly explicit about the date, so this gathering must be distinguished from the council that convened in Rome on 19 November. The business transacted in the 19 November synod does, however, indicate some of the other concerns that pressed on the papal court in autumn 1078. According to the papal register (VI.5b), the synod excommunicated the emperor of Constantinople, received legates from Henry and Rudolf, and enacted a variety of decrees touching the condition of the church; among these decrees were warnings to the German kings against seizing church property, the ex-

---

18. See Robinson's comments, *Authority and Resistance*, pp. 29–30.
19. Robinson, "Friendship network," p. 6.
20. The status of this gathering has occasioned some discussion because Bernold in *De veritate corporis* states that Berengar appeared before two "general synods" presided over by Gregory VII. *Serta Mediaevalia*, p. 251 ll. 99–102. Matronola, p. 23 n. 1, doubts that the All Saints gathering can correctly be termed a "general council," but that problem need not concern us here. See also the bibliography cited by Vogel, *Gregor VII. und Heinrich IV.*, p. 126. We shall see that it is also possible that Bernold's statement referred to the 19 November council. For a useful overview of how Gregory VII's councils functioned and the documentation they produced, see Robert Somerville, "The Councils of Gregory VII," *Studi gregoriani* 13 (1989): 33–53.

communication of the archbishop of Narbonne and the count of St. Gilles, protection for Monte Cassino from the Normans, and ordinances touching a number of matters of church discipline.

Virtually all our information about the All Saints council comes from Berengar's own account in his apologia. Meeting in the Lateran, it was attended by bishops, abbots, clergy, and monks from all over. According to Berengar, Gregory suggested the following oath as a statement with which everyone could agree:

> I profess that the bread on the altar after consecration is the true body of Christ, which was born from the Virgin, which suffered on the cross, which sits at the right hand of the Father, and that the wine on the altar, after it is consecrated, is the true blood which flowed from the side of Christ, and just as I pronounce with my lips so I affirm that I hold in my heart. So help me God, and these holy things.

> ———

> [Profiteor panem altaris post consecrationem esse verum corpus Christi, quod natum est de Virgine, quod passum est in cruce, quod sedet ad dexteram Patris, et vinum altaris, postquam consecratum est, esse verum sanguinem qui manavit de latere Christi, et sicut ore pronuntio, ita me in corde habere confirmo. Sic me adiuvet deus, et haec sacra.][21]

The pope, Berengar says, believed that this oath would be acceptable to everyone;[22] indeed, it sidestepped the difficult issue of whether the substance of the bread survived the consecration. In favor of this oath, moreover, Gregory noted the examples of Augustine and Peter Damian, and brought books that dealt with the Eucharist by Augustine, Jerome, and Ambrose. The pope's suggestion won support from many there, Berengar says, among whom he named specifically Bishops John of Porto, Bonizo of Sutri, and Ambrose of Terracina, Cardinal-Archbishop Atto of Milan, Cardinal Deusdedit, the papal chancellor Peter, and a handful of lesser figures. But others in attendance, notably Bishops Ulrich of Padua and Landulf of Pisa, prevailed with the suggestion that the matter be deferred to the council that would meet the following Lent.

---

21. *Serta Mediaevalia*, p. 256 ll. 4–9; see also Cowdrey's analysis, *Pope Gregory VII*, pp. 497–98.

22. Montclos believes that the oath was written by Berengar, and that the statement about its acceptability expresses Berengar's views rather than those of Gregory VII, p. 222; he himself notices, however, that the oath borrows much of the language of Berengar's opponent Lanfranc.

The *Iuramentum* suggests that Gregory's strategy was to smother debate by finding an innocuous formula every word of which was well supported by authority. Had he succeeded, he would at once have asserted papal control of this kind of issue and laid to rest a possible source of division within the church. In other issues, as Cowdrey observed, Gregory was prepared to adopt "a conciliatory approach to liturgical and sacramental matters," and his desire for *concordia* "may help explain his patient and conciliatory dealings with Berengar";[23] in this, he observes, Gregory was acting "toward Berengar much as he did in other liturgical and sacramental matters: not by trying to establish and impose a single ruling but by exploring which varieties of usage were and were not acceptable in the light of traditional authorities."[24] In this regard, it may be significant that all the men Berengar mentions as having supported the pope were Gregory's intimates and participants in the reform movement.[25] But the council's decision to defer judgment was not necessarily a serious defeat for the pope. Lively discussion was common in his councils, with debate among bishops rather than papal decree the general rule.[26]

Potentially more threatening to Gregory than the council's specific action was the confluence of forces that had come together in rejecting the compromise he proposed. The background of the two bishops who took the lead against Berengar in November indicates the danger that the pope's other supporters may have seen. Ulrich seems essentially to have been more a politician than a theologian, and not a very reputable one.[27] He first appears in surviving records as bishop in 1064; soon afterward Mainardus, cardinal bishop of Silva Candida, wrote Henry IV warning him that the bishop of Padua was dissipating the goods of his church.[28] By the late 1070s, however, Ulrich had thrown

---

23. "The Papacy and the Berengarian Controversy," p. 132.

24. *Pope Gregory VII*, p. 500.

25. For John of Porto, see Klewitz, *Reformpapsttum*, pp. 35–36, where he notes that John was described as "intimus . . . secretis Hildebrandi" by Beno, *Gesta Romane Ecclesiae contra Hildebrandum MGH*, Libelli de Lite 2: 371. Deusdedit was the leading canonist of the papal court; Cowdrey, *Age of Desiderius*, pp. 99–102 and bibliography there. Ambrose of Terracina was a former monk of Monte Cassino; Cowdrey, *Age of Desiderius*, pp. 65, 92.

26. Robinson, *Papacy*, p. 124; Somerville, "Councils," pp. 52–53.

27. The available information on Ulrich has been collected by G. B. Borino, "Odelrico vescovo di Padova (1064–80). Legato di Gregorio VII in Germania (1079)" (*Miscellanea in onore di Roberto Cessi*, vol. 1) [Storia e letteratura: 71] (Rome, 1958), pp. 63–79.

28. The letter is included in Erdmann, *Briefsammlung*, p. 67.

his lot in with the emperor. Bonizo of Sutri described Ulrich as "a more than eloquent man and one more than loyal to King Henry" [vir valde eloquentissimus et Heinrico regi satis fidelissimus],[29] and one can only suspect that his lively interest in the Eucharist reflects his service to his master. Borino suggested that Gregory may have been so impressed with Ulrich's service against Berengar that he named him as legate to Germany in 1079, but it is more likely that his selection was an effort to avoid confrontation with Henry IV in dealing with Germany. It was, in any case, an unhappy choice: Ulrich rapidly betrayed his oath to the pope, and Gregory's enemies seized upon the appointment of one known "for all the vices" as another mark against him.[30] Ulrich died as he lived, apparently killed by one of his company in returning to Rome, still in the service of Henry IV.[31]

Yet if Ulrich was more thug than priest, Landulf of Pisa cannot be dismissed so easily. Little is known about him or his brief episcopate (1077–1079), but the few facts we have are suggestive.[32] Landulf was elected bishop in what Gregory VII described as a return to canonical procedures, apparently with the support of the pope and of Matilda of Canossa; during his reign, moreover, Matilda made a generous gift to the canons of Pisa, which is regarded as evidence of her favor toward Landulf.[33] Virtually his only other appearance in the historical record comes shortly after the November 1078 synod, when Gregory named him legate over Corsica.[34]

Landulf's attack on Berengar thus raises a number of questions that there is really no way of answering. Did he represent his own views only or those of Matilda of Canossa, a patron who certainly had opinions on religious issues?[35] Was the pope's gift of rights over Corsica

---

29. Cited by Vogel, *Gregor VII. und Heinrich IV.*, p. 143, who comments that "In der historischen Rückschau mußte Udalrich als Anhänger des salischen Königs gelten."

30. Wido de Ferrara, *De schismate Hildebrandi, Libelli de Lite*, 1: 558.

31. Cowdrey, *Gregory VII*, p. 195.

32. For a detailed discussion and references to older bibliography, see C. Violante, "Cronotasi dei vescovi e degli arcivescovi di Pisa dalle origini all'inizio del secolo XIII. Primo contributo ad una nuova 'Italia Sacra,'" in *Miscellanea Gilles Gérard Meersseman*, vol. 1 (Padua, 1970). Additional context is provided by Fabrizio Foggi, "Pisa e Enrico IV," *Bollettino storico Pisano* 57 (1988): 1–10.

33. On this, see also Matilde Tirelli Carli, "La donazione di Matilde di Canossa all'Episcopato pisano," *Boll. Storico Pisano* 46 (1977): 139–59.

34. *Reg*, VI.12, 30 Nov. 1078; C. Violante, "Le concessioni ponteficie alla Chiesa di Pisa riguardanti la Corsica alla fine del secolo XI," *Bulletino dell'Istituto Storico Italiano per il Medio Evo* 75 (1963): 43–56.

35. See the discussion of works produced with Matilda's patronage by Giampaolo Ropa, "Testimonianze di vita culturale nei monasteri matildici nei secoli xi–xii," *Studi Matildici. Atti e memorie*

intended to regain Landulf's support after the debates over the Eucharist a few weeks earlier? or, conversely, did Landulf take the occasion of the discussion of Berengar to demonstrate to the pope how troublesome he could be if he did not receive authority over Corsica? But such unsolvable problems do not obscure the main point: Berengar's case had given Henry's supporters an occasion to make common cause with those concerned with matters of the faith. This inference, moreover, is confirmed by the fact that, despite the condemnation of Berengar, when Henry's supporters announced the deposition of Gregory in 1080 they gave as one of their reasons the pope's supposed support of Berengar's heresy.[36]

As for the All Saints council itself, two details mentioned elsewhere by Berengar hint at what may have been left out of his account in the *Iuramentum*. In the first place, the discussion in November clearly extended beyond what Berengar admitted in his apologia. There was certainly some discussion of whether the word *substantialiter* should be included in Berengar's profession, because in the Monte Cassino text published by Matronola, Berengar or his supporter mentions that Alberic and Bonifiglio "reproached me that at the first synod in the Chapel of St. Lawrence I conceded that the bread was in substance and in reality changed into the body of Christ" [increpaverat me quod in prima sinedo in cappella sancti laurentii concesseram panem substantialiter fieri corpus cristi et realiter]. (ll. 210–13) Berengar does not deny this charge, but instead attempts to explain it away with the observation that there are visible and invisible substances.

Berengar also mentions in the *Iuramentum* that the All Saints council had decided that Berengar's faith should be put to the ordeal of hot iron.[37] Testing the faith by ordeal is reminiscent of a miracle worked in the presence of Hildebrand in the 1050s, when a prelate suspected of simony was unable to repeat a prayer.[38] The day before the test was to occur, however, as Berengar was preparing himself for the judgment by fasting and prayer, he received news that it had been put off. Since

---

del II convegno di studi matildici. Modena-Reggio E., 1–2–3 maggio 1970 (Modena, 1971), pp. 231–80; Silvia Cantelli, "Il commento al Cantico dei Cantici di Giovanni da Mantova," *Studi medievali* 3a ser., 26,1 (1985): 101–84.

36. The decree of deposition is given in *MGH, Const.* I, p. 118–20; p. 119 ll. 39–41 contains the passage on Berengar. See also Beno, *Gesta Romanae Ecclesiae I, MGH Libelli de Lite* I, p. 370.

37. *Serta Mediaevalia*, p. 267.

38. Robinson, "Friendship network," p. 7.

the council of 19 November would have been an appropriate occasion for the ordeal, this anecdote may explain why Bernold writes of that council having "conceded" a delay to Berengar.[39]

The news of the postponement of the ordeal was brought to Berengar by Desiderius, whom Berengar described as "then of the greatest authority in the palace" [summae tunc in palatio auctoritatis].[40] Over the winter Monte Cassino would move from a supporting role to a leading one in the drama.

Alberic and Berengar

What was at stake in the period between 1 November 1078 and the opening of the Lenten council of 11 February 1079 is indicated by a subsequent mission to Berengar consisting of Desiderius and another Cassinese monk, Petrus Neapolitanus.[41] This Petrus appears to be identical with the Petrus Neapolitanus who participated in the 1083 ordeal by water held in Santa Maria in Pallara to judge the dispute between Gregory VII and Henry IV;[42] he was thus an intimate of Desiderius and Gregorian circles generally. The abbot and the monk brought Berengar a message from Gregory VII that he should desist from public discussion and, especially, that he must cease claiming that the pope shared his views. Berengar, of course, paid no attention to the warning. But that it was given at all, and conveyed by such important messengers, suggests that the reform party was concerned that Gregory's enemies could use his tolerance of Berengar as a bridge to those such as Landulf of Pisa and the house of Canossa whose previous support of the reform movement had been critical.

This politicization of the theological dispute, and Monte Cassino's effort to protect Gregory from charges of being "soft on Berengarianism," form the background necessary to understanding Alberic's pivotal role in the winter of 1078–79. Skilled though he was in curial politics, Desiderius was not scholar enough to respond to Berengar

---

39. Bernold, *Chronicon*, ed. G. Waitz, *MGH SS* 5.385–487, at p. 435.

40. *Serta Mediaevalia*, p. 267 ll. 253–54.

41. *Serta Mediaevalia*, p. 269 ll. 310–11. The incident is discussed by Lentini, "Alberico di Montecassino," pp. 68–70; Lentini is followed by Montclos, p. 219, and Cowdrey, *Age of Desiderius*, p. 93. MacDonald, however, places this incident during the Lenten council, *Berengar*, p. 194.

42. Montclos, p. 219 n. 4.

himself: if Monte Cassino was to influence the debate itself, Alberic would have been the obvious choice to take the lead. Such a collaboration, moreover, is entirely consistent with the circumstance that the two men worked together closely on at least one other occasion as well. Alberic was the coauthor of Desiderius's book, *Dialogi de Miraculis S. Benedicti*, of which books 1–3 are preserved in the unique and contemporary Monte Cassino MS Vat. lat. 1203. The work was produced in the years 1076–1079.[43] It is possible to see therefore how, in the same period, Alberic worked with his abbot both for the goals of the monastery, to further the glory of St. Benedict and the house he founded, and for the goals of the wider church, to deal with a doctrine that was seen as potentially dangerous and a political situation that could undermine the process of reform.[44] The identification of Alberic's treatise and the conclusion that it was dedicated to Desiderius confirm what otherwise could reasonably have been surmised, that the scholar's intervention in the Eucharistic Controversy grew out of his ongoing cooperation in the project of his abbot and their monastery.

It does not necessarily follow that Alberic began work on his treatise immediately after the November 19 council. The legend at Monte Cassino was that it had been written quickly, and we have seen that a writer with Alberic's skill and experience could have produced it quickly, despite the polish of the work itself. The existence of the dossier of *praetermissae,* as we have called the further collection of sources that follows the treatise in the Aberdeen manuscript, would also have facilitated Alberic's making quick work of the actual treatise. At whatever moment the treatise was actually written, however, the importance attributed at the time to Alberic's eventual intervention is confirmed by the only other contribution apparently dating from this winter of 1078–79, the text in Monte Cassino 276 published by Matronola. This document is difficult to interpret, but it deserves attention here as a significant expression of Berengar's attitudes. We would conclude that: (a) it reflects the state of affairs between November 1078 and February 1079, and perhaps was actually written in that period; and (b) it records an exchange or exchanges, not necessarily face-to-face, among Berengar, Alberic, and an unknown Bonifilius that occurred at

---

43. Newton, *Scriptorium,* pp. 67 and 337, and pl. 28.

44. For the most recent discussion, see H. Bloch, vol. 1, pp. 80–81; and idem, pp. 597–98 and the fundamental discoveries of Meyvaert and Lentini cited there.

that time. As far as Alberic is concerned, it agrees with the later brief statement by Berengar indicating that there had been contact between the two scholars before Lent 1079 and before Alberic's treatise attacking Berengar's treatise.

Berengar's opening remarks mark the purpose of the treatise: "That the bread of the Lord's Table upon consecration by the priest becomes the most true body of Christ, the nature of the bread being seen to be in it" [Quod panis mense dominice consecratione sacerdotis fiat verissimum corpus christi. visa (videtur *coni. Matronola*) esse natura panis in eo.][45] The reader is reminded of the confession that he had been prepared to make at the All Saints council, that the bread becomes the "verum corpus Christi"; the specifics of that oath, that it was the flesh born of the virgin and crucified, are repeated in a later quotation from Augustine (ll. 49–53). But Berengar cannot leave the matter there. He presses on to argue that the bread itself survives the blessing, as the exterior man survives the blessing of baptism (ll. 19–21). He also argues that the bread is *spiritualiter* made into the body of Christ (ll. 45–46). These points, all carefully supported by patristic quotations, are consistent with the concerns Berengar expressed in his stay in Rome. He also acknowledges the growing importance of *substantia* as an aspect of the discussion of the Eucharist by arguing that the bread can "be converted spiritually into the substance of the body of Christ" [verti in substantia corporis christi spiritaliter] (ll. 182–83), but the sources cited for his philosophical learning, here as in the *Rescriptum*, were Augustine, not Aristotle. (ll. 171–79; 193–98)

In this text, the principal adversary was clearly Alberic, who held in the Aberdeen treatise that the conversion of the bread and wine into Christ's body and blood was accomplished "carnally" [carnaliter] (l. 202) or "according to some physical reason" [secundum quandam fisice rationem] (l. 203). Both he and Bonifilius, moreover, reproached Berengar for having withdrawn from his earlier concession, apparently on 1 November 1078, that the bread was *substantialiter* or *realiter* transformed into Christ's body. (ll. 212–13)[46] Yet Berengar was apparently cheered by the fact that "Yet neither before this nor afterwards did Alberic assert that the essence of the bread perishes; nor did he disagree

45. Matronola, p. 109. We translate without Matronola's emendation.
46. The word *realis* appears in our treatise at l. 489.

with me in any way" [Albericus tamen nec prius nec postea perire essentiam panis asseruit. nec ullo modo a me discensit]. (ll. 221–22) Despite a characteristically acid remark about Bonifilius, "a hundred-year-old child" [puer centum annorum],[47] Berengar is quite detached in regard to Alberic and registers his dissenting opinion in a matter-of-fact way. Berengar's discussions with Alberic, and the fact that he thought them worth recording, point to Alberic's central role in this period. Berengar sought his support, while the community of Monte Cassino eventually claimed his intervention on the other side.

Berengar's cautious handling of Alberic in this text makes it unlikely that he knew the content of Alberic's own treatise, which was not yet begun or still perhaps in preparation. The treatise itself, therefore, must have come as a serious disappointment to the aged *scholasticus* from Tours. While we have emphasized the detached tone of its opening, and the absence of personal attacks on the man Berengar (in this respect quite different from the treatises of Lanfranc and Guitmund), the treatise from the first is strong and unequivocal in its condemnation of the essence of Berengar's teaching. That is pronounced at the outset (l. 10) "contrary to Catholic faith." The word *substantialiter* is missing, but the argument is based on a change in the *substance* of the bread and the wine. The key passage is that already quoted[48] beginning (ll. 505–6) "Substance is changed into substance" [Mutatur enim substantia in substantiam], and this theme recurs at ll. 606–8, and in the dossier in a quotation from Ps. Euseb. Emesin. (App. ll. 104–8), "For the invisible priest by secret power converts the visible creatures with his word into the substance of his own body and blood, saying: TAKE AND EAT, THIS IS MY BODY" [Nam invisibilis sacerdos visibiles creaturas in substantiam corporis et sanguinis sui verbo suo secreta potestate convertit dicens: ACCIPITE ET COMEDITE, HOC EST CORPUS MEUM]. Not to believe in this change is heresy; after a passage from Ambrose, *De Sacramentis*, on the miracles accomplished by the Word of God, our author (ll. 236–39) says: "I think that the words of the blessed Ambrose are sufficient of themselves to refute all the heretics who deny that that sacrament of which we speak is the true flesh and blood of Christ" [Puto quod haec verba beati Ambrosii ad

---

47. "A hundred-year-old child," Matronola, *Un testo*, p. 117.
48. See above, pp. 80–81.

omnes hereticos convincendos, qui illud de quo loquimur sacramentum veram Christi carnem et sanguinem negant esse, sola sufficiant].
Berengar's name, as we have said, is used only once—in the proem—
but the implication for his teaching is plain and emphatic throughout. Even more pointed is the quotation twice (in ch. 7 and again in
ch. 16) of John Chrysostom's eloquent denunciation of Judas—a passage that clearly appealed to our rhetorician-author. Judas is by implication the type of those who ate Christ's flesh and drank his blood *ore
sed non corde.*[49]

Knowing the content of Alberic's treatise lifts some of the mystery
surrounding the discussions that settled the Eucharistic Controversy.
The other, mostly French, treatises written against Berengar chal-
lenged him on difficult philosophical and theological issues: the relation between reason and authority, the question of how one interprets
texts and physical reality, or the relation between *sacramentum* as sign
and the *res sacramenti.* Lacking Alberic's text, scholars have naturally
assumed that his treatise was in the same spirit. Montclos, for example, believed that Alberic's treatise would explain what *substantialiter*
meant in 1079,[50] a suggestion recently reaffirmed by Hélène Toubert.[51]
But the reality of the text is quite different. Cutting across these issues,
even departing from a different definition of *sacramentum,* Alberic's
treatise did not so much overthrow Berengar's arguments as build the
basis for a consensus to reject him. The question of whether the bread
and wine were altered *substantialiter,* so offensive to Berengar, is barely
discussed apart from the passages already quoted; instead, Alberic insists that the bread becomes the *vera caro Christi,* the true flesh of
Christ.[52] This is so, however, only for the believer: "Christ's flesh
would never be eaten corporeally, unless the substance of the bread
were changed into it spiritually" [Christi caro numquam corporaliter
commederetur, nisi panis substantia spiritualiter mutaretur]. (ll. 606–8)
Such arguments might not have convinced masters of dialectic, and

---

49. Judas is prominent in the scene of the *cena* depicted in Desiderius's church of S. Angelo in Formis
(built 1072–86). [See our frontispiece.] Hélène Toubert has suggested (*Un art dirigé. Réforme grégorienne et iconographie* [Paris, 1990], pp. 162–66) that the famous frescoes reflect the Eucharistic Controversy of 1078–79. The references to Judas in our libellus and his striking appearance
in the beautiful fresco would fit such an interpretation.

50. Montclos, p. 233; see also Matronola, p. 39.

51. *Art dirigé,* p. 163.

52. For example, ll. 175, 356–57.

certainly did not satisfy Berengar; but by 1079 the audience that mattered consisted not of trained scholars but of prelates: the bishops gathering for the Lenten synod. One is reminded of the comments of Bruno of Segni, that it was impossible to refute Berengar philosophically, that he had instead to be resisted by faith, authority, and the fire of charity.[53] This is precisely what Alberic did. Unlike Berengar, or Lanfranc and Guitmund, Alberic was not writing for other masters. He was writing to sway the mood of a church council most of whose members, however devout (and not all were), were little interested in grappling with the finer issues of philosophy and hermeneutics.

At the same time, the treatise implicitly rejects some of the grosser charges to which the position of Lanfranc and Alberic might be exposed. A passage already quoted[54] including (ll. 586–87) the words, "It shall not be as you suppose; my flesh will not be torn, etc." with its graphic physical imagery should be read in the light of the drastic statement composed by Humbert of Silva Candida and forced upon Berengar in 1059.[55] Also, a passage from Remigius/Haimo quoted at ll. 630–33, "That flesh which Christ assumed and this bread are not two bodies, but one body of Christ; so that while that is broken and eaten, Christ is sacrificed and taken and yet remains living and whole" [Non sunt, inquit, duo corpora, illa caro quam Christus assumpsit, et iste panis, sed unum corpus Christi; in tantum, ut, dum ille frangitur et comeditur, Christus immolatur et sumitur, et tamen vivus et integer manet] indirectly responds to Berengar's argument that Lanfranc's in-

---

53. "Berengar . . . who in disputing in philosophical fashion the subject of the body and blood of Christ, was drawing us into impossibilities. Yet we take in by the fire of the spirit and of charity that which we do not comprehend by reason, and we believe not so much arguments as the faith of the saints and authorities. . . . In cases in which we cannot resist heretics by reason and arguments, we resist them by faith and authority and the fire of charity" [Berengarius . . . qui de corpore et sanguine Christi philosophice disputando ad impossibilia nos ducebat. Nos tamen, quod ratione non comprehendimus, igne spiritus et charitatis absumimus, et non tantum argumentis, quam sanctorum fidei et auctoritatibus credimus. . . . In quibus enim haereticis ratione et argumentis resistere non possumus, fide, et auctoritate, et charitatis igne resistimus]. PL 164: 404C, quoted by Meyvaert, p. 326. We give the text found in the Monte Cassino manuscript of Bruno, MC 195, p. 43. Could Bruno have been inspired at this moment in his commentary (on Leviticus 7:17, ending "ignis absumet") to refer to the Berengarian Controversy by the citation near the end of our libellus at the climax of the catena of biblical passages on acceptance of the incomprehensibilia (l. 660) of the words from Exodus 12:10, "Si quid residuum fuerit, igne comburatur" (ll. 662–63)? On the catena see pp. 83–84.

54. See pp. 63–65 above.

55. See Macy, Theologies, pp. 36 and 38 for a summary of the problems caused by this confession and Humbert's possible motives.

terpretation would affect the body of Christ.[56] This aspect of the treatise confirms Chadwick's observation that the debate had moved much closer to Berengar's position since the 1059 council and its oath, leaving little but the word *substantialiter* for him to disagree with.[57]

The treatise has its elements of dialectic, for example, in the discussion of *substantia, species,* and *res.*[58] The *auctoritas* of the fathers is everywhere crucial. It must be observed, however, that the experience of the mass itself is a living presence. From the quotation from the *Sacramentarium Gregorianum* at the end of the second or definition paragraph, to the quotations from John 6 at the end, the treatise is close to the practice of liturgical celebration. We are reminded of the fact that a miracle was said to have occurred at a mass celebrated by the monk Theodemar at Monte Cassino at a critical moment in the Controversy: "the aforesaid oblation was changed into flesh" [praedictam oblationem in carnem mutatam].[59] The importance of the mass in Alberic's spiritual environment is underscored in the treatise by the repeated reference to *daily* celebration; *cotidie* and *cotidianus* are key thematic words, as we see, for example, at the climactic point in chapter II (ll. 362–99). The accompanying dossier includes more than one discussion of the verse on *panis cotidianus* in the Lord's Prayer.[60]

It will be obvious, from what has already been said, that Augustine is quoted more than any other single author. The treatise thus reflects the same intense interest in this father that is evidenced in book production at Monte Cassino in this period.[61] Indeed, the Eucharistic Controversy will have contributed to the enthusiasm for the campaign of Augustine book production already two decades old by the time of the Synod. But another father appears at a number of critical moments in the treatise; it is Gregory the Great. In addition to the central com-

---

56. Macy, *Theologies,* p. 40.

57. "Ego Berengarius," *Journal of Theological Studies* n.s. 40 (1989): 414–45, at pp. 434–35.

58. See the passage beginning at l. 505, discussed in ch. 2 at pp. 44–45 and ch. 3 at pp. 80–82.

59. Peter the Deacon, *Ortus et Vita Iustorum Cenobii Casinensis,* ed. Robert H. Rodgers [University of California Publications: Classical Studies, vol. 10] (Berkeley and Los Angeles, 1972), pp. 71–73. See Lentini's comments, "Alberico di Montecassino nel quadro," p. 74–75.

60. See Appendix.

61. For specific information on the copying of Augustine texts under Abbots Desiderius and Oderisius, see the article of F. Newton, "Due tipi di manoscritti ed il rinnovamento culturale nell'epoca di Desiderio," in F. Avagliano and O. Pecere, eds. *L'età dell'abate Desiderio. III.1: storia arte e cultura, Atti del IV Convegno di studi sul medioevo meridionale (Monte Cassino, 4–8 ottobre, 1987), Miscellanea Cassinese* 67 (1992), 467–81; and in his *Scriptorium and Library,* pp. 79–86.

parison discussed above,[62] between Gregory the Great and Gregory VII (ll. 362–69), he is called on to dispose of a major difficulty. Structurally, the argument falls into two major parts: the demonstration that the eucharistic elements are transformed into the body and blood of Christ (ll. 39–502), and the discussion of the nature of the change (ll. 503–666), the end of the body of the work, which is followed by the "brief epilogue."[63] Both major sections are filled with patristic citations. In the first, there are no disagreements among them, but in the second the fathers divide on the question whether it is the same blood that we drink that was shed on the point of the soldier's lance. Four authorities (Ambrose, Gregory, Remigius/Haimo, and Johannes Constantinopolitanus/Chrysostom) are found to be in agreement that it was, while two (Jerome and Augustine) "seem to sound a different note." (ll. 640–43) The entire conflict is resolved ("cuncta solvuntur," ll. 649–52) by quoting Gregory I (*Dialogi*, 4.58) "Who though RISING FROM THE DEAD NOW DOES NOT DIE, AND DEATH SHALL HAVE NO MORE DOMINION OVER HIM, nevertheless living immortally and incorruptible in himself, for us again in this mystery of his sacred sacrifice is he sacrificed" [Qui licet SURGENS A MORTUIS IAM NON MORITUR, ET MORS ILLI ULTRA NON DOMINABITUR, tamen in se ipso immortaliter atque incorruptibiliter vivens, pro nobis iterum in hoc misterio sacrae immolationis immolatur]. A few lines later, the mystery of the *how* of the transformation is summed up by Alberic at the climax of this section, and thus of the work, in the words (ll. 664–65): "For he is changed as he will, he is sacrificed as he will, he is eaten and drunk as he will" [Mutatur enim quomodo vult, immolatur quomodo vult, manducatur et bibitur quomodo vult].

Although Alberic's treatise was designed to appeal to the broad constituency that would be represented at the Lenten council, the prominent role of Gregory the Great suggests that he also had a more particular audience in mind: Gregory VII himself. Not only would the pope have appreciated the comparison between himself and his great namesake in paragraph 11, but the passage from the *Dialogi* to which it immediately leads is one that Gregory VII himself had cited in a let-

---

62. See ch. 2, pp. 40–41.

63. The breaks are marked, at l. 502 and l. 666, by the structural expression "Sed de his hactenus." The introduction and definition sections (chs. 1–2) similarly ended (l. 38), "De his autem hactenus; nunc vero ad ipsius rei seriem veniamus." See pp. 61–62, 65–68.

ter to Matilda of Canossa on daily communion.[64] Even without knowing the author or the precise circumstances in which the treatise was
composed, Capitani suggested the possibility that it was directed personally to the pope; now that Alberic's identity has been established,
that possibility becomes a near certainty. An address to the pope may
also be seen in the prominence of Marian themes, as in the quotations
from Remigius/Haimo at l. 426 and in the dossier that ascribed to
Jerome at Appendix, ll. 1–8: "Indeed that body of Christ, which the
most blessed Virgin bore, which she cradled in her lap, which she
bound in swaddling-clothes . . ." [Illud siquidem corpus Christi, quod
beatissima virgo genuit, quod gremio fovit, quod fasciis cinxit . . .].
Although of wide appeal, these images would have had a special meaning to the pope; according to the *Iuramentum*, at some time in the
winter between the two councils, Gregory told Berengar that "as is
my custom" he had appealed to the Virgin for enlightenment on the
Eucharist.[65] The final formulation of the oath that Berengar took laid
stress upon her as well.[66]

Scholars have assumed that Alberic's treatise must have been similar to those of Lanfranc or Guitmund. The text we have, however, is
closer to the *Libelli de lite*. Like Alberic's treatise, those polemics were
addressed to a specific person.[67] They also were rhetorically sophisticated works—so much so, indeed, that most of them survived only because preserved in twelfth-century collections for the study of writing.[68] Certain libelli even take up the *topos* with which Alberic begins
his treatise: as Robinson notes, the charge that an author's opinions
were discussed among the general public "was equivalent to accusing
him of 'giving that which is holy to the dogs'" (Matt. 7:6).[69] Alberic's

---

64. "Rapporti," p. 129 n. 62; the letter to Matilda is *Register Gregors VII*, I.47, pp. 71–73. The passage, from book 4 of the *Dialogues*, appears in the treatise at ll. 369–84.

65. *Serta Mediaevalia*, p. 268 ll. 279–80.

66. See below pp. 106–7.

67. Thus Robinson observes: "Most of the *Libelli de Lite* were written to convince a great magnate of the righteousness or injustice of the papal or anti-papal cause—as, for example, the *libelli* which adherents of both parties addressed to the Countess Matilda of Tuscany—or to justify the conduct of a particular bishop to other churchmen of the province." *Authority and Resistance*, p. 9; see pp. 101–3 and 153–79 for specific examples.

68. I. S. Robinson, "*Colores rhetorici* in the Investiture Contest," *Traditio* 32 (1976): 209–38.

69. *Authority and Resistance*, p. 8, citing specifically Manegold, *Liber ad Gebhardum*, MGH *Libelli de Lite* 1.420, and Sigebert of Gembloux, *Apologia contra eos qui calumniantur missas coniugatorum sacerdotem*, MGH, *Libelli de Lite* 2.438.

treatise pre-dates these other works, however; in that sense, he was a pioneer in a powerful new literary form.

Berengar and Alberic at the Lenten Council, 1079

We know nothing at all about the circulation of the treatise during the period between the councils, or the course of debate more generally during the winter of 1078–79, but we are somewhat better informed about the Lenten council itself. It drew partisans from both sides of the Investiture Contest. Bernold, who attended the council personally, noted the presence of Henry patriarch of Aquileia, the bishops of Lucca, Pisa, Florence, Die, Passau, Metz, "and of the other 150 bishops and abbots and countless clerics" [et reliquorum CL episcoporum et abbatum et innumerabilium clericorum].[70] Henry of Aquileia, like Ulrich of Padua, was an appointee of the emperor; even as the council confirmed his election, it reprimanded him for improper investitures.[71] The bishop of Albano, on the other hand, was Petrus Igneus, the Vallombrosan monk who in 1068 had walked through fire to convict a bishop of Florence of simony;[72] Anselm of Lucca was one of the principal canonists of the reform movement; Altmann of Passau was a leader of the papal party in Germany;[73] and Hugh of Die, as already noticed, was one of Gregory's closest associates.

Berengar's oath was just one of the items on the synod's agenda. The struggles of the Investiture Contest were at a peak in the winter of 1078–79, and the record of the synod in the Register of Gregory VII lists several actions related to this crisis: representatives of Henry IV and the anti-king Rudolf appeared and swore oaths; the archbishop of Aquileia and the bishop of Reggio swore different oaths of loyalty to Gregory VII; and several prelates were excommunicated.[74] Separate letters contained in the papal register reprimanded Eberhard bishop of

---

70. *Serta Mediaevalia*, p. 252 ll. 121–25; the presence of the bishop of Metz is mentioned in Bertold, *Chronicon*, ed. G. H. Pertz, *MGH SS* 5.264–326, at p. 316.

71. Vogel, *Gregor VII. und Heinrich IV.*, pp. 39–40; Bertold, *Chronicon*, p. 317.

72. Vogel, p. 143.

73. I. S. Robinson, "Pope Gregory VII, the Princes, and the Pactum 1077–1080," *EHR* 94 (1979): 721–56, at p. 740.

74. *Register Gregors VII*, 6.17a, pp. 425–29.

Parma for preventing the abbot of Reichenau from reaching Rome for the synod and threatened the *ministeriales* of the Bamberg church with excommunication.[75] Bertold of Reichenau's account in the *Chronicon* similarly emphasizes political issues, especially a debate between the representatives of Henry IV and Rudolf of Swabia; he passes over Berengar's appearance in a sentence.[76]

The entry in the papal register regarding the discussion of the Eucharist is brief but suggestive. It reads:

> When all then were gathered in the Church of the Savior, a discussion was held regarding the body and blood of our Lord Jesus Christ, with many espousing the one belief, and some, in advance, the other. Indeed the greatest part were asserting that the bread and wine through the words of the sacred prayer and consecration by the priest, by the invisible work of the Holy Spirit, were converted in substance into the Lord's body born from the Virgin, which hung on the cross, and into the blood which was shed from his side by the lance of the soldier, and [they] defended this assertion in every way by citations from the holy orthodox Fathers, both Greek and Latin. But certain ones, being struck with exceedingly great and long-continued blindness, deceiving themselves and others, were attempting by certain sophistries to establish †that it was only a figure†. But when they began to debate the matter, even before they entered the synod on its third day, the second group ceased to struggle against the truth. For indeed the fire of the Holy Spirit, consuming their resources of chaff and with his brilliance slashing to bits and darkening their false light, turned the gloom of their night into light. Finally Beringarius, who had taught this error, confessing before the full council, after the impiety that he had long espoused as doctrine, that he had erred, and, asking and begging forgiveness, won it as a result of apostolic clemency. And he swore an oath such as is comprised in the following.

> ——

> [Omnibus igitur in ecclesia Salvatoris congregatis habitus est sermo de corpore et sanguine domini nostri Iesu Christi multis hec, nonnullis illa prius sentientibus. Maxima siquidem pars panem et vinum per sacre orationis verba et sacerdotis consecrationem Spiritu sancto invisibiliter operante converti substantialiter in corpus Dominicum de virgine natum, quod et in cruce pependit, et in sanguinem, qui de eius latere militis effusus est lancea, asserebat atque auctoritatibus orthodoxorum sanctorum

---

75. *Register Gregors VII*, 6.18–20, pp. 429–32.
76. Bertold, *Chronicon*, pp. 316–18.

patrum tam Grecorum quam Latinorum modis omnibus defendebat. Quidam vero cecitate nimia et longa perculsi †figura tantum† se et alios decipientes quibusdam cavillationibus conabantur astruere. Verum ubi caepit res agi, prius etiam quam tertia die ventum fuerit in synodum, defecit contra veritatem niti pars altera. Nempe sancti Spiritus ignis emolumenta palearum consumens et fulgore suo falsam lucem diverberando obtenebrans noctis caliginem vertit in lucem. Denique Beringarius, huius erroris magister, post longo tempore dogmatizatam impietatem errasse se coram concilio frequenti confessus veniamque postulans et orans ex apostolica clementia meruit. Iuravitque sicut in consequentibus continetur.][77]

While asserting that from the very beginning of the council the *maxima pars* had held that the bread and wine on the altar were converted *substantialiter* into the body and blood of Christ, the entry conceded that there were also those who defended Berengar's views: much the same situation as that which had existed in the fall. "But when they began to debate the matter," according to the register, "even before they entered the synod on its third day" the opposition collapsed entirely. The Register gives the oath he swore as follows:

> I Berengar believe in my heart and confess with my lips that the bread and the wine that are placed upon the altar, through the mystery of the sacred prayer and the words of our redeemer are converted in substance into the true and proper and life-giving flesh and blood of Jesus Christ our Lord, and after consecration are the true body of Christ, which was born of the Virgin and which for the salvation of the world hung upon the cross and which sits at the right hand of the Father, and the true blood of Christ, which was shed from his side, not only through the sign and force of a sacrament, but in its natural property and in the truth of its substance. Just as it is contained in this brief, and as I have read and you understand, so I believe and I shall not any longer teach contrary to this faith. So help me God and these holy Gospels.

———

> [Ego Beringarius corde credo et ore confiteor panem et vinum, quae ponuntur in altari, per mysterium sacrae orationis et verba nostri redemptoris *substantialiter* converti in veram et propriam ac vivificatricem carnem et sanguinem Iesu Christi domini nostri et post consecrationem esse verum Christi corpus, quod natum est de virgine et quod pro salute

———

77. *Register Gregors VII*, ed. Erich Caspar, *MGH Epistolae selectae*, 2nd ed. (Berlin, 1955), 6.17a, pp. 425–26.

mundi oblatum in cruce pependit et quod sedet ad dexteram patris, et verum sanguinem Christi, qui de latere eius effusus est, non tantum per signum et virtutem sacramenti, sed in proprietate naturae et veritate substantiae. Sicut in hoc brevi continetur et ego legi et vos intelligitis, sic credo nec contra hanc fidem ulterius docebo. Sic me Deus adjuvet et haec sacra evangelia.]⁷⁸

Afterward, according to the papal register, Gregory ordered Berengar to refrain from discussing the Eucharist except to bring back to the faith those whom he had led away from it. This same version of Berengar's oath was subsequently incorporated into Lanfranc's treatise, winning a wide circulation for this account of how the eleventh-century discussion of eucharistic theology was finally resolved.

Brief Epilogue: Berengar Remembers

Berengar's *Iuramentum* provides a more detailed account of the Lenten synod. According to Berengar, discussions in Lent began when Landulf of Pisa presented him with an oath to read that he had not written nor the pope approved; the key phrase of this oath read: "I believe in my heart and I confess with my lips that the bread and wine that are put upon the altar, through the mystery of the sacred prayer and the words of our Redeemer are *in their true substance* converted into the true and proper and life-giving flesh and blood of Jesus Christ" [Corde credo et ore confiteor, panem et vinum, quae ponuntur in altari, per misterium sacrae orationis et verba nostri Redemptoris *substantialiter* converti in veram et propriam ac vivificatricem carnem et sanguinem Iesu Christi]. After realizing that this oath did not exclude the possibility that the substance of the bread remained after consecration, Berengar prepared to read it, only to be stopped by a demand that he stipulate that in swearing this oath he accepted the council's interpretation of what the oath meant. This demand he resisted as unnecessary, citing at this time his private conversation with Gregory VII in which the pope told him of his prayer to the Virgin and her answer that what mattered was consistency with Scripture; the pope agreed, Berengar claimed, that Berengar's position met this criterion. The pope, however, angrily denied this report, and Berengar's resistance

---

78. *Register Gregors VII*, 6.17a, pp. 426–27.

collapsed: remembering the message earlier brought him by Desiderius to be quiet or face imprisonment, he fell to the ground and, at the pope's command, confessed his error.[79]

None of the accounts discussed so far mentions Alberic, but the brief Subiaco text focuses climactically on him and leaves no doubt that he was instrumental in arriving at the final consensus. Berengar begins by observing that if it is wrong to say that the consecrated bread on the altar is the body of Christ without adding the word *substantialiter,* then Christ himself erred in the words he spoke in the gospels, as did the Apostle Paul, Ambrose, Augustine, and Jerome. But, he continues, none of them erred, not Paul, not the Fathers, and certainly not Truth himself when he did not judge it necessary to add *realiter* or *substantialiter.*[80]

> Rather it was he who erred, who (more simply put) plainly erred, that Cassinese not-monastic-but-DEMONastic Alberic, who with keen intelligence perceiving the obvious truth with me (whence Augustine says in the book *De vera religione:* "human authority is by no means valued above the reasoning of the more finely-tuned spirit which has arrived at clear truth"; and the apostle: "if anything be revealed to one who is sitting near at hand, let the first one hold his peace"), and at the same time observing the incontrovertible truth of the texts regarding the sacrifice of the Church, nevertheless did not remain steadfast in the truth: what things he had destroyed, he did not scruple to build up again in unholy collusion;[81] though he had publicly proclaimed that my understanding of the Lord's Table was correct and that in the perception of truth concerning the scriptures the opinions that I held were in keeping with the divine, he, seeking glory from men and not seeking the glory that is from God alone, fell away from that one who for the glory that was set before him bore the cross and despised the shame; and he falsely asserted in regard to the Lord's Table that if when I said "the consecrated bread on the altar is the body of Christ," I did not add "substantially," I was in error; so as to ingratiate himself with, and (so to speak) make victors out of, those who were really in error regarding the Sacrifice of the Church, if he might assume that I should take away from my statement about the Sacrifice of Christ, or perchance add something.

———

79. *Serta Mediaevalia,* pp. 268–69; Cowdrey, *Gregory VII,* p. 499–500.
80. Because we are proposing a new interpretation of this text, we give it in both Latin and English.
81. Cf. Gal. 2:18.

[Erravit potius, facilius plane erravit Cassinus ille non monachus sed daemoniacus Albricus, qui mentis acie perspicuam mecum intuens veritatem
(unde Augustinus in libro *de Vera Religione:* "rationi purgatioris animae,
quae ad perspicuam veritatem pervenit, nullo modo auctoritas humana
praeponitur." Et Apostolus: "Si cui revelatum fuerit sedenti, prior taceat")
simul impervertibilem de Sacrificio Ecclesiae scripturarum auctoritatem
attendens, in veritate tamen non perstitit: *quae destruxerat, praevaricatione*
sacrilega *iterum reaedificare* non horruit; cum publice praeconatus fuisset
recta me de mensa sentire dominica, in perceptione veritatis de scripturis
me habere Deo digna, gloriam ab hominibus quaerens, gloriam quae a solo
Deo est non quaerens, defecit ab eo qui proposito sibi gaudio sustinuit
Crucem, confusione contempta; mentitusque est errare me de mensa dominica, nisi cum dicerem "panis sacratus in altari est corpus Christi"
adderem "substantialiter": ut in eo sibi conciliaret, et quasi victores con-
stitueret errantes de sacrificio Ecclesiae, si effectum daret, ut ego enuntia-
tioni de Christi sacrificio meae demerem aliquid forte vel adderem.][82]

It is likely that this denunciation of Alberic refers to his role in the ma-
neuvering that produced the sudden, perhaps overnight, erosion of
support for Berengar's position described by the register with curious
precision "even before they came into the synod on the third day" [prius
etiam quam tertia die ventum fuerit in synodum].

Precisely what Alberic did we can only guess. It is possible that Alberic worked principally by assisting Desiderius's own lobbying on the
issue, both in person and by circulating his treatise from hand to hand
among the participants in the council. It is also possible that he addressed the council in the course of its debates, and although our other
sources leave no trace of such public activities, a possible clue to them
comes from the splendid Ottoboni manuscript (Vatican Library, Ottobonianus lat. 1406) already mentioned here. The contents of this
manuscript, a collection of classical dialectical texts, are not excep-
tional, but the manuscript as a whole certainly is.[83] To begin with, although most eleventh-century manuscripts of the liberal arts are mod-
estly prepared volumes meant for private study, the Ottobonianus
manuscript is a deluxe codex on fine white parchment, containing
many elaborate initials, charts, and illustrations and using gold on

82. Maurer, "Berengarii ut videtur," p. 205.
83. For its splendid frontispiece, see Figure 2, p. 67. For discussion of the influence of the style of its
    texts upon the style of Alberic's libellus, see ch. 3, pp. 65–68.

nearly every page. It is, in short, a manuscript intended for display. Confirming this impression, moreover, is the second unusual feature of the volume: in violation of the normal rules of South Italian book production, and especially as pertains to display manuscripts, the Ottobonianus mixes scripts, using Beneventan for the text but Caroline minuscule in the charts and diagrams. The 1079 synod is an obvious occasion when tables legible to a public not accustomed to Beneventan script would have been useful for a Cassinese scholar, and that hypothesis receives some support from two of the tables. One of them (see Fig. 3), an impressive *arbor Porphyriana,* shows at the top "Substantia" with three figures at the bottom (Socrates and Plato standing and a horseman with the mysterious name Arfastus, clearly to be identified with Aristotle); the other, showing "Schemata praedicatorum," similarly is headed "Substantia."[84]

---

84. For a detailed discussion of this manuscript, see F. Newton, *Scriptorium* (Cambridge, 1999), pp. 114–18. It is perhaps significant that Bruno of Segni, the later Cassinese abbot who left us his interpretation of the philosophical dispute and its response in the Berengarian Controversy, in his commentary on Leviticus (partly quoted above, n. 53), two pages later says of the various uses that sacrificial fat and blood might have, "hereticorum et philosophorum scientia sepe nobis in multis utilis est. Sepe enim nobis Aristotelis, Prisciani et Origenis scientia necessaria est" [the knowledge of heretics and philosophers is often useful to us in many instances. For often the knowledge of Aristotle, Priscian, and Origen is necessary]. This makes us think of the homage paid to Aristotle in the Ottobonianus. Bruno's language may even reflect that book; the last two

---

FIGURE 3

Vatican City, Biblioteca Apostolica Vaticana, MS Ottobonianus latinus 1406, fol. 11r, logical chart, showing changes of *Substantia* (cf. libellus, ch. 14).

The manuscript (see also Fig. 2, p. 67) was a product of Monte Cassino under Abbot Desiderius (1058–1087). Like all the decoration in the volume, this chart is splendid with colors and gold. Delicate tendrils link the stages of the tree (an "Arbor Porphyriana") from "Substantia" at the top to the central "HOMO" face, below which are figures labeled "Socrates" and "Plato" flanking the figure "Arfastus" (the name is enigmatic, but this figure must represent Aristotle) mounted on the "equus ratio" = the "horse reason." The chart faces the opening of Aristotle's Categories. It is striking that this chart and one other in the book are headed "Substantia," the concept-word which, in the adverbial form "substantialiter," was a key factor in the oath that Berengar was required to swear in 1079. Was the Ottoboni book connected with Monte Cassino's role at the February Synod? One extraordinary aspect of the volume is its princely magnificence—unparalleled in eleventh-century manuscripts of the classics—and another is that, unlike the text, which is written in handsome Beneventan, all the charts are labeled in the superlatively clear ordinary minuscule. These extraordinary factors suggest that this display manuscript, including its charts, was intended to be shown at the monastery to visitors from all over Europe. For such visitors Caroline (chart hand) 𝖲𝗎𝖻𝗌𝗍𝖺𝗇𝗍𝗂𝖺, for example, would have been more readily legible than Beneventan (text hand) 𝖲𝗎𝖻𝗌𝗍𝖺𝗇𝗍𝗂𝖺 .

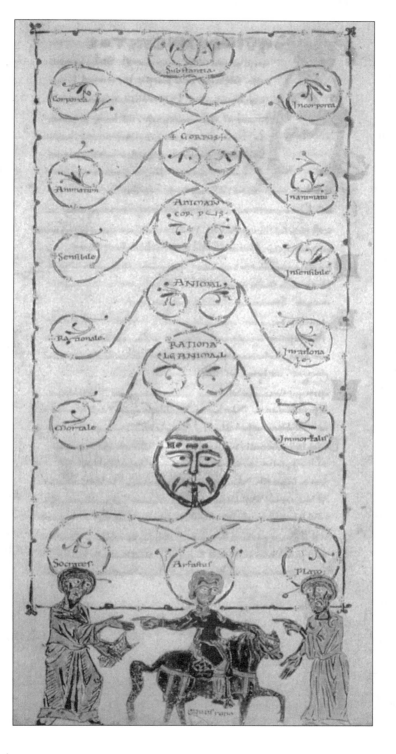

Although these tables, in the context of an entire book suited to Abbot Desiderius's princely magnificence, hint at the tantalizing possibility that Alberic addressed the meeting in his capacity of *grammaticus* with the Ottobonianus in his hand, there are aesthetic, or perhaps subjective, reasons and there are also practical reasons for placing the production of this stunning book in the aftermath of the synod and Berengar's decisive defeat. The volume has about it a celebratory air. There is in it a decidedly festive aspect, which is seen, for example, in the opening initial where on a sumptuous gold ground philosophers converse while embowered in the intricacies of the great initial C (*Cum* sit necessarium . . .), or in the logical charts, which here are decorated in colors and gold so that they seem like lovely flower trellises. There is in the book, besides, a definite triumphal feeling. The frontispiece (see Fig. 2, p. 67) shows Dialectica awarding a prize to one of her pupils (Alberic, as we propose); and the "Substantia" chart that we have illustrated (Fig. 3) depicts Aristotle—it is he, since he faces the opening of the philosopher's *Categories*—mounted on a horse ("Equus ratio") as though to make a triumphal entrance, and attended by Plato and Socrates on foot.[85] On the practical side, such a display manuscript as this, written throughout in a single hand, and decorated on every page, would have required a considerable amount of time for its execution, and a date just after the resolution of the controversy would in many ways be preferable to a date in the course of the urgent and probably fevered activity that led up to the February synod.

If this is indeed the time period in which to set the copying and decoration of such a notable volume, the book would perhaps reflect the sense of accomplishment that Alberic and Desiderius carried away from the Roman synod and back to their abbey. There the charts could have been shown to visitors—Monte Cassino was thronged with them throughout the second half of Desiderius's abbacy—who would have come from all over Europe. For the northern visitors especially, the charts with their Caroline labels—quite anomalous in such a handsome Beneventan book—would have been accessible to an extraordinary degree.

---

words of his sentence *(necessaria est)* echo the opening of the first treatise of the Ottobonianus, with its superb initial *C* showing on a gold ground philosophers debating: "Cum *sit necessarium* . . ." (Vat. Ottobon. lat. 1406, fol. 2v, the beginning of Boethius on Porphyry's *Isagoge*).

85. For the reminder of the aristocratic connotations of the horse, we are endebted to Annabel Wharton.

And here was a body of (largely) pagan philosophical texts that had been executed in a style usually reserved for the most sacred of sacred texts. These philosophical texts were important. They had made it possible for Alberic to confront and defeat the scholar from Tours, defending the appropriateness of seeing the transformation worked in the Eucharist as one of *substantia*. We cannot repeat too often, however, that what Alberic learned from the Latin treatises of Aristotle, Cicero, Porphyry, Boethius, and the rest, that enabled him to win the controversy was not skill in classical logic; it was the skillful manipulation of prose style that is seen in his libellus.[86] It is the fair Dialectica who is enthroned on the frontispiece of Vat. Ottobon. lat. 1406, but it was the fair Rhetorica who was enthroned in Alberic's heart.

If the book really played a role of this kind, then the Subiaco fragment can be read as a kind of counterpoint to it. The aspect of the Subiaco fragment that has attracted the most discussion is Berengar's statement that Alberic once supported him publicly. Lentini saw no possibility of any real agreement between them at any time: "In the grip of the able dialectician Berengar, Alberic might at some point have found himself uncertain or embarrassed in a way that his adversary interpreted as consent; but that does not authorize us to think that there was a true assent, and even less lasting assent." For him it was in Berengar's interest here and in the Matronola text, which Lentini ascribes to Berengar, "to show himself consenting to his doctrine."[87] More recent studies, however, have emphasized what Meyvaert called an *évolution* in Alberic's understanding of the Eucharist and of his view of Berengar's teaching.[88] Cowdrey took a similar position, noting that "the implication is that at some earlier gathering, perhaps that of 1 November 1078, Alberic had publicly agreed that Berengar's teaching was admissible";[89] in a similar spirit, Montclos suggested that Berengar referred to support Alberic had given to the pope at the All Saints council. In this case, Alberic's evolution would have been moved more by a recognition of what was possible and acceptable in a shifting political situation than by a change in his theology. When pushed, however, Alberic was prepared to add the adverb *substantialiter* with the impli-

---

86. See the discussion on pp. 65–68.
87. A. Lentini, in *Aspren*, p. 73.
88. Meyvaert, "Bérenger de Tours," p. 330.
89. Cowdrey, *Age of Desiderius*, p. 94.

cation that the matter of the bread was entirely transformed; Berengar was not.

The identification and analysis of Alberic's treatise clarify some of the reasons for Berengar's anger. Its main argument is that the Eucharist is the *verum corpus et sanguis Christi,* a statement of doctrine that had been acceptable to Berengar at the All Saints council. In the context of our libellus, however, where the technical-sounding term *substantialiter* would have been inconsistent with the rest of the language, *verum* was clearly intended to convey a meaning unacceptable to Berengar. The passage (ch. 14) that insists upon the transformation of the *substantia* of the bread and wine is, moreover, subject to every kind of objection: vinegar can hardly be said to retain the *species* of wine unless that is understood in a purely visual sense; and the claim that the appearance of the bread and wine has, in fact, changed due to consecration but the change is not perceived owing to Ambrose's *horror cruoris* certainly would seem to merit some attempt at explanation. Alberic concedes that Augustine and Jerome sometimes "seem to utter something that sounds different," a concession that perhaps would have been enough to save Berengar except that Alberic immediately brushes it aside by wrapping the whole problem up in the language of mystery. Even at the highly rhetorical end, as he urged that views like Berengar's were heretical, Alberic was not really prepared to offer an alternate reading either of the physical facts or of key patristic texts.

But the Subiaco fragment raises questions that go beyond whether Alberic shifted his position over time. The passage as a whole is typically Berengarian. The vitriolic tone reminds the reader of Huygens's remark, that the author "is never at a loss for terms of invective."[90] The style too is characteristic, the very opposite of the lucid and moderate prose of Alberic but in its strange way just as subtle; Berengar's sentences here as elsewhere are rambling and elaborate, filled with wordplay and lengthy parentheses, and decidedly obscure.[91] Yet this is very interesting prose, and we may not ignore or dismiss a single word of it. Even the tiniest stroke contributes to the picture of Alberic that Berengar paints.

---

90. *Serta Mediaevalia,* p. 259 note on 66–67.
91. Huygens, *Serta Mediaevalia,* p. 225, "le style de Bérenger est abominable et sa pensée souvent très difficile à suivre."

For example, the seemingly otiose parenthesis is premature, but its quotation from Augustine forces the reader to ask specifically, Who is the human authority, whom *Alberic* should not prefer to the light of reason? The answer, of course, is Desiderius, his abbot. The second quotation in the parenthesis, that from I Corinthians 14:30, reinforces this impression of a specific reference: the "first one," who is to hold his peace when inspiration comes to a subordinate, is a *prior*, and in the context it is clear that Berengar is thinking of Alberic's relation to a monastic superior *(monachus/prior)*. As the sentence makes its tortuous way forward, the character of Alberic grows steadily darker and his motives worse: in addition to colluding with the enemy *(praevaricatio)*, he seeks glory from men, and if the reader's identification of *auctoritas humana* is correct, then the men *(homines)* from whom Alberic seeks it are in reality one man: Desiderius; and (more depraved still) Alberic curries favor *(conciliare)* with, and makes a species of winner out of *(quasi victores constituere)* those who are, in reality, in error in their perception of the Eucharist. It is the words *quasi victores* that provide the key to the entire passage; *quasi*, as so often, is a marker to signal to the reader that the following word is used in a sense not wholly literal and, as such, can often be rendered with modern quotation marks: Alberic is depicted as "ingratiating himself with those who are in error concerning the Sacrifice of the Church, and making 'Victors' out of them."[92] The use of Desiderius's papal name (Victor III) is decisive.[93] It fully confirms the reader's identification, tentatively formulated in the course of the sentence.

In this astonishing passage Berengar, of course, refers to more than the outcome of the Eucharistic Controversy. Looking back from the vantage point of a number of years, he sees Desiderius as a "winner" in the Controversy; indeed, a major winner. The whole process, in Beren-

---

92. Berengar's trenchant rhythmical poem, "Iuste Iudex, Iesu Christe," written before his final condemnation at the 1079 synod, shows powerfully his anxieties in the face of his enemies *(hostes, inimici, mihi detrahentes, odientes me)*. He prays in language to be echoed in the Subiaco document and in the *Iuramentum:* "Sanctae crucis tuae signum sensus meos muniat / Et vexillo triumphali me *victorem* faciat, / Ut *devictus* inimicus viribus deficiat" [May the sign of Holy Cross strengthen my senses / And under its triumphant banner make me the *victor, / That my enemy, defeated,* may lose all strength]. The whole of this remarkable poetic prayer should be studied in the light of Berengar's long travail.

93. Berengar's use of *quasi* as a marker of wordplay is parallel to Guitmund's use of "quodammodo, ut ita dixerim" to mark his wordplay regarding certain Berengarians who believed the Real Presence to be *impanari* [to be breaded] like a *coteletta alla Milanese*. See pp. 24–26 and n. 72.

gar's eyes, gained him the papacy, and it was Alberic's kowtowing to human authority and his *volte-face*[94] that guaranteed Desiderius the "*victoria*" in two senses.

Berengar liked this particular *antanaclasis* that he had found so much that he used it on another occasion as well. In the *Iuramentum* he prefaces it with a similar quotation—this time from Horace—to set the stage:[95]

> This text [i.e., the oath that it was proposed that Berengar swear], changed to suit the pleasure of those who, as the pagan poet says, *think it a disgrace to obey those who are younger, and to confess in their old age that what they learned in their beardless youth deserves to be discarded,* in order to seem to be "Victors."

> [Hoc scriptum, mutatum ad placitum eorum, qui, ut ait poeta gentilis, *turpe putant parere minoribus et quae inberbes didicere, senes perdenda fateri* (Hor. *Ep.* 2.1.84–85), ut quasi victores viderentur.]

Berengar's complaint is the same as before, and he mentally sees a parallel in his own case to Augustine's objection to blind following of human authority (in interpretation) and Horace's objection to the refusal of the elderly to admit the value of younger poets and their work. Again, the wordplay serves Berengar's purpose by allowing him to criticize, but covertly, the role of a man now pope for his actions in the outcome of the Controversy. All this throws light on the two other, open references to Desiderius in the *Iuramentum*.

Desiderius was made pope and given the name Victor on 24 May 1086. Berengar died on 6 January 1088. Both the Mabillon–Meyvaert–Maurer text (the Subiaco one) and the Martène–Huygens text (the *Iuramentum*) are thus to be dated in the last biennium or less of Berengar's life.[96] Their tone, especially that of the former, reveals a bitterness and a haunted insistence on reliving the author's traumatic experiences at the synods in Rome, now more than seven years behind him. Berengar, a natural-born teacher now debarred from teaching,

94. We borrow the term from Meyvaert, "Bérenger," p. 326.
95. *Serta Mediaevalia*, p. 261 ll. 88–91.
96. Meyvaert thought the text that he published, like that of Matronola, probably dated from the beginning of Berengar's stay in Rome. See "Bérenger," p. 329.

achieved, it would seem, no serenity of spirit in his last years, at least not in his contemplation of this issue. But this obsession of Berengar with the Controversy, long after it was over, provides the student of Alberic's treatise with a valuable glimpse into the way in which the loser perceived the roles of Alberic and Desiderius in its resolution.[97]

97. The word *substantialiter,* already used in Guitmund's treatise and in the Poitiers Council, was known in more than one context in this period. The contemporary translation of a medical treatise of Hunayn ibn Ishaq's, known in the Latin tradition as the *Isagoge* and perhaps made by Constantine the African, who worked at Monte Cassino before the death of Desiderius, contains near its opening this word in the sentence "Est colera rubea clara naturaliter et substantialiter. . . ." We quote this from the late eleventh-century manuscript Monte Cassino 225, p. 129, ll. 27–28. This manuscript may not have been produced at the monastery, but it was there before 1100, as the heading of the *Isagoge* shows. On Monte Cassino 225, see F. Newton, "Constantine the African and Monte Cassino: New Elements and the Text of the *Isagoge,*" in *Constantine the African and Ali ibn Al-Abbas Al-Magusi. The Pantegni and Related Texts,* ed. Charles Burnett and Danielle Jacquart (Leiden/New York/Cologne, 1994), pp. 16–47.

Conclusion

Several scholars have had occasion recently to observe that the condemnation of Berengar appears to have done little actually to settle eucharistic doctrine. Miriam Rubin and H. Chadwick have noted that, in the early twelfth century, Rupert of Deutz and Alger of Liège were able to propose widely varying interpretations of the mass,[1] while Gary Macy, especially, has shown that a wide range of opinions continued to thrive throughout the twelfth century. Even the Fourth Lateran's affirmation of "transubstantiation," Macy argues, should not be seen as enunciating a clear doctrine so much as a condemnation of the clearly heretical Cathars.[2] This impression that the question was still open after 1079 is confirmed by the content of Alberic's treatise. Not only was Alberic able to unite the council without offering a clear doctrine of his own—one might almost write: *by* not offering a clear doctrine of his own—but he is never specific about which aspects of Berengar's position required condemnation. Understandably, Berengar was not convinced by this result, and though silenced he remained unreconciled to it, apparently until the end of his life.

Because of the many gaps and omissions in our knowledge about the eleventh century, scholars have often succumbed to the temptation

---

1. Rubin, *Corpus Christi*, pp. 20–21; Chadwick, "Ego Berengarius." For the later impact of the Berengarian controversy, see also Macy, "Berengar's Legacy as Heresiarch," and Ludwig Hödl, "Die theologische Auseinandersetzung mit Berengar von Tours," both in *Auctoritas und Ratio*, pp. 47–88.
2. *Theologies*, esp. pp. 2–10, where he argued that it is a mistake to see early theology as pointing inevitably toward Thomas Aquinas, and pp. 140–41.

to illuminate its darknesses by using the comparatively brighter light cast by our much greater knowledge of the twelfth and thirteenth centuries. That light, unfortunately, has often done more to cast misleading shadows than it has to illuminate actual events of the eleventh century. Thus Berengar's own position, and the theological discussion as a whole, has been seen as a consequence of the growing interest of the French schools in the study of dialectic and speculative grammar, while the Lenten council of 1079 has often been considered a crucial step toward the doctrine of transubstantiation. Neither interpretation survives careful study of the eleventh-century evidence.

Attributing a coherent theology to the 1079 council is not the only error scholars have made in grappling with this dispute. We have also seen that the Berengarian controversy in fact owed very little to new studies in logic and grammar. Berengar's own position seems to have arisen from his interest in the theological issues and the problems of interpreting theological texts: a pattern not greatly different, except in its outcome, from that of his own master, Fulbert of Chartres. The liberal arts played only a peripheral role in his considerations, so much so that he himself did not cite Aristotle or other works on either logic or grammar in support of his position. The position of Berengar's critic Guitmund of Aversa is similar, for Guitmund's discussion of *substantia* likewise appears to have been inspired not by Aristotle but by the language of the Arian controversy. The exception, of course, is Lanfranc, who does explicitly employ dialectical analysis in answering Berengar. But that exception itself proves how different the cultural formation received before 1050 was from what we are accustomed to thinking of as the norm for the central Middle Ages, because Lanfranc's mastery of dialectic—and we must remember that it seemed like mastery to his contemporaries—was acquired not in France but in Italy and was based on Cicero rather than on Aristotle. The dialectical revival did come to France in the later eleventh century, but it is more likely that this study was inspired by the increasing philosophical and interpretative complexities of the Eucharistic Controversy than that it contributed much to its outcome.

The modest role in the Berengarian debate of dialectic and speculative grammar is confirmed by the new piece of evidence that we have to offer, that of the Aberdeen treatise. This libellus was written in 1078 or 1079 by a central or Southern Italian monk with an unusually strong background in the liberal arts. No master by the name of Berengar, the name that stands in an obvious addition at the head of the text, is known for this region and time; and Berengar of Venosa, to whom Morin attributed the treatise, is not known to have been a master or to have written at all. Instead, stylistic evidence overwhelmingly supports attribution of this work to Alberic of Monte Cassino, who was the leading master of Southern Italy in the late eleventh century, and who moreover is known to have written a work against Berengar of Tours. Had the treatise come down to us anonymously, without the spurious and misleading rubric, it would certainly have been assigned to Alberic when originally discovered.

The treatise is not precisely what the *Chronicle* described, however, for it was written at the urging of Alberic's fellow monks and presented to Desiderius rather than written in a week at the request of the Lenten council. Clearing up this misconception permits us to make better sense of the 1079 council and the period leading up to it than has previously been possible. Berengar, it would seem, was condemned not on the basis of compelling new arguments that answered his claims, and certainly not because of a convincing use of dialectic, but as a result of a polished and graceful articulation of opposing views supported by passages drawn from the Fathers. The political intent of the treatise, moreover, becomes clear when we place the Eucharistic Controversy in the context of the ongoing struggle between Gregory VII and Henry IV. The alliance against Berengar between the reformer Landulf of Pisa and Henry's supporter Ulrich of Padua in the All Saints council spelled danger to Gregory's supporters. Desiderius, especially, apparently was active throughout the winter of 1078–79 trying to contain the damage. It was during this same period that Alberic's own position was crucial, his support being enlisted by his fellow monks and sought by Berengar himself or a close supporter, who wrote the text published by Matronola. As events played out, however, it was Berengar's hopes that were disappointed. Alberic's treatise both provided the basis for a broad consensus condemning Berengar and equipped Desiderius to play a major role at the council itself. When Berengar's support in the Lenten council collapsed, evidently as a result of efforts in which Desiderius and Alberic played central roles, it was clear even to Berengar that further resistance was hopeless, but to the last years of his life he harbored a bitterness against those he felt had betrayed the truth (and him).

Finally, it must be noted that the treatise provides us with new information about a major eleventh-century scholar, Alberic of Monte Cassino. Alberic's work in *ars dictaminis* is of the highest importance, and his hagiographical works are among the most interesting examples of the genre, but the treatise against Berengar is the only work in which we can observe Alberic's rhetorical training placed in the service of debate in an argument whose outcome was still uncertain. The effect is impressive. Even Alberic's choice of words is careful and exact with respect to sound, phrasing, and rhythm as well as meaning and the visual images conveyed. He draws easily upon his classical learning, with a passing reference to Cicero's *Topica* as in other works he paraphrases Virgil and Horace, and especially upon his study of the classical prose of dialectic found in such collections as the Ottobonianus. Nor should the gracefulness of the prose distract us from the intelligence with which the whole work is shaped, for Alberic moves easily, effortlessly, from point to point, leading the listener and the reader along. So much is this in contrast to the French contributions to the Eucharistic Controversy, in which the doctrinal issues are accentuated and debated *seriatim* in the manner of the schools, that one is tempted to describe the treatise as the work not just of a master but of a master in the Italian tradition of the *artes,* a hint of the differences between the learned cultures of the two societies that would become still clearer in the twelfth century.

The Text and Translation of the Libellus

Introduction

Dom Germain Morin's publication of 1932 has the distinction of being the *editio princeps* of our text. Morin also served the text well by making good the deficiencies of the unique manuscript, at Aberdeen, Department of Manuscripts and Archives, Aberdeen University Library, King's College, manuscript 106, our text being on fols. 55v–61v through the penultimate line. He provided a series of excellent emendations (l. 15 *si lectio*, l. 73 *in visu*, l. 441 *tunc*, l. 504 *Nunc*, l. 564 *cum ore*, l. 568 *et panis*, l. 586 *fiet* , l. 587 *in frusta*, l. 615 *ad Ephesios*, l. 647 *biberetur*, l. 656 *quid*, and l. 679 *corde;* most of these are adopted in the present edition), and notes identifying in large part the citations. Morin's useful division of the text into chapters, which has no support in the manuscript, is retained in this edition.

Despite the excellences of Morin's work, we have concluded that a fresh edition is needed. Morin's text has a series of omissions, some sizable, such as the lines at 408–10, or the phrase at ll. 435; others involve only a single word, but a significant one for the style and the shape of the argument, as, for example, l. 239 *tamen*, l. 499 *a*, and l. 521 *adhuc*. Some verb endings in the manuscript are misread; in it the addressee is consistently in the second-person singular, and a number of citations begin with the subjunctive as the various Fathers are called on to speak (*Dicat* or *audiamus*). Morin ignored the manuscript's punctuation signs in the important series of rhetorical questions at ll. 120–22. A number of other readings of the manuscript go un-reported, and there are a few obvious typographical errors. Perhaps most important of all, Morin had no clear sense of the end point of the treatise. It is true that the conclusion is not marked in any way in the manuscript, and other *sententiae* follow without interruption on the bottom line of fol. 61v and the following leaves; these most valuable pieces we think of as the "Praetermissae of the Dossier" (see introduction to the Appendix). A close examination of the text, however, permits one to see the natural point of conclusion, and in this present edition, for the first time (we believe), the rhetorical structure of the libellus and its argument is visible.

Our text was copied by two hands: one on 55v through 58r l. 5 *nec eius sanguinem bibit* (in our l. 267), and a second who takes up at this point and continues through the remainder of the treatise and beyond. The scribe of the first 5+ pages has a rounded hand with low center of gravity and no Beneventan ligatures or striking abbreviations (both scribes, for example, abbreviate *autem* as *aut* with macron above); the one example of the 2-shaped Beneventan suprascript sign over *Quis* in his section on 57v l. 13 demonstrates that this feature, occurring in a hand that lacks Beneventan characteristics, is copied from an exemplar in Beneventan. The first scribe also marks citations with names of Fathers so far out in the margins that the binder's knife has trimmed most away; he also uses crosses in the margins for this purpose. The hand that continues the work is more upright, with generally finer strokes and more pronounced finials at the top of ascenders. He often shows the Beneventan (and Central Italian) *ri* ligature. References to the citations of the Fathers are frequent, in the margins and within the text. His small initials are heavier. It is in his part of the text, on 58v, that the quotation from Gregory the Great and the tribute to Gregory VII occurs, and its beginning is marked by a triangle of points over the first letter. Accents are few; they mark the exclamatory word *O* at ll. 182–83: *O Christi misericordia! O Iudae dementia!*

We have generally followed the readings of the manuscript, even in citations from the Fathers, unless these latter were nonsense in the context. Scriptural references quoted by the author of the libellus are identified in the source notes; those quoted by his patristic sources are identified in the text, in parentheses, immediately before the quotation. The manuscript is reasonably careful in the orthography of words containing *ae;* this we have usually regularized. Other spellings vary, following the manuscript: *intellegere* or *intelligere, praetermissus* or *praetermisus.* The title that we have proposed for the treatise, in brackets, is adopted on the basis of the passage from the *Chronicle* of Monte Cassino that we have discussed on pages 47–49. The apparatus criticus shows the few places in which the present editor has proposed an emendation.

In the apparatus criticus, A (Aberdonensis) stands for the first hand in the text (either scribe) and A¹ for that scribe correcting his own work.

[Adversus Berengarium Diaconum de Corpore et Sanguine Domini]

1. Noviter ad nos, beatissime pater, de corpore et sanguine domini exortae quaestionis allata relatio sic totam subito hanc terram
replevit, ut non solum clerici ac monachi, quorum intentio in talibus invigilare debet, verum etiam ipsi laici de hoc inter se in plateis
5 confabulentur. Aiunt enim Beringarium quendam Turonensem
magni ingenii profundaeque scientiae virum Romam advenisse,
qui eam cui quondam abrenuntiaverat sententiam velit iterum renovare; asserens, ut dicunt, quod in sacramento nostrae redemptionis nec panis in carnem nec vinum mutatur in sanguinem. Quod
10 quantum catholicae fidei contrarium sit, norunt illi quorum cibus
est lectio sacra. Unde factum est ut fratres et confinitimi nostri, qui
me ut ita dixerim saepe mihi praeponunt, ad hoc meum animum
excitarent, quatinus quid de his potissimum sentiam eis propalarem. Collegi igitur has sanctorum patrum, quae in hoc libello
15 continentur sententiae, pluribus tamen praetermissis; ne, si lectio
prolixa foret, animum lectoris fortasse gravaret. Volui autem non
prius haec illorum infundere mentibus, quam tibi legata qualiacunque sint tuo examine iudicentur.

2. Quoniam autem de sacramento locuturi sumus, prius quid
20 sit ipsum sacramentum audiamus. *Est autem sacramentum,* ut Ysi-
dorus ait, *cum aliqua celebratione res ita fit, ut aliquid significare intelligatur; dicitur autem sacramentum a sacris vel secretis virtutibus.*
Fit autem sacramentum aliquando in figura, ut illius agni in veteri
lege immolati; aliquando in re, ut istius qui cotidie in ecclesia man-
25 ducatur. Unde beatus Ambrosius: *Ut scias,* inquit, *hoc esse sacramentum, huius figura ante praecessit.* Hoc igitur modo dicitur sacramentum, non quod aliquid significet, sed quod ab aliquo
significatum sit: sicut e contra illud vetus, non quod ab aliquo significatum fuerit, sed, quoniam huius figuram gerebat, sacramen-
30 tum dicebatur. Haec autem ideo dicta sunt, ne quis ecclesiae sacramentum tipice intelligere velit. Nichil est autem aliud dicere: *Ut*

Titulum Domino sancto ac venerabili. G. Summo pontifici. Berengarius servus eius. *add. A²*
(manus coaeva Beneventana); vide tabulam 1 et quae diximus supra, pp. 32–40.   7 velit] velit e *A,*
corr. A¹.   15 si lectio] silentio *A,* si lectio *coniecit Morin.*   20 audiamus] audiamus *A,*
dicamus *A¹.*

20–22 Est . . . virtutibus] Isidor. *Etymol.* 6.19.39,40.   25–26 Ut . . . praecessit] Ambros. *De
sacram.* 4.5.25, *CSEL* 73, p. 57 [*PL* 16: 464A].

[Against Berengar the Deacon, On the Body and Blood of the Lord]

1. The report recently brought to us, O most blessed Father, of the questioning that has arisen in regard to the body and blood of the Lord, has suddenly filled all this land to such an extent that not only clerics and monks, whose watchful attention should be devoted to such matters, but even the very laymen are chattering about it among themselves in the town squares. What they say is that a certain Berengar of Tours, a man of great talent and profound knowledge, has come to Rome and wishes to revive anew the interpretation which he had once renounced: asserting, as they say, that in the sacrament of our redemption neither is the bread turned into flesh nor the wine into blood. How contrary this is to the Catholic Faith is well known to those whose food consists of the reading of sacred texts. The result of this has been that my brothers and neighbors, who (so to speak) often set me above myself, have stirred up my spirit to this undertaking, that I should lay out for them my own particular views on these matters. Therefore I have gathered together these sentences of the holy Fathers that are contained in this little tract, yet with the omission of many, so that the reading might not be burdensome to the spirit of my reader, as it would perchance be if it were too long. Moreover, I have chosen not to pour these teachings into *their* minds until they might, such as they are, be presented to *you* and be weighed and judged on your own balance-scales.

2. Now since we are to speak of the sacrament, let us first hear what a sacrament is in itself. *A sacrament is,* as Isidore says, *when a thing is done with some celebration in such a way that it is understood to signify something; and a sacrament is called after sacred or hidden forces.* Now a sacrament takes place at times figuratively, as the sacrament of the well-known lamb sacrificed under the Old Law; and at times in reality, as the sacrament of him who is daily eaten in the Church. Whence the blessed Ambrose says, *That you may know that this is a sacrament, the figure of it preceded it and came before.* Therefore it is called a sacrament in this way, not because it points to something, but because it has been pointed to by something; just as on the other hand that former thing was called a sacrament not because it was pointed to by something, but because it carried the prefiguring of this present one. These things have been said to this end, that no one should choose to understand the sacrament of the Church typologically. And it is just the same to say, *That*

scias hoc esse sacramentum, huius figura ante praecessit, quam si diceret: Ut scias autem hoc esse in re, iam aliud praecessit in specie. Illud enim quod beatus Gregorius deprecatur dicens: *ut quod specie ger-*
35 *imus, rerum veritate capiamus,* ad hoc nobis valere debet, ut in cuius commemoratione haec agimus, eius revera carnem et sanguinem esse credamus. In specie quidem agitur, quia quod est non videtur. De his autem hactenus; nunc vero ad ipsius rei seriem veniamus.

3. AMEN AMEN DICO VOBIS NISI MANDUCAVERITIS CARNEM
40 FILII HOMINIS ET BIBERITIS. E. S. N. V. IN VOBIS. Haec verba illius sunt, qui mentiri non potuit. Ille ea scripsit cuius testimonium verum est. Haec beatus Augustinus exponens, quasi aquila post aquilam volans, divina et spiritali utitur locutione. Ait ergo: *Hunc itaque cibum et potum societatem vult intelligi corporis et membrorum*
45 *suorum, quod est sancta ecclesia, in praedestinatis et vocatis et iustificatis sanctis et fidelibus suis.* Et paulo post: *Huius,* inquit, *rei sacramentum, id est, unitatis corporis et sanguinis Christi alicubi quotidie, alicubi certis intervallis dierum in dominica mensa praeparatur* [56ʳ] *et de mensa dominica sumitur, quibusdam ad vitam, quibusdam ad ex-*
50 *itium; res vero ipsa, cuius sacramentum est, omni homini ad vitam, nulli ad exitium, quicunque eius particeps fuerit.* Aliud igitur est sacramentum, aliud virtus sacramenti; siquidem omnibus haec dat vitam, illud autem aliis sumitur ad mortem, aliis ad vitam. Unde idem ipse ait: *Hic est ergo* (Ioan. 6:51-52) PANIS VIVUS, QUI DE
55 CAELO DESCENDIT, UT, SI QUIS EX IPSO MANDUCAVERIT, NON MORIATUR; *sed quod pertinet ad virtutem sacramenti, non quia pertinet ad visibile sacramentum: qui manducat intus, non foris: qui manducat corde, non qui premit dente.*

4. Sed quid est visibile sacramentum? Dicat Ambrosius, fons
60 scientiae, clavis secretorum, cuius flores, ut aiunt, in ecclesia redolent: (Matt. 24:28; Luc. 17:37) UBI, inquit, CORPUS, IBI ET AQUILAE. *Forma corporis altare est, et corpus Christi est in altari. Aquilae vos es-*

---

49 exitium] exitum *A.*   51 exitium] exitum *A.*   54 vivus] vius *A.*   58 dente] dentem *A.*
62 altari] altaris *A.*

34–35 ut . . . capiamus] *Das Sacramentarium Gregorianum nach dem Aachener Urexemplar,* ed. D. Hans Lietzmann [Liturgiewissenschaftliche Quellen und Forschungen Heft 3] (Münster in Westf., 1921), Mensis septimi orationes die dominico, Sabbato ad sanctum Petrum XII Lectiones, p. 95.   39–40 Amen . . . vobis] Ioh. 6:53.   43–51 Hunc . . . fuerit] Aug. *Tract. 26 in Ioh.* c. 15, *CC* 36, pp. 267–68 [*PL* 35: 1614].   54–58 Hic . . . dente] Aug. *Tract. 26 in Ioh.* c. 12, *CC* 36, p. 266 [*PL* 35: 1612].   61–65 ubi . . . nota] Ambros. *De sacram.* 4.2.7, 4.3.8, *CSEL* 73, p. 49 [*PL* 16: 456D–457A].

*you may know that this is a sacrament, the figure of it preceded it and
came before,* as if one said, "that you may know that this is true in
reality, another thing has preceded it in seeming." For this which
the blessed Gregory prays for, saying that *that which we do in outward seeming, we should take in real truth,* ought to have such force
with us that we should believe that it is in reality the flesh and
blood of him in whose commemoration we do these things. It is
done in seeming indeed, because what is, is not seen. So much,
then, for these matters for the moment; now let us come to the orderly laying out of the subject itself.

    3. VERILY, VERILY I SAY UNTO YOU, UNLESS YOU SHALL EAT
THE FLESH OF THE SON OF MAN, AND DRINK HIS BLOOD, YOU
WILL NOT HAVE LIFE IN YOU. These are the words of him who
could not lie. He wrote these words whose testimony is true. In his
exposition of them, the blessed Augustine, like an eagle following
an eagle, uses divine and spiritual language. Therefore he says, *And
so this food and drink he wishes to be understood as the union of his body
and limbs, which is the holy church, in those who are predestined and
called and justified as his saints and his faithful.* And, a little later, he
said, *The sacrament of this, that is, of the unity of the body and blood
of Christ, is prepared on the Lord's Table in some places every day, and
in some places at a fixed interval of days, and taken from the Lord's
table, by some people for life and by others for destruction; but the thing
itself, of which this is the sacrament, is taken by every man who participates in it for life and by no-one for destruction.* Therefore the sacrament is one thing, and the force of the sacrament is another; inasmuch as this [force] gives life to all, that [sacrament] is taken by
some for death, by others for life. Whence Augustine himself says,
This is therefore THE LIVING BREAD, WHICH DESCENDS FROM
HEAVEN, SO THAT, IF ANYONE SHALL EAT OF IT, HE MAY NOT
DIE; *but what pertains to the force of the sacrament, not what pertains
to the visible sacrament; he who eats it within, not without; who eats
it in his heart, not who grinds it with his tooth.*

    4. But what is the visible sacrament? Let Ambrose speak, the
fountain of knowledge, the key to hidden stores, whose flowers, as
they say, perfume the Church; he says, WHERE THERE IS A BODY,
THERE ALSO ARE EAGLES. *The form of the body is the altar, and the
body of Christ is upon the altar. You all are*

tis, renovatae ablutione delicti. Venisti ad altare; vidisti sacramenta posita super altare; et ipsam quidem miratus es creaturam, tamen crea-
65 *tura sollemnis, et nota.* Audisti quid dixerit: *Vidisti,* inquit, *sacramenta posita super altare.* Quod enim videtur, visibile est. Sed *vidisti,* inquit; hoc est igitur quod dicimus visibile sacramentum. Sed dicis: Cur ergo, qui vinum video, sanguinem non video? Audi itaque quid idem doctor in eodem sacramentorum libro dixerit: *Si-*
70 *cut,* inquit, *mortis similitudinem sumpsisti, ita etiam similitudinem pretiosi sanguinis bibis. Sed quare similitudinem? Ut nullus horror cruoris sit, et pretium tamen operetur redemptionis.* Ac si diceret: Nisi horror esset in visu, et carnem utique quam manducas, et sanguinem videres quod bibis. Hoc autem visibile sacramentum alii
75 ad vitam, alii ad iudicium manducant et bibunt. Unde apostolus ait: QUICUNQUE AUTEM MANDUCAVERIT ET BIBERIT INDIGNE, IUDICIUM SIBI MANDUCAT ET BIBIT, NON DIIUDICANS CORPUS DOMINI. Sed audi quid Augustinus de visibili, quid de spiritali cibo in expositione supra Iohannem dixerit: (Ioan. 6:49) PATRES
80 VESTRI MANDUCAVERUNT MANNA, ET MORTUI SUNT. *Quid est,* inquit, *unde superbitis?* MANDUCAVERUNT MANNA, ET MORTUI SUNT. *Quare manducaverunt, et mortui sunt? Quia quod videbant credebant, quod non videbant non intellegebant. Ideo patres vestri, quia similes estis illorum. Nam quantum attinet, fratres mei, ad*
85 *mortem istam visibilem et corporalem, numquid nos non morimur, qui manducamus panem de caelo descendentem? Sic sunt mortui et illi, quem ad modum et nos sumus morituri, quantum attinet, ut dixi, ad mortem huius corporis visibilem atque carnalem. Manducavit manna et Moises, manducavit et Aaron, manducavit et Finees, mandu-*
90 *caverunt ibi et alii multi, qui domino placuerunt, et mortui non sunt. Quare? Quia visibilem cibum spiritaliter intellexerunt, spiritaliter esurierunt, spiritaliter gustaverunt, ut spiritaliter satiarentur. Nam et nos hodie accipimus visibilem cibum: sed aliud est sacramentum, aliud virtus sacramenti. Quam multi de altari accipiunt, et moriuntur, et ac-*

---

63 ablutione] oblatione *A.*   73 in visu] in usu *A,* in visu *coniecit Morin.*   73 sanguinem] vinum *A,* sanguinem *coniecit* FN.   88 corporis] *post* corporis *rasura unius verbi A.*

69–72 Sicut . . . redemptionis] Ambros. *De sacram.* 4.4.20, *CSEL* 73, p. 54 [*PL* 16: 462B].
76–78 quicunque . . . domini] I Cor. 11:27.   **80–96** Quid . . . bibit] Aug. *Tract. 26 in Ioh.* c. 11, *CC* 36, pp. 264–65 [*PL* 35: 1611].

the eagles, renewed by the washing away of sin. You have come to the altar; *you have seen the sacraments laid upon the altar: and you have marveled at the creature itself, yet [it is] the accustomed creature, and the one well known.* You have heard what he said, *you have seen,* he says, *the sacraments laid upon the altar.* For what is seen is visible. But *you have seen,* he says; this is therefore what we call the visible sacrament. But you say, "Why then do I who see the wine, not see the blood?" And so hear what the same doctor says in the same book of sacraments. He says, *Just as you have taken the likeness of his death, so also you drink the likeness of his precious blood. But why the likeness? That there may not be the revulsion of [seeing] blood, and yet that it might accomplish the price of redemption.* As if he said, "If it were not for the revulsion caused by seeing [it], you would see both the flesh that you eat and the blood that you drink." Now this visible sacrament some eat and drink to their [souls'] life, but others to their [souls'] judgment. Whence the Apostle says, WHOSOEVER SHALL HAVE EATEN AND DRUNK UNWORTHILY EATS AND DRINKS JUDGMENT UPON HIMSELF, NOT JUDGING RIGHTLY THE BODY OF THE LORD. But hear what Augustine has said about the visible and about the spiritual food in his exposition of John: YOUR FATHERS ATE MANNA AND DIED. *On what basis,* he says, *do you feel pride?* THEY ATE MANNA AND DIED. *Why did they eat and die? Because they believed what they saw, and did not understand what they did not see. Therefore [they are] your fathers, because you are like them. For as regards what pertains, my brothers, to that visible and corporeal death, surely we do not die, who eat the bread that descends from heaven? So they also died, just as we are to die, as far as what pertains to the visible and carnal death of this body goes. Moses also ate the manna, Aaron ate it, Phineas ate it, and many others there besides, who pleased the Lord and did not die. Why [was this]? Because they understood the visible food spiritually they hungered spiritually, they tasted spiritually, that they might be filled spiritually. For we also today receive a visible food; but the sacrament is one thing, the force of the sacrament another. How many receive from the altar and die, and*

95 *cipiendo moriuntur! Unde dicit apostolus:* IUDICIUM SIBI MANDU-
CAT ET BIBIT. Quid est autem, quod hic egregius expositor nos hoc
in loco intelligere persuadet, nisi ut ea quae videmus non credamus,
et ea quae non videmus intellegamus? Panem vides, intellige
carnem; vinum vides, intellige sanguinem. Intellegendo crede, cre-
100 dendo manduca, manducando imitare; id est, Christus in te, et tu
in Christo maneas. Unde et supra memoratus Augustinus ait: [56ᵛ]
*Hoc est ergo manducare illam escam, et illum bibere potum, in Christo
manere, Christum manentem in se habere. Ac per hoc, qui non manet
in Christo, et in quo non manet Christus, procul dubio nec manducat*
105 *eius carnem, nec bibit eius sanguinem, etiam si tantae rei sacramentum
ad iudicium sibi manducat et bibit.*
    5. Si igitur hanc carnem et sanguinem nemo, qui non manet in
Christo, et in quo non manet Christus, manducat et bibit, quid est
quod apostolus ait: QUI MANDUCAT ET BIBIT INDIGNE, IUDI-
110 CIUM SIBI MANDUCAT ET BIBIT? Aut enim nullus manducat indigne, aut indigne manducans manet in Christo. Quod si indigne
manducans manet in Christo, non utique ad iudicium, sed ad vitam manducat. Ipse enim dominus ait: QUI MANDUCAT CARNEM
MEAM, ET BIBIT SANGUINEM MEUM, IN ME MANET, ET EGO IN
115 ILLO. Hoc et Augustinus subsequenter exponens dixit: *Signum
quia manducavit et bibit, hoc est: si manet, et manetur; si habitat, et
inhabitatur; si haeret, ut non deseratur.* Ecce Augustinus cum
Christo concordat; idem enim uterque dicit. Sed quid dicit? QUI
MANDUCAT CARNEM MEAM, ET BIBIT SANGUINEM MEUM, IN
120 ME MANET, ET EGO IN EO. Currant ergo heretici? Currant homi-
cidae? Currant quicumque facinorosi? Comedant carnem Christi,
ut et ipsi in Christo, et Christus in eis maneat? Si enim Christus
in eis manserit, sancti erunt: TEMPLUM ENIM DEI SANCTUM EST,
QUOD ESTIS VOS. Et psalmista: TU AUTEM, inquit, IN SANCTO
125 HABITAS. His et his similibus omni auctoritate scripturarum ad

---

100 id est] id est *in ras. A.*   107 carnem] carnem qui *A, corr. A¹.*   117 haeret] *post* haeret
rasura duarum litterarum A.   120 eo] eum *A.*   125 His . . . similibus] His et enim similibus
A, His et horum similibus *proposuit Morin,* His et his similibus *coniecit FN (vide supra p. 61).*

102–6 Hoc . . . bibit] Aug. *Tract. 26 in Ioh.* c. 18, *CC* 36, p. 268 [*PL* 35: 1614].   109–10 Qui . . .
bibit] I Cor. 11:29.   113–15 qui . . . illo] Ioh. 6:56.   115–17 Signum . . . deseratur] Aug.
Tract. 27 in Ioh. c. 1, *CC* 36, p. 270 [*PL* 35: 1616].   123–24 templum . . . vos] I Cor. 3:17.
124–25 tu . . . habitas] Ps. 24:4.

die receiving! Whence the Apostle says, HE EATS AND DRINKS JUDG-
MENT FOR HIMSELF. Now what is it that this noble expounder
urges us to understand in this passage, if not that we not believe
those things that we see, and that we understand those things that
we do not see? You see bread: understand flesh; you see wine: understand blood. Understanding, believe; believing, eat; eating, imitate; that is, let Christ remain in you, and you are to remain in
Christ. Whence also the same Augustine says, *This is then eating
that food and drinking that drink: to remain in Christ, and to have
Christ remaining in one. And because of this, one who does not remain
in Christ, and in whom Christ does not remain, without a doubt does
not eat his flesh or drink his blood, even if he eats and drinks the sacrament of this mighty thing for judgment upon himself.*

5. Therefore if no one eats this flesh and blood who does not
remain in Christ, and in whom Christ does not remain, why is it
that the Apostle says, HE WHO EATS AND DRINKS UNWORTHILY,
EATS AND DRINKS JUDGMENT UPON HIMSELF? For either no one
eats unworthily, or, eating unworthily, he remains in Christ. But if,
eating unworthily, he remains in Christ, then he eats not to judgment, but to life. For the Lord himself says, HE WHO EATS MY
FLESH, AND DRINKS MY BLOOD, REMAINS IN ME, AND I IN HIM.
Augustine in his exposition of this also continues by saying: *A sign
that he has eaten and drunk, is this: if he remains, and one remains in
him; if he dwells and is dwelt in; if he clings fast, so that he is not de-
serted.* Behold, Augustine is in harmony with Christ, for each says
the same thing. But what does he say: HE WHO EATS MY FLESH,
AND DRINKS MY BLOOD, REMAINS IN ME, AND I IN HIM. Well
then, are heretics to come running? Are murderers to come running? Are criminals of every kind to come running? Are they to
eat the flesh of Christ, that they may remain in Christ, and Christ
in them? For if Christ remains in them, they will be holy: FOR THE
TEMPLE OF GOD—WHICH YOU ARE—IS HOLY. And the Psalmist
says, NOW YOU DWELL IN THE HOLY ONE. For these and those
like them it is forbidden in all the authority of the scriptures

hoc sacramentum accedere interdictum est. Unde consequens esse
videtur, ut nullus hanc carnem indigne manducet: nullus enim
manducat, nisi in quo manet Christus, et qui manet in Christo.
Quid est igitur, beate Paule, quid est, o doctor gentium, quod di-
130 cis? Christus enim carnem suam indigne manducari posse negat;
tu autem indigne manducari posse confirmas. Dicis enim: IDEO
INTER VOS MULTI INFIRMI ET INBECILLES, ET DORMIUNT
MULTI. Quare IDEO? Quoniam hanc carnem indigne manducant.
    6. Determinandum est igitur quod dicitur: QUI MANDUCAT
135 CARNEM MEAM, ET BIBIT SANGUINEM MEUM, IN ME MANET ET
EGO IN EO. Alii enim ore et corde, alii corde et non ore, alii ore et
non corde manducant. Ore namque et corde, id est, interiori
homine et exteriori apostoli manducaverunt; nec non et ceteri fideles post eos, qui fuerunt, et sunt, et qui futuri sunt, manducaverunt,
140 manducant, et manducabunt. Unde scriptum est: CENANTIBUS IL-
LIS ACCEPIT IESUS PANEM, BENEDIXIT, AC FREGIT, ET DEDIT
DISCIPULIS SUIS DICENS: ACCIPITE ET COMMEDITE, HOC EST
CORPUS MEUM. SIMILITER ET CALICEM POSTQUAM CENAVIT
DICENS: ACCIPITE ET BIBITE EX EO OMNES, HIC EST ENIM SAN-
145 GUIS MEUS. Quod beatus Ieronimus exponens ait: *postquam
tipicum pascha fuerat impletum, et agni carnes cum apostolis comederat,
assumpsit panem qui confortat cor hominis, et ad verum paschae trans-
grediens sacramentum, ut quo modo in praefiguratione eius
Melchisedech summi dei sacerdos panem et vinum offerens fecerat, ipse
150 quoque in veritate sui corporis et sanguinis repraesentaret.* Notandum
autem quod ait, *postquam tipicum pascha impletum fuerat.* Si enim
tipicum pascha impletum erat, illud quidem, quod iam tunc a
Christo agebatur, tipicum non erat. Tipico igitur impleto, ad
verum paschae transgreditur sacramentum. Non autem ideo verum
155 dixit, quod falsa praecesserint sacramenta; alioquin nec sacramenta
quidem fuissent. Surgit igitur verum quia iam non tipicum: non
figura, sed veritas. Unde Augustinus in expositione psalmi [57ʳ] ubi

---

136 eo] eum *A.*   **147** hominis] hominis *corr. ex ? A.*

131–32 Ideo . . . multi] I Cor. 11:30.   **134–36** qui . . . eo] Ioh. 6:56.   **140–45** cenantibus . . .
meus] Matt. 26:26–28.   **145–50** postquam . . . repraesentaret] Hieron. *Comment. in Matt. lib.
IV* [*PL* 26: 202C–203A].

that they should approach this sacrament. From this, the consequence seems to be that none should eat this flesh unworthily; for
no one eats it except one in whom Christ remains, and who remains in Christ. What then is it, O Blessed Paul; what is it, O
Teacher of the Gentiles, that you say? For Christ denies that his
flesh can be eaten unworthily, but you assert that it can be eaten
unworthily. For you say, THEREFORE THERE ARE MANY INFIRM
AND WEAK AMONG YOU, AND MANY SLEEP. Why THEREFORE?
Because they eat this flesh unworthily.

6. And so we must determine what the saying means: HE WHO
EATS MY FLESH AND DRINKS MY BLOOD, REMAINS IN ME, AND
I IN HIM. For some eat with lips and with heart; others with heart
and not with lips; others with lips and not with heart. The apostles ate with lips and with heart, that is, with the inner and outer
man, and the rest of the faithful after them, those faithful who
were and are and are to be, so ate, eat, and will eat. Hence it is written: AS THEY WERE AT DINNER, JESUS TOOK BREAD, BLESSED
IT, AND BROKE IT, AND GAVE IT TO HIS DISCIPLES, SAYING,
"TAKE AND EAT; THIS IS MY BODY." LIKEWISE ALSO THE CUP
AFTER HE HAD SUPPED, SAYING: "TAKE AND DRINK OF THIS,
ALL OF YOU, FOR THIS IS MY BLOOD." The blessed Jerome in expounding this says, *After completing the Passover, which was the type,
and eating the flesh of the lamb with the apostles, he took up the bread
which strengthens the heart of man, and passing to the true paschal
sacrament, so that, as Melchisedek, the priest of the supreme God, had
done in offering bread and wine, in prefiguration of him, he might show
it forth in the truth of his body and blood.* It is notable that he says
After completing the Passover, which was the type. For if the Passover
that was the type was completed, that which was even then carried
out by Christ was not the type. Therefore, having completed the
type, he passes over to the true paschal sacrament. Now he did not
call it true because the sacraments that had gone before were false;
otherwise they would not even have been sacraments. Therefore
the true one arises, because it is now not the type: it is not a figure,
but truth. Hence Augustine, in the exposition of the Psalm verse,

scriptum est SACRIFICIUM ET OBLATIONEM NOLUISTI, CORPUS
AUTEM APTASTI MIHI: *Perfectio,* inquit, *promissorum abstulit verba*
160 *promittentia. Nam si adhuc sunt promittentia, nondum impletum est
quod promissum est. Hoc promittebatur quibusdam signis: ablata sunt
signa promittentia, quia exhibita est veritas promissa. In hoc corpore
sumus, huius corporis participes sumus.* Quod accipimus novimus; et qui
non nostis, noveritis; et cum didiceritis, non ad iudicium accipietis. QUI
165 ENIM MANDUCAT ET BIBIT INDIGNE, IUDICIUM SIBI MANDU-
CAT ET BIBIT. Liquido igitur his verbis comprehendi potest, quoniam ecclesiae sacramentum non figura, non promissio, non significatio, immo ipsa veritas est. Sed considerandum quod modo ait:
QUI ENIM MANDUCAT ET BIBIT INDIGNE, IUDICIUM SIBI MAN-
170 DUCAT ET BIBIT. Superius enim dixerat: *Qui non manet in Christo,
et in quo non manet Christus, procul dubio non manducat eius carnem,
nec bibit eius sanguinem, etiam et tantae rei sacramentum ad iudicium
sibi manducat et bibit.*

7. Quod autem hoc sacramentum, id est, panis et vinum, quod
175 a sacerdotibus in sancta ecclesia consecratur, vera Christi caro fiat
et sanguis, audi quid Iohannes episcopus Constantinopolitanus in
eo sermone, quem de cena domini edidit, dicat: (Matt. 26:26) AC-
CEPIT IESUS, inquit, PANEM, BENEDIXIT ET FREGIT, ET DEDIT
DISCIPULIS SUIS, DICENS: ACCIPITE ET COMEDITE, HOC EST
180 CORPUS MEUM. *Praesens,* inquit, *Iudas erat, ista Christo dicente. Iste
est sanguis, dicit, Iudas, quem XXX denariis vendidisti; iste est sanguis,
de quo ante cum phariseis pactum fecisti. O Christi misericordia! O Iudae dementia! Ille eum XXX denariis paciscebatur ut venderet, et
Christus ei sanguinem quem vendidit offerebat. Et nunc ille praesto est
185 Christus, qui illam ornavit mensam, ipse istum consecrat panem. Non
enim homo est, qui proposita corpus Christi facit et sanguinem, sed ille
qui crucifixus est Christus. Ore sacerdotis verba proferuntur, et dei vir-*

159 Perfectio] Profectio *A, corr. A*¹.   164 accipietis] accipiatis *A.*   174 sacramentum]
sacramento *A.*   177 edidit] et *A,* edidit *statim A*¹. | Accepit] accipite *A, corr. A*¹.
178 panem] panem inquit *A, corr. A*¹.   187 dei] de *A.*

158–59 sacrificium . . . mihi] Heb. 10:5.   159–64 Perfectio . . . bibit] Aug. *In Psalmum XXXIX
Enarratio,* c. 12 [*PL* 36: 442].   164–66 qui . . . sibi manducat et bibit] I Cor. 11:29.
169–73 Qui . . . bibit] Aug. *Tract. 26 in Ioh.* c. 18, *CC* 36, p. 268 [*PL* 35: 1614].
180–94 Praesens . . . firmitatem] Ioh. Chrys. *Sermones panegyrici. De proditione Judae,* hom. 1, c. 5
[*PG* 49: 380—but from the translation published Basil., 1525, fol. 45v–46r].

YOU DESIRED NOT SACRIFICE AND OBLATION, BUT YOU HAVE
PREPARED A BODY FOR ME, says, *The fulfillment of the promises has
done away with the promising words. For if they are still promising,
that which is promised is not yet fulfilled. This was being promised by
certain signs: the signs that promised have been taken away, because the
truth that was promised has been revealed. We are in this body, we share
in this body. What we receive, we know; and you who do not know will
know; and when you will have learned, you will receive it not towards
judgment.* FOR HE WHO EATS AND DRINKS UNWORTHILY, EATS
AND DRINKS JUDGMENT UPON HIMSELF. Therefore it can be
clearly understood in these words that the sacrament of the church
is not a figure, not a promise, not a signifying; it is the truth. But
we must ponder how he says, FOR HE THAT EATS AND DRINKS
UNWORTHILY, EATS AND DRINKS JUDGMENT UPON HIMSELF.
For earlier he had said, *One who does not remain in Christ, and in
whom Christ does not remain—have no doubt—does not eat his flesh,
nor drink his blood, and even eats and drinks the sacrament of this
mighty thing as a judgment upon himself.*

7. Now as to the fact that this sacrament, that is, the bread and
wine, which is consecrated by the priests in the holy church, becomes the true flesh and blood of Christ, hear what John, the
bishop of Constantinople, says in that sermon that he wrote on the
Lord's Supper: he says, JESUS TOOK BREAD, BLESSED IT, AND
BROKE IT, AND GAVE IT TO HIS DISCIPLES, SAYING, TAKE AND
EAT, THIS IS MY BODY. *Judas was present, as Christ said these words.
"This is the blood," he says, "O Judas, that you have sold for thirty
denarii; this is the blood that you bargained away to the Pharisees." Oh
the mercy of Christ! Oh the madness of Judas! He was bargaining to sell
it for thirty denarii, and Christ was offering him the blood that he sold.
And now that Christ is present, who set that table, he himself conse-
crates this bread. For it is not a human being who makes the things set
forth here the body and blood of Christ, but it is that Christ who was
crucified who does it. The words are brought forth by the lips of the
priest, and by the power*

tute consecrantur eius gratia. HOC EST, *ait,* CORPUS MEUM. *Hoc verbo proposita consecrantur; et sicut illa vox, quae dixit* (Gen. 1:22)
190 CRESCITE ET MULTIPLICAMINI ET REPLETE TERRAM, *semel quidem dicta est, sed omni tempore sentit effectum ad generationem operante natura, ita et vox illa semel quidem dicta est, sed per omnes mensas ecclesiae usque ad hodiernum et usque ad eius adventum praestat sacrificio firmitatem.* Quid autem planius, quid apertius, quid evi-
195 dentius dici potest? *Iudas, inquit, XXX denariis Christum paciscebatur ut venderet; Christus ei sanguinem quem vendidit offerebat.* Si igitur et verum sanguinem vendidit Iudas, constat quia verum sanguinem ei ad bibendum dominus optulit. Unde et Augustinus in expositione psalmi XXXIII, in cuius titulo legitur quod David (Ps.
200 33:1) MUTAVIT VULTUM SUUM CORAM ABIMELECH, ET FEREBATUR IN MANIBUS SUIS, sic ait: *Hoc vero, fratres, quomodo posset fieri in homine quis intelligebat? Quis enim portatur in manibus suis? Manibus alienis portari potest homo: manibus suis nemo portatur. Quomodo ergo intelligatur in ipso David secundum litteram non in-*
205 *venimus: in Christo autem invenimus. Ferebatur enim Christus in manibus suis, quando commendans ipsum corpus suum ait:* HOC EST CORPUS MEUM. *Ferebatur enim illud in manibus suis.* Ecce habes quod Augustinus iam non panem, non vinum, non figuram, non sacramentum dicit sed *corpus,* inquit, *suum ferebat in manibus suis.*
210 Hoc est [57ᵛ] ergo quod Christus ferebat, hoc est quod secundum ordinem Melchisedech discipulis offerebat: panem utique et vinum iam in suam carnem et sanguinem commutata. Unde Ambrosius: (Ps. 109:4) TU ES, inquit, SACERDOS IN AETERNUM SECUNDUM ORDINEM MELCHISEDECH. *Ergo auctor sacramentorum*
215 *quis est, nisi dominus Iesus? De caelo ista sacramenta venerunt: consilium enim omne de caelo est. Vere autem magnum et divinum est miraculum, quod populo pluit manna de caelo, et non laborabat populus, et manducabat. Tu forte dicis: "Meus panis est usitatus." Sed panis iste pa-*

---

189 proposita] proposito *A.*   198 optulit] optolit *A, corr. A*¹.   199 expositione] exposio *A, statim corr. A*¹.   203 portari] portatur *A, corr. A*¹.

200–7 Mutavit . . . suis] Aug. *In Psalmum XXXIII Enarratio,* sermo 1 c. 10 [*PL* 36: 306].
213–36 Tu . . . Christi] Ambros. *De sacram.* 4.3.12–4.4.16, *CSEL* 73, pp. 51–53 [*PL* 16: 458C–461A].

of God they are consecrated through his grace. THIS IS, *he says,* MY
BODY. *With this word the offerings are consecrated; and just as that
word, which said,* GROW AND MULTIPLY AND FILL THE EARTH,
*was spoken only once but feels its effect upon the work of generation
throughout all time, by the operation of nature, so also that other word
was spoken only once, but upon all the tables of the Church down to today, and even on until his coming, offers a foundation for sacrifice.* Now
what can be said more plainly, what more openly, what more evidently? He says, *Judas was bargaining to sell Christ for thirty denarii;
Christ was offering to him the blood that he sold.* If therefore Judas
sold the true blood, it is established that the Lord offered him true
blood to drink. Whence Augustine in his exposition upon Psalm
XXXIII, in whose heading one reads that David CHANGED HIS
FACE BEFORE ABIMELECH, AND WAS CARRIED IN HIS HANDS,
says this: *Who, O brethren, might understand how this can be done in
the case of a man? For who is carried in his own hands? Another's hands
might carry a man, but no one is carried in his own hands. How then
this may be understood literally in the case of David himself we do not
find; but we find it in Christ. For Christ was being carried in his own
hands, when, commending his very body, he said,* THIS IS MY BODY.
For that was being carried in his own hands. Behold, you have what
Augustine says is now not bread, not wine, not a figure, not a sacrament, but, he says, *he was carrying his own body in his hands.* This
is then what Christ was carrying, this is what he was offering, after the order of Melchisedech, to his disciples; namely, the bread
and wine now transformed into his own flesh and blood. Whence
Ambrose says, THOU ART A PRIEST FOREVER, AFTER THE OR-
DER OF MELCHISEDECH. *Therefore who is the author of sacraments,
if not the Lord Jesus? These sacraments have come from heaven; for all
counsel is from heaven. It is truly a great and divine miracle, that
manna rained down from heaven upon the people, and the people did
no work and ate. You perchance say, "My bread is the common kind."
But this bread you*

220 *nis est ante verba sacramentorum; ubi accesserit consecratio, de pane*
fit caro Christi. Hoc igitur astruamus, quomodo potest, qui panis est,
corpus esse Christi. Consecratio igitur quibus verbis est et cuius ser-
monibus? Domini Iesu. Nam reliqua omnia dicuntur: laus deo fertur;
oratio petitur pro populo, pro regibus, pro caeteris. Ubi venitur ut con-
225 *ficiatur venerabile sacramentum, iam non suis sermonibus utitur sac-*
erdos, sed utitur sermonibus Christi. Ergo sermo Christi hoc conficit
sacramentum. Quis sermo Christi? Nempe is quo facta sunt omnia.
Iussit dominus, et factum est caelum: iussit dominus, et facta est terra:
iussit dominus, et facta sunt maria: iussit dominus et omnis creatura
230 *generata est. Vides igitur quam operatorius sit sermo Christi? Si ergo*
tanta vis est in sermone domini Iesu, ut inciperent esse quae non erant,
quanto magis operatorius est, ut sint quae erant, et in aliud commu-
tentur? Caelum non erat, mare non erat, terra non erat; sed audi di-
centem: (Ps. 32:9) IPSE DIXIT ET FACTA SUNT, MANDAVIT ET CRE-
235 ATA SUNT. *Ergo ut tibi respondeam, non erat corpus Christi ante*
consecrationem; dico tibi quia iam corpus est Christi. Puto quod haec
verba beati Ambrosii ad omnes hereticos convincendos, qui illud
de quo loquimur sacramentum veram Christi carnem et sanguinem negant esse, sola sufficiant; verum tamen ut maiori confu-
240 sione digni habeantur, plurima ad haec sanctorum patrum argu-
menta subdemus.

8. Sed prius eam, quam supra fecimus, exponamus divisionem.
Memores igitur esse debemus quod sanguis agni, qui super
utrumque postem in veteri lege positus est, hoc praefiguraverit,
245 quod Christi sanguinem, quem agnus ille significabat, ore carnis et
cordis bibituri eramus. Unde beatus Gregorius in suis homeliis ita
testatus est, dicens: *Quis namque sit sanguis agni, iam non audiendo*
sed bibendo didicistis: Qui sanguis super utrumque postem ponitur,
quando non solum ore corporis, sed etiam ore cordis hauritur. In utroque
250 *etenim poste sanguis est positus, quando sacramentum passionis illius*
cum ore ad redemptionem sumitur, ad imitationem quoque intenta
mente cogitatur. Quo modo igitur ore et corde Christi caro et san-

---

244 veteri] veteris *A, corr. A*[1].   247 audiendo] audiendun? *A, corr. A*[1].
249 corporis] corporis auritur *A, corr. A*[1].

247–52 Quis . . . cogitatur] Greg. M. *Homiliarum in Evangelia libri duo,* lib. 2 hom. 22 c. 7 [*PL* 76: 1178B].

speak of is the bread before the words of sacrament; when the consecra-
tion is added, from bread it becomes the flesh of Christ. Let us establish
this then, how that which is bread can be the body of Christ. Therefore
the consecration takes place in what words and in whose language? The
Lord Jesus's. For all the rest is said: praise is offered to God; prayer is
made for the people, for the rulers, for the rest. [But] when it comes to
the point of carrying out the venerable sacrament, the priest no longer
uses his own language, but uses the language of Christ. Therefore the
language of Christ carries out this sacrament. What language of Christ?
Why, that by which all things were created. The Lord commanded, and
the heavens were made; the Lord commanded, and the earth was made;
the Lord commanded, and the seas were made; the Lord commanded,
and every creature was generated. Do you see then how effective is the
language of Christ? If therefore there is such power in the language of
the Lord Jesus that what was not should begin to be, how much more
effective it is that that which was, should be changed into something
else. The heavens were not, the sea was not, the earth was not; but hear
the one who says, HE SPOKE AND IT WAS DONE, HE GAVE COM-
MAND AND IT WAS CREATED. *Therefore, to reply to you, it was not*
the body of Christ before consecration; I say to you that now it is the body
of Christ. I think that these words of Blessed Ambrose alone would
be sufficient to convict as heretics all who deny that that sacrament
of which we speak is the true flesh and blood of Christ; but that
they may be deemed worthy of further confounding, I shall add to
these yet further arguments of the holy Fathers.

8. But first, let us explain the distinction that we set up earlier.
We ought then to be mindful that the blood of the lamb, which
under the Old Law was placed on both doorposts, prefigured this,
that we were to drink, with lips of flesh and with lips of the heart,
the blood of Christ, for whom that lamb was a sign. Whence
Blessed Gregory in his homilies testified as follows, saying, *For you*
have now learned what the blood of the lamb is, not by hearing but by
drinking—this blood which is placed on both doorposts—since it is
drunk not only with the lips of the body but also by the lips of the heart.
For indeed the blood is placed on both doorposts, since the sacrament of
his passion, while it is taken upon the lips for redemption, is also pon-
dered in the attentive mind for imitation. How then the flesh and
blood of Christ are eaten and drunk by the lips and in the heart,

guis manducatur et bibitur, in hac expositione beati Gregorii evi-
dentissime dictum est. Nunc autem quis ore et non corde suscip-
255 iat, eumdem ipsum audi dicentem: *Nam qui sic,* inquit, *redemptoris
sui sanguinem accipit, ut imitari passionem illius necdum velit, in
unum postem sanguinem posuit.* Et paulo post: *Quid enim prodest corpus et sanguinem illius ore percipere, et ei insuper moribus contraire?*
Unde et apostolus Corinthios increpat dicens: CONVENIENTIBUS
260 VOBIS IN UNUM IAM NON EST DOMINICAM [58ʳ] CENAM MAN-
DUCARE. UNUSQUISQUE ENIM SUAM CENAM PRAESUMIT AD
MANDUCANDUM, et caetera quae secuntur. De his igitur, quoniam
Christi sacramentum indigne suscipiebant, subinferens ait: IDEO
INTER VOS MULTI INFIRMI ET INBECILLES, ET DORMIUNT
265 MULTI. De talibus ergo dicit beatus Augustinus: *Qui non manet in
Christo, et in quo non manet Christus, procul dubio nec eius carnem
manducat, nec eius sanguinem bibit*—subauditur ore cordis (sive, ut
Pascasius ait, *ad vitam*)—*etiam si tantae rei sacramentum ore carnis
ad iudicium sibi manducat et bibit.*
270   9. His igitur ita dispositis, quid sit corde et non ore manducare
dicamus. Qua in re solius Augustini sententiae sufficere possent:
in hac enim spiritali manducatione et bibitione plurimum quidem
ipse laborat. Hoc autem modo priusquam de virgine nasceretur,
Christus a sanctis patribus olim manducabatur; hoc et nunc a
275 fidelibus et bibitur et manducatur. Quod ut planius fiat, ipsius
quem modo diximus Augustini verba ponamus: (I Cor. 10:1-3)
NOLO ENIM VOS IGNORARE, FRATRES, inquit, QUIA PATRES
NOSTRI OMNES SUB NUBE FUERUNT, ET OMNES PER MARE
TRANSIERUNT, ET OMNES PER MOYSEN BAPTIZATI SUNT IN
280 NUBE ET IN MARI, ET OMNES EANDEM ESCAM SPIRITUALEM
MANDUCAVERUNT. *Spiritualem utique eandem, nam corporalem al-
teram: quia illi manna, nos aliud.* Breviter autem hic Augustinum
interrogare volo, quare dixerit, *illi manna, nos aliud.* Ut quid enim

---

255 redemptoris] redeptoris *A.*   259 apostolus] p *A,* apostolus *A*¹.

255–57 Nam . . . posuit] *Ibid.*   257–58 Quid . . . contraire] Greg. M. *Homiliarum in Evangelia
libri duo,* lib. 2 hom. 22 c. 8 [*PL* 76: 1178D–1179A].   259–62 convenientibus . . . manducandum]
I Cor. 11:20–21.   263–65 ideo . . . dormiunt multi] I Cor. 11:30.   265–69 Qui . . . bibit] Aug.
Tract. 26 in Ioh. c. 18, *CC* 36, p. 268 [*PL* 35: 1614].   268 ad vitam] Pascas. *De corp. et sang. domini*
c. 6:3 [*CCCM* 16, p. 36]   277–91 nolo . . . spirituali] Aug. *Tract. 26 in Ioh.* c. 12, *CC* 36, p. 265
[*PL* 35: 1612].

is most clearly explained in this exposition of the blessed Gregory. Now then, listen to the same one as he says who it is who takes it with his lips but not his heart: *For,* he says, *one who takes the blood of his Redeemer in such a way that he does not yet choose to imitate his passion, has placed the blood upon only a single doorpost.* And, a little after that, *For what does it avail to take his body and blood in one's mouth and then to contradict him in one's ways?* Whence the Apostle rebukes the Corinthians, saying, WHEN YOU COME TOGETHER AS ONE, IT IS NOT TO EAT THE LORD'S SUPPER. FOR EACH INDIVIDUAL TAKES HIS OWN SUPPER TO EAT, and the rest that follows. Regarding these then, since they took the sacrament of Christ unworthily, he says in interpretation, THEREFORE MANY AMONG YOU ARE INFIRM AND WEAK, AND MANY SLEEP. Regarding such as these, then, the blessed Augustine says, *Who does not remain in Christ, and in whom Christ does not remain, without a doubt does not eat his flesh or drink his blood*—one understands "with the lips of the heart," (or, as Paschasius says, *for life*)—*even if he eats and drinks the sacrament of this great thing with the lips of his flesh for judgment upon himself.*

9. Having settled these matters in this fashion, let us declare what it is to eat with the heart and not with the lips. On this subject the statements of Augustine alone would be sufficient, for he himself takes great pains over this spiritual eating and drinking. In this manner, even before he was born of the Virgin, Christ was formerly eaten by the holy Fathers; in this manner he is both drunk and eaten even now by the faithful. To make this plainer, let us set down the words of the very Augustine whom I have just now mentioned; he says, I WOULD NOT HAVE YOU IGNORANT, BROTHERS, THAT OUR FATHERS WERE ALL UNDER THE CLOUD, AND ALL PASSED OVER THE SEA, AND ALL WERE BAPTIZED BY MOSES IN THE CLOUD AND IN THE SEA, AND ALL ATE THE SAME SPIRITUAL FOOD, *namely, the same spiritual [food], for the bodily one was different, since they ate manna, while we [eat] something else.* But at this point I wish briefly to question Augustine, as to why he said, *they [ate] manna, while we [eat] something else.*

non dixit: illi manna, nos panem? Hoc enim modo verborum ordo
285 rectius procederet. Cur autem illud dixit, et hoc non dixit? Quia
videlicet, quod nos sumimus, nec panis est, nec manna, immo
Christi caro et sanguis. Sequitur in eodem: *Spiritualem vero, quam
nos. Sed patres nostri, non patres illorum; quibus nos similes sumus, non
quibus illi similes fuerunt.* Et adiungit: (I Cor. 10:4) ET OMNES EU-
290 NDEM POTUM SPIRITUALEM BIBERUNT. *Aliud illi, aliud nos: sed
specie visibile, quod tamen hoc idem significaret veritate spirituali.* Id
ipsum autem et alibi exponens prope eisdem utitur verbis: EUN-
DEM, inquit, POTUM SPIRITUALEM BIBERUNT. *Spiritualem eundem, nam corporalem non eundem. Quid enim illi bibebant?* (I Cor.
295 10:4) BIBEBANT AUTEM DE SPIRITUALI CONSEQUENTI EOS PE-
TRA. PETRA AUTEM ERAT CHRISTUS. *Videte ergo fidem manentem,
signa variata. Ibi petra Christus: nobis Christus, quod in altari dei
ponitur. Et illi pro magno sacramento eiusdem Christi biberunt aquam
profluentem de petra; nos quid bibamus norunt fideles. Si speciem visi-
300 bilem adtendas, aliud est; si intelligibilem significationem, eum potum
biberunt spiritualem.* Idem ipse in psalmo, ubi dicitur (Ps. 21:26)
VOTA MEA REDDAM IN CONSPECTU TIMENTIUM EUM: *id est,
sacramenta corporis et sanguinis mei reddam coram timentibus eum.*
(Ps. 21:26) EDENT PAUPERES ET SATURABUNTUR: *Edent humiles
305 et contemptores saeculi, et mutabuntur.* (Ps. 21:27) VIVENT CORDA
EORUM IN SAECULUM SAECULI: *nam cibus ille cordis est.* Item Augustinus de eo quod dicitur: (Ioan. 6:56) CARO MEA VERE EST
CIBUS, ET SANGUIS MEUS VERE EST POTUS: *cum enim cibo,* inquit,
*ac potu id appetant homines, ut neque esuriant neque sitiant, hoc ve-
310 raciter non praestat nisi iste cibus et potus, qui eos a quibus sumitur immortales et incorruptibiles facit, id est, societas ipsa sanctorum, ubi pax
erit, et unitas plena atque perfecta. Propterea quippe, sicut etiam ante
nos hoc intellexerunt homines dei, dominus noster Iesus Christus corpus
et sanguinem suum in his rebus commendavit, quae ad unum aliquid
315 rediguntur ex multis; namque aliud in unum ex multis granis confici-
tur, aliud in unum ex multis acinis confluit.* [58ᵛ]

---

297 quod . . . altari] quia in altari *A.*

292–301 Eundem . . . spiritualem] Aug. *Tract. 45 in Ioh.* c. 9, *CC* 36, p. 393 [*PL* 35: 1723].
302–6 vota . . . cordis est] Aug. *In Psalmum XXI Enarratio I* c. 26–27 [*PL* 36: 170].
307–16 Caro . . . confluit] Aug. *Tract. 26 in Ioh.* c. 17, *CC* 36, p. 268 [*PL* 35: 1614].

For why did he not say, "they [ate] manna, while we [eat] bread"? For in this way the order of the words would run more straight-forwardly. So why did he say that, and not this? Because, to be exact, what we take is not bread and not manna; no, it is the flesh and blood of Christ. The same writer continues, *The spiritual [food], which we eat. But our fathers, not their fathers; ones whom we resemble, not ones whom they resembled.* And he adds, AND ALL DRANK THE SAME SPIRITUAL DRINK. *They [drank] one thing, we another; but visible in its outward seeming, yet one which could be a sign of this same thing through spiritual truth.* And, expounding this very thing elsewhere, he uses virtually the same words: THEY DRANK, he says, THE SAME SPIRITUAL DRINK. *The same spiritual drink, for [it was] not the same bodily one. But what did they drink?* NOW THEY DRANK FROM THE SPIRITUAL ROCK THAT FOLLOWED THEM. AND THE ROCK WAS CHRIST. *So observe the faith that abides [and] the signs that are varied. There the rock is Christ; for us it is Christ that is placed upon the altar of God. And they, for a great sacrament of the same Christ, drank water flowing from the rock; the faithful know what we drink. If you should attend to the visible outward seeming, it is something else; if you attend to the intelligible signification, they drank that spiritual drink.* The very same one [says], regarding the Psalm that reads, I SHALL PAY MY VOWS IN THE SIGHT OF THOSE THAT FEAR HIM: *that is, I shall offer the sacraments of my body and blood before the face of those who fear him.* THE POOR SHALL EAT AND THEY SHALL BE FILLED: *the humble and those who despise the world shall eat, and shall be changed.* THEIR HEARTS SHALL LIVE FOR-EVER: *for that is the food of the heart.* Likewise Augustine says on the passage in which it is said, MY FLESH IS TRULY FOOD, AND MY BLOOD IS TRULY DRINK: *For while men with food and drink seek to avoid being hungry or thirsty, in truth that is guaranteed only by this food and drink, which renders immortal and incorruptible those by whom it is taken, that is, the very communion of the saints, wherein will be peace, and a unity full and perfected. Indeed, for this reason, as men of God have understood this subject even before us, our Lord Jesus Christ has commended his body and blood in these objects, which out of many things are fashioned into some one thing; for the one element is kneaded into one out of many grains, the other is strained into one out of many grapes.*

10. Quid autem nos aliud beatus Augustinus in his verbis intelligere ammonet, immo quasi vi quadam id sentire cogit? Ut Christi corpus et sanguinem sumendo unitatem et caritatem te-
320 neamus; quatenus et ipsum, cuius sanguinem bibimus, toto corde, tota anima omnibusque viribus, et proximos nostros tamquam nos ipsos diligamus. In cuius assertione sententiae eleganti panis et vini utitur similitudine, quae sic ex pluribus unita sunt, ut iam nullo modo singula a se vel discerni vel sequestrari possint. Quod si mihi
325 non credis, ipse Augustinus suam tibi voluntatem innotescat: *Diximus enim, fratres,* inquit, *hoc dominum commendasse in manducatione carnis suae, et potatione sanguinis sui, ut in illo maneamus, et ipse in nobis. Manemus autem in illo, cum sumus membra eius; manet autem ipse in nobis, cum sumus templum eius. Ut autem simus membra*
330 *eius, unitas nos compaginat; ut compaginet unitas, quae facit nisi caritas? Et caritas dei unde? Apostolum interroga.* (Rom. 5:5) CARITAS, *inquit,* DEI DIFFUSA EST IN CORDIBUS NOSTRIS PER SPIRITUM SANCTUM QUI DATUS EST NOBIS. *Ergo* (Ioan. 6:64) SPIRITUS EST QUI VIVIFICAT. *Spiritus enim facit viva membra; nec viva membra*
335 *spiritus facit, nisi quae in corpore quod vegetat ipse spiritus invenerit. Nam spiritus qui est in te, o homo, quo constat ut homo sis, numquid vivificat membrum quod separatum invenerit a carne tua? Spiritum tuum dico animam tuam; anima tua non vivificat nisi membra quae sunt in carne tua. Unum si tollas, iam ex anima tua non vivificatur,*
340 *quia unitati corporis tui non copulatur. Haec dicuntur, ut amemus unitatem, et timeamus separationem. Nichil enim sic debet timere christianus, quam separari a corpore Christi. Si enim separatur a corpore Christi, non est membrum eius; si non est membrum eius, non vegetatur spiritu eius.* De hoc autem et in sequentibus ipse sic loquitur: *Hoc*
345 *totum, quod de carne et sanguine suo dominus locutus est, et quod in eius distributionis gratia vitam nobis promisit aeternam, et quod hinc voluit intellegi manducatores et potatores carnis et sanguinis sui, ut in illo maneant, et ipse in illis; hoc ergo totum ad hoc nobis valeat, dilectissimi, ut carnem et sanguinem Christi non edamus tantum in sacra-*

330–31 nisi . . . interroga] nisi caritas, et caritas Dei? Unde apostolum interroga *A*.
335 quae] *om. A, restituit Morin.* 340 unitati] veritati *A, corr. A*[1]. | dicuntur] Dominus *A*.
344 spiritu] spiritus *A*. 345 quod in eius] quid in eius *A*. 346 hinc] hunc *A*.
349 sacramento] sacramentum *A, corr. A*[1].

325–44 Diximus . . . spiritu eius] Aug. *Tract. 27 in Ioh.* c. 6, *CC* 36, pp. 272–73 [*PL* 35:1618].
344–54 Hoc . . . tormenta] Aug. *Tract. 27 in Ioh.* c. 11, *CC* 36, pp. 275–76 [*PL* 35: 1620–21].

10. Now what else does the blessed Augustine advise us to understand in these words, nay rather compels us to feel with, as it were, a kind of force? That in taking the body and blood of Christ we should hold unity and charity; so that we may love him, whose blood we drink, with all our heart, with all our soul, with all our strength, and love our neighbors as ourselves. In the assertion of this position he uses the elegant simile of bread and wine, which are brought together out of many things in such a way that the individual elements can by no means be separated or taken apart. If you do not believe me, let Augustine himself make his intention known to you: *For we have said, my brothers,* he says, *that the Lord commended this in the eating of his flesh, and in the drinking of his blood, that we should remain in him, and he in us. Now we remain in him, when we are his members; and he remains in us, when we are his temple. And that we may be his members, unity binds us together; what causes unity to bind us together, if it is not charity? and whence comes God's charity? Ask the Apostle.* THE CHARITY OF GOD, *he says,* IS SPREAD ABROAD IN OUR HEARTS THROUGH THE HOLY SPIRIT WHO IS GIVEN TO US. *Therefore,* THE SPIRIT IS HE WHO CAUSES ONE TO LIVE. *For the spirit makes living members: nor does the Spirit make members live except those that he shall have found in the body to which the Spirit himself imparts vigor. For the spirit that is in you, O Man, which guarantees that you are a man, surely does not impart life, does it, to a limb which it finds separated from your flesh? I say that your breath is your spirit: your breath does not impart vigor to any limbs except those that are in your flesh. If you should take away a limb, it is no longer given vigor by your breath, because it is not joined to the unity of your body. These things are said that we may love unity and fear separation. For a Christian ought not to fear anything as much as being separated from the body of Christ. For if he is separated from the body of Christ, he is not his member; if he is not his member, he is not given vigor by his Spirit.* Furthermore, on this subject he has this to say also in the following: *This whole saying which the Lord gave us regarding his flesh and blood, both that he has promised us eternal life in the grace of its distribution, and that in this passage he wished us to understand a reference to those who eat and drink his flesh and blood, that they should remain in him and he in them: this whole statement then should have this force for us, dearly beloved, that we should not eat the*

350 *mento, quod et multi sic accipiunt, sed usque ad spiritus participationem*
manducemus et bibamus; ut in domini corpore tamquam membra
maneamus, ut in eius spiritu vegetemur, et non scandalizemur, etiam si
multi modo nobiscum manducant et bibunt temporaliter sacramenta,
qui habebunt in fine aeterna tormenta. Illud quo modo beatus Au-
355 gustinus ait, ut carnem et sanguinem Christi non edamus tantum
in sacramento, valde nobis considerandum est; in hoc enim veram
Christi carnem et sanguinem in hoc esse sacramento innuit, et non
tantum ore corporis suscipi debere demonstrat.

    11. Fortasse ista Augustini verba sufficerent; sed melius est se-
360 cundum Tullium *aliquid* superesse *reliquiarum, quam non saciatum*
aliquem hinc abire patiamur. Age ergo, nunc alii loquantur, inter
quos eiusdem tamen testimonia misceamus. Dicat igitur beatus
Gregorius papa Romanus—diiudicet iste, qui nunc eiusdem nominis eiusdemque spiritus eiusdem Gregorii, et ipse Gregorius,
365 possidet locum; cui, ut credimus, divinitus reservatum est [59ʳ] ut,
quod ille dixerat, iste confirmet; haec autem, quae dicturi sumus,
beati Gregorii verba sic istius, qui nunc mundum illustrat, pectori
insita sunt, ut, quod ille cotidie fieri debere dixit, iste cotidie agere
non praetermittat—*debemus,* inquit Gregorius, *praesens saeculum,*
370 *vel quia iam conspicimus defluxisse, tota mente contempnere, cotidiana*
deo lacrimarum sacrificia, cotidianas carnis eius et sanguinis hostias
immolare. Haec namque singulariter victima ab aeterno interitu ani-
mam salvat, quae illam nobis mortem unigeniti per misterium reparat.
Qui licet (Rom. 6:9) SURGENS A MORTUIS IAM NON MORITUR,
375 ET MORS ILLI ULTRA NON DOMINABITUR, *tamen in se ipso im-*
mortaliter atque incorruptibiliter vivens, pro nobis iterum in hoc mis-
terio sacrae oblationis immolatur. Eius corpus quippe ibi sumitur, eius
caro in populi salute partitur, eius sanguis non iam in manus in-
fidelium, sed in ora fidelium funditur. Hinc ergo pensemus, quale sit pro
380 *nobis hoc sacrificium, quod pro absolutione nostra passionem unigeniti*
filii semper imitatur. Quis enim habere fidelium dubium possit, in ipsa
immolationis hora ad sacerdotis vocem caelos aperiri, in illo Iesu Christi

---

378 populi] populis *A.*   381 fidelium] filium *A.*

360–61 aliquid . . . patiamur] Cic. *Topica* 25–26.   **369–84** debemus . . . fieri] Greg. M. *Dial.,*
4.58 [*PL* 77: 425C–428A].

flesh and blood of Christ only in a sacrament, as many take it, but that we may eat and drink even to the sharing of the Spirit, that we may remain as limbs in the Lord's body, that we may be invigorated in his Spirit and not be offended, even if many now eat and drink the sacraments temporally with us who in the end will have eternal punishment. This we must ponder deeply, as the blessed Augustine says, that we should not eat the flesh and blood of Christ only in a sacrament: for in this he indicates that the true flesh and blood of Christ is in this sacrament, and he shows that one should not receive it only with the bodily lips.

II. Perchance these words of Augustine would suffice; but according to Cicero it is better for *some remnants* to be left over, *than for us to allow* anyone *to go away from here unfilled.* Come then, let others now speak; and yet let us mix in among them passages that bear witness from the same Augustine. Let then the blessed Gregory, the Roman pope, speak—and let the present one pass judgment who, now endowed with the same name and the same spirit, himself a Gregory, holds the place of the same Gregory; for the present Gregory, as we believe, it was reserved by divine providence that he should carry out what the former one had said; moreover, these words of the blessed Gregory, which I am about to rehearse, are so deeply implanted in the heart of the present Gregory, who now gives light to the world, that he unfailingly carries out daily what the former one said should be done daily—*we ought,* says Gregory, *with all our minds to despise the world that is present now, precisely because we see that already it has slipped away, and to yield up to God the daily sacrifice of tears, the daily offering of his flesh and blood. For this victim uniquely saves the soul from eternal destruction, making good for us that death of the only-begotten one, through a mystery. Who, though* RISING FROM THE DEAD NOW NO LONGER DIES, AND DEATH SHALL HAVE NO MORE DOMINION OVER HIM, *yet in his very self living immortally and incorruptibly, he is sacrificed for us again in this mystery of the sacred oblation. Indeed his body is there taken, his flesh is divided in the salvation of the people, his blood is poured out, no longer upon the hands of the faithless but upon the lips of the faithful. Therefore, from this let us consider the nature of this sacrifice made for us, which for our absolution forever imitates the passion of the only-begotten son. For who among the faithful could have any doubt that in the very hour of immolation at the word of the priest the heavens are opened, that in that mystery*

misterio angelorum choros adesse, summis ima sociari, terram cae-
lestibus iungi, unumque ex visibilibus atque invisibilibus fieri? Haec
385 igitur beatus Gregorius dixit. Nunc autem quid Ambrosius dixerit
audiamus: *Accipe,* inquit, *quomodo sermo Christi creaturam omnem*
mutare consueverit, et mutat, quando vult, instituta naturae. Deinde
enumerat, quomodo virgo Maria contra naturam peperit; quomodo Moyses aquas virga tetigit, et ad se undam divisit; quomodo
390 lignum in fontem amarum miserit, et dulcoratus est; quomodo fer-
rum Elisei super aquas nataverit. Ac deinde subinferens ait: *Ex his*
igitur omnibus non intelligis quantum operetur sermo caelestis? Si op-
eratus est in fonte terreno, si operatus est sermo caelestis in aliis rebus,
non operatur in caelestibus sacramentis? Ergo didicisti quod ex pane
395 *corpus Christi fiat. Et quidem vinum cum aqua in calicem mittitur; sed*
fit sanguis consecratione verbi caelestis. Didicisti ergo quia, quod ac-
cipis, corpus est Christi. Vis scire quia verbis caelestibus consecratur?
Accipe quae sunt verba. Dicit sacerdos: "Fac nobis hanc oblationem as-
criptam, rationabilem, quod est figura corporis et sanguinis domini nos-
400 *tri Iesu Christi. Qui pridie quam pateretur, in sanctis manibus suis ac-*
cepit panem, respexit ad caelum, ad te, sancte pater omnipotens aeterne
deus, gratias agens, benedixit, fregit, fractumque apostolis et discipulis
suis tradidit dicens: ACCIPITE, ET EDITE EX EO OMNES; HOC EST
CORPUS MEUM, QUOD PRO MULTIS CONFRINGITUR." *"Similiter et*
405 *calicem, postquam cenatum est, pridie quam pateretur, accepit, respexit ad*
caelum, ad te, sancte pater omnipotens aeterne deus, gratias agens,
benedixit, apostolis et discipulis suis tradidit dicens: ACCIPITE, ET BIB-
ITE EX EO OMNES; HIC EST ENIM SANGUIS MEUS." *Vide: omnia illa*
verba evangelistae sunt usque ad "accipite," sive corpus, sive sanguinem;
410 *inde verba sunt Christi: "Accipite et bibite ex eo omnes; hic est enim san-*
guis meus." Et vide singula. "Qui pridie," inquit, "quam pateretur, in
sanctis manibus suis accepit panem." Antequam consecretur, panis est; ubi
autem verba Christi accesserint, corpus est Christi. Denique audi dicen-
tem: (Matt. 26:26; cf. Marc. 14:22, Luc. 22:19, I Cor. 11:24) ACCIPITE

384 unumque] unum quod *A*.   394 in caelestibus sacramentis] caelestibus sacramentis *A*.

386–87 Accipe . . . naturae] Ambros. *De sacram.,* 4.4.17, CSEL 73, p. 53 [*PL* 16: 461A].
391–418 Ex . . . redemit] Ambros. *De sacram.* 4.4.19–4.4.20, CSEL 73, pp. 54–56 [*PL* 16: 462A–463B].

of Jesus Christ the choirs of angels appear, that depths are linked with heights, earth joined to heavenly regions, and the visible and the invisible are made one? These then are the words of the blessed Gregory. Now let us hear what Ambrose said: *Hear* (he said) *how the word of Christ has repeatedly changed all creation, and changes, when he will, the dispositions of nature.* Then he counts them up: how the Virgin Mary bore a child contrary to nature; how Moses touched the waters with his rod and divided the wave upon itself; how he threw the wood into the brackish fountain and the water was made sweet; how Elisha's iron floated on the water. And then, giving his inference, he said, *On the basis of all these then do you not understand the great effectiveness of the heavenly word? If the heavenly word produced its effect upon an earthly spring, if it produced its effect upon other things, does it not produce its effect upon heavenly sacraments? Therefore you have learned that from bread it becomes the body of Christ. And indeed it is wine that is put with water into the chalice, but it becomes blood by the consecration of the heavenly word. You have learned then that what you receive is the body of Christ. Do you want to know that it is consecrated with heavenly words? Listen to what the words are. The priest says, Make this to be our appointed and reasonable offering, for it is a figure of the body and blood of our Lord Jesus Christ. Who, on the day before he suffered, took bread in his holy hands, looked towards heaven, giving thanks to you, Holy Father, omnipotent and eternal God, blessed it, broke it, and when he had broken it gave it to his apostles and disciples, saying,* TAKE, AND EAT OF IT, ALL OF YOU; THIS IS MY BODY, WHICH IS BROKEN FOR MANY. *Likewise, after supper on the day before he suffered, he took the cup, looked towards heaven, giving thanks to you, Holy Father, omnipotent and eternal God, blessed it, and gave it to his apostles and disciples, saying,* TAKE THIS AND DRINK OF IT, ALL OF YOU; FOR THIS IS MY BLOOD. *Observe this: all those words are the words of the evangelist, down to "take," whether the body or the blood; after that the words are the words of Christ:* TAKE THIS AND DRINK OF IT, ALL OF YOU; FOR THIS IS MY BLOOD. *And observe the individual points. He says, "Who, on the day before he suffered, took bread in his holy hands." Before it can be consecrated, it is bread; but when the words of Christ are added, it is the body of Christ. Then hear him as he says,* TAKE AND EAT

415 ET COMEDITE EX EO OMNES: HOC EST ENIM CORPUS MEUM. *Et ante verba Christi calix est vini et [59ᵛ] aquae plenus; ubi verba Christi operata fuerint, ibi sanguis efficitur, qui plebem redemit.* Nota quae dicuntur: *qui plebem redemit.* Sequitur: *Ergo videte quantis generibus potens est sermo Christi universa convertere. Deinde ipse dominus Iesus* 420 *testificatur nobis, quod corpus suum accipiamus et sanguinem. Numquid debemus de eius fide et testificatione dubitare?* Vide refugium, vide probationem, vide argumentum, vide sillogismum insuperabilia.

12. His autem ita dispositis, quid etiam Remigius episcopus dixerit audiamus. Quaere hoc in epistola ad Corinthios, ubi dici-425 tur (I Cor. 11:24) ACCIPITE ET COMEDITE; HOC EST CORPUS MEUM. *Sicut caro,* inquit, *Christi, quam assumpsit in utero virginali, verum corpus Christi est, et pro nostra salute crucifixum atque occisum, ita panis, quem Christus tradidit suis discipulis omnibusque praedestinatis ad vitam aeternam, et quem consecrant sacerdotes in ecclesia cum* 430 *virtute divinitatis, quae illum panem replet, verum est corpus Christi. Nec sunt duo corpora, illa caro quam assumpsit et iste panis, sed unum corpus Christi; in tantum ut, dum ille frangitur et comeditur, Christus immolatur et sumitur, et tamen vivus et integer manet. Et sicut illud corpus, quod in cruce depositum pro nostra salute et redemptione im-435 molatum est, ita ad nostram salutem atque redemptionem cotidie iste panis deo offertur; qui licet panis videatur, corpus est Christi.* Item in epistola ad Ebreos: *Sacerdotes,* inquit, *Iudaeorum exemplari, id est, figurae et umbrae caelestium misteriorum serviebant, quia omnia similitudines et figurae istorum erant, quae modo in ecclesia in veritate* 440 *aguntur.* Vides igitur quantum melior est ista celebratio illa, quae tunc temporis agebatur; siquidem illa exemplar et figura est, ista veritas. Idem in eodem: *Sacrificia,* inquit, *legalia, exemplaria, id est, figuram et similitudinem vocat; ista autem, quae modo in ecclesia in veritate aguntur, caelestia appellat, id est, spiritalia; siquidem et spir-*

428 omnibusque] que *om. A.*   429 quem] quae *A.*   433 vivus et] vivus et et *A.*
434 quod] quia *A.*   441 tunc] *om. A, supplevit Morin.*

418–21 Ergo . . . dubitare] Ambros. *De sacram.* 4.5.23, *CSEL* 73, p. 56 [*PL* 16: 463B].
425–36 Accipite . . . Christi] Haimo (Remigius) *In epistolam I ad Corinthios* c. 11 [*PL* 117: 572C]. This work is now attributed to Haimo of Auxerre. See Dominique Iogna-Prat, "L'oeuvre d'Haymon d'Auxerre: État de la question," in *L'école carolingienne d'Auxerre de Murethach à Rémi 830–908*, ed. Dominique Iogna-Prat, Colette Jeudy, Guy Lobrichon (Paris, 1991).   437–40 Sacerdotes . . . aguntur] Haimo (Remigius) *In epistolam ad Hebraeos*, c. 8 [*PL* 117: 874D]. This work is now attributed to Haimo of Auxerre.   442–45 Sacrificia . . . sunt] Haimo *In epistolam ad Hebraeos*, c. 9 [*PL* 117: 886C].

OF THIS, ALL OF YOU, FOR THIS IS MY BODY. *And before the words of Christ the cup is full of wine and water; when the words of Christ have had their effect, then it is made the blood that redeemed the people.* Note that it is said, *that redeemed the people.* Then follows, *Therefore see in what ways the word of Christ is powerful to transform all things. Then too the Lord Jesus himself testifies for us that we receive his body and blood. Surely we ought not to doubt his faith and testimony, should we?* Observe the recourse, observe the proof, observe the argument, observe the syllogism—all elements that are quite unassailable.

12. Now, with these aspects dealt with in this fashion, let us hear also what the bishop Remigius has said. Look for this in the Epistle to the Corinthians, at the verse, TAKE AND EAT, THIS IS MY BODY. *As the flesh of Christ* (he said), *which he assumed in the Virgin's womb and which was crucified and slain for our salvation, is the true body of Christ, so the bread, which Christ handed over to his disciples and to all those predestined to eternal life and which the priests consecrate in church with the power of divinity, which fills that bread, is the true body of Christ. And there are not two bodies, that fleshly one which he assumed and this bread, but one body of Christ; to such an extent that, while that one is broken and eaten, Christ is sacrificed and taken, and yet remains living and entire. And just as that body, which he laid on the cross for our salvation and redemption, was sacrificed, so for our salvation and redemption daily this bread is offered to God; which, though it seems to be bread, is the body of Christ.* Likewise in the Epistle to the Hebrews: *The priests of the Jews* (he said) *served as an exemplification, that is, a figure and shadow of the heavenly mysteries, because all their actions were likenesses and figures of the actions which now are carried out in the church in truth.* You see therefore how much better this celebration is than that which was being carried out at that time, inasmuch as that one is an exemplification and a figure, while this one is truth. The same authority in the same work says: *He calls the sacrifices legalistic and illustrative, that is, figure and likeness; these however, that are carried out in the church in truth, he calls heavenly, that is, spiritual, inasmuch as they are spiritual*

445 *italia sunt, et spiritaliter agenda sunt. In hoc enim differt ab illo veteri sacrificio saepius repetito istud nostrum, quod similiter repetitur,
quoniam hoc est veritas, illud figura; hoc perfectum dedit hominem, illud minime. Et istud quidem non infirmitatis suae causa repetitur,
quod non possit videlicet perfectam conferre salutem; sed in Christi pas-*
450 *sionis commemorationem, sicut ipse dixit:* (I Cor. 11:24) HOC FACITE,
inquiens, IN MEAM COMMEMORATIONEM. *Et una quidem est haec
hostia, non autem multae, sicut illae erant. Quomodo, inquam, una et
non multae, cum et a multis diversisque in locis diversisque temporibus
offeratur? Attentissime ergo animadvertendum, quia divinitas verbi*
455 *dei, quae una est, et omnia replet, et tota ubique est, ipsa facit ut non
sint plura, sed unum sacrificium, licet offeratur a multis, et sit unum
corpus Christi cum illo, quod in utero virginali suscepit, non multa corpora. Nec dum quidem aliud maius, aliud minus, aliud hodie, aliud cras
offerimus; sed semper idipsum aequam magnitudinem habens. Proinde*
460 *unum est hoc Christi sacrificium, non diversa, sicut illorum erant. Nam
si aliter esset, quoniam multis in locis offertur, multi essent Christi.
Unus ergo Christus ubique est, et hic plenus existens, et illic plenus:
unum corpus ubique habens; et sicut quod ubique offertur unum corpus
est, non multa, ita et unum est sacrificium.*

465   13. Videamus etiam quid de his sanctus Leo papa dixerit: *Sic
sacrae,* inquit, *mensae communicare debetis, ut nichil prorsus de veritate corporis Christi et sanguinis ambigatis. Hoc enim ore sumitur quod
fide creditur; et frustra ab illis "Amen" respondetur, a quibus contra id
quod accipitur disputatur.* Cui et illud Ambrosii simile est: *Ergo non*
470 *otiose,* inquit, *dicis tu "Amen," iam in spiritu confidens quod accipias
corpus Christi. Dicit sacerdos:* [60ᵣ] *"Corpus domini nostri Iesu Christi
det tibi vitam aeternam;" et tu dicis "Amen," hoc est, verum. Quod
confitetur lingua, teneat affectus.* O miser, et per omnia infelix, qui
Christi corpus accipiens dubitat, manducans ambigit, et contra id
475 quod accipit incredulus disputat; qui lingua dicit, "Verum est," et
corde, "Quomodo est?" Sic enim interpretatur ille Chus, qui dis-

452 inquam una] inquam unam *A.*   475 lingua] lingua lingua *A.*

445–64 In . . . sacrificium] Haimo *In epistolam ad Hebraeos,* c. 10 [*PL* 117: 889BC].
465–69 Sic . . . disputatur] Leo I, *Sermo* 91 c. 3 [*PL* 54: 452B].   469–73 Ergo . . . affectus]
Ambros. *De sacram.* 4.5.25, *CSEL* 73, pp. 56–57 [*PL* 16: 463C–464A].

and are to be performed in spiritual manner. For in this there is a difference between that old sacrifice often repeated and this of ours, which is similarly repeated, that this is truth, that was a figure; this gave the perfect man, that did not. And this is not repeated by reason of its weakness, that is, because it cannot confer perfect salvation, but rather as a commemoration of Christ's passion, as he himself said: DO THIS IN REMEMBRANCE OF ME. *And this is one victim not many, as those were. How, I say, one and not many, since it is offered both by many and in diverse places and at diverse times? Well then, one must observe most carefully that the divinity of the word of God, which is one, and fills the world, and is wholly present everywhere, causes it to be not many sacrifices but a single sacrifice, though it is offered by many, and to be one body of Christ with that one which he took on in the Virgin's womb, not many bodies. Nor do we offer one greater, and another smaller, or one thing today and another tomorrow, but always one having an equal magnitude. Further, this is a single sacrifice of Christ, not different ones, as were theirs. For if it were otherwise, seeing that it is offered in many places, there would be many Christs. Therefore there is one single Christ everywhere, existing in all his plenitude here and in all his plenitude there, having one body everywhere; and just as what is offered everywhere is one body, not many, so there is also one sacrifice.*

13. Let us see also what the holy Pope Leo said about this subject: *You ought* (he said) *to share in the holy table in such a way that you have no doubt at all regarding the verity of Christ's body and blood. For that is taken in by the lips which is believed by faith; and it is vain for those to respond "Amen" who are disputing against what they receive.* Ambrose's statement is also similar to that: *Therefore it is not idly that you say "Amen,"' being confident in spirit as you now are that you receive the body of Christ. The priest says, "May the body of our Lord Jesus Christ give to you eternal life," and you say "Amen," that is true. What the tongue confesses, let feeling retain.* Oh wretched the man and unfortunate every way, who receiving Christ's body doubts, who eating is of two minds, and who unbelievingly disputes that which he receives; one who says with his tongue, "It is true," and with his heart, "How can that be so?" For so is that Cush interpreted, who prefigured

cipulos illos figurabat qui de Christi sermone scandalizati abiere retrorsum. Adtende et quid Augustinus in primo sermone super epistolam Iohannis dixerit: *Multi,* inquit, *ex Iudaeis crediderunt, et*
480 *dimissus est eis sanguis fusus Christi. Quem primum fuderunt, cum sae-virent; postea biberunt, cum crediderunt.* Scio enim, quoniam beati Augustini verba multipliciter exponi possunt, hoc etiam in loco hereticorum non deesse astutiam. Dicent enim Christi sanguinem eos tantum corde et fide bibisse, quoniam dixit *biberunt cum cre-*
485 *diderunt.* Nec vero nos dicimus quod ex fide et corde non bibamus. Scimus enim eundem Augustinum, cum de cibo qui non perit lo-queretur, dixisse: *Ut quid paras dentes et ventrem? Crede, et mandu-casti;* itemque: *Credere,* inquit, *in eum, hoc est manducare panem vi-tae.* Sed cum modo de reali sanguine manifestissime loqueretur,
490 quomodo tam cito ad spiritualem converti posse credatur? Video autem et aliam mihi nasci quaestionem, quoniam idem doctor al-ibi ait: *Non hoc corpus, quod videtis, manducaturi estis; nec bibituri illum sanguinem, quem fusuri sunt qui me crucifigent.* Hoc autem in sequentibus exponemus. Sed si forte superiori capitulo istud se-
495 cundum nostram intellegentiam concordari non posset, nonne potius hoc quam illud abiciendum esset? Sicut enim illud, quod pluribus sanctorum patrum sententiis confirmatur, magis am-plexandum est, ita etiam quod ab eis dissidet, si quid forte dissidet, tenendum non est. Absit autem quod a sanctis patribus, qui in hoc
500 libello referuntur, beatum Augustinum diversa sensisse credamus. Namque et ipsi evangelistae, cum eadem dixerint, tamen sibi con-traria dixisse a quibusdam crediti sunt. Sed de his hactenus.

14. Constat igitur tot sanctorum patrum auctoritatibus quod et panis mutetur in carnem, et vinum mutetur in sanguinem. Nunc
505 autem de ipsa mutatione aliquid dicamus. Mutatur enim substan-tia in substantiam aut specie et re, aut specie et non re, aut re et non specie. Specie quidem mutatur et re, ut terra in hominem et caetera animalia; similiter et aqua in sal, et glacies in cristallum, et multa quidem huius generis repperire poteris. Specie autem et non

---

492 quod] quia *A.*   504 Nunc] Non *A,* Nunc *coniecit Morin.*

479–81 Multi . . . crediderunt] Aug. *In epistolam Ioh. ad Parthos,* Tract. 1 c. 9 [*PL* 35: 1985].
487–88 Ut . . . manducasti] Aug. *Tract. 25 in Ioh.,* c. 12, *CC* 36, p. 254 [*PL* 35: 1602].
488–89 Credere . . . vitae] Aug. *Tract. 26 in Ioh.,* c. 1, *CC* 36, p. 260 [*PL* 35: 1607].
492–93 Non . . . crucifigent] Aug. *In Psalmum 98 Enarratio,* c. 9 [*PL* 37: 1265].

those disciples who were scandalized by Christ's words and departed and went back. Observe also what Augustine said in the first sermon on the Epistle of John: *Many of the Jews believed,* (he said) *and the shedding of Christ's blood was forgiven them. That which they shed at first, in rage, they afterwards drank, in faith.* For I know that the words of the blessed Augustine can be interpreted in many ways, and that even on this subject the cleverness of the heretics does not fail them. For they will say that they drank Christ's blood in their hearts and by faith only, since he said, *they drank, in faith.* And we do not say that we do not drink in our hearts and by faith. For we know that the same Augustine, in speaking of the food that does not perish, said, *Why do you ready your teeth and your belly? Believe and you have eaten.* And likewise, he said, *To believe in him is to eat the bread of life.* But when he was most obviously speaking just now of real blood, how might it be believed that it could so quickly be turned into the spiritual? Now I see that another question arises before me, since the same doctor elsewhere says, *You will not eat this body which you see; nor drink that blood which they who shall crucify me will shed.* And this we shall explain in what follows. But if perchance this present chapter could not be reconciled with the former one according to our understanding, is it not rather this one that should be rejected instead of the other? For just as the former one, which is confirmed by many statements of the holy Fathers, is the more to be embraced, so also that which is in disagreement with them— if perchance there is any disagreement—is not to be retained. Far be it from us to believe that the blessed Augustine's position was different from that of the holy Fathers who are cited in this little treatise. For indeed even the Evangelists themselves, though they said the same things, have nevertheless been supposed by some to have said things that conflicted. But enough on this subject for now.

14. Therefore it is established in the authoritative statements of so many holy Fathers, both that the bread is changed into flesh, and that the wine is changed into blood. Now then, let us say something about the change itself. For substance is changed into substance either in seeming [*species*] and in reality [*res*], or in seeming and not in reality, or in reality and not in seeming. It is changed in seeming and in reality, to be sure, as earth is [changed] into mankind and the other animate creatures; similarly also water into salt, and ice into crystal; and you will be able to find many examples of this kind. Moreover, change takes place in seeming and not

510 re mutatio fit, ut ipse angelus satanae transfigurat se in angelum
lucis; necnon et ab artificibus ita quaedam saepe mutantur, ut,
quamvis propriam naturam non amiserint, omnino tamen aliud
esse credatur. Re autem et non specie mutatur substantia, ut vinum
in acetum, nam et si res alia sit, species tamen nisi vel odore vel
515 gustu facile discerni non potest; res autem in tantum diversa est,
ut illud calidae, istud frigidae sit naturae. Quam igitur harum
trium mutationem suscipit panis et vinum in sacrificio commutata?
Eam utique, quam et specie et re fieri diximus. Nisi enim, ut beatus Ambrosius ait, horror esset cruoris, vera carnis et sanguinis ap-
520 pareret figura. Sed ne quis fortasse post hanc mutationem panis
adhuc et vini substantiam remansisse opinetur, introducamus et
alias mutationes, quae ad divinae virtutis comprobationem factae
sunt [f. 60ᵛ]. Uxorem namque Loth in salis statuam conversam ac-
cepimus, quae utique carnis proprietatem funditus amisit. Virga
525 Moysi in serpentem mutata, rursus de serpente in virgam conversa
est; sed sicut serpentis substantiam in virgam mutata perdidit, ita
etiam ligni naturam, cum in serpentem mutaretur, amisit. Flumina
Egipti domino iubente Moyses mutavit in sanguinem; in quibus
pariter et aquae peremit naturam; nisi enim aquae natura defecis-
530 set, nequaquam pisces mortui fuissent; non possunt enim pati naturam sanguinis, quorum generatio coepit ab aquis. CONVERTIT,
inquit propheta, AQUAS EORUM IN SANGUINEM, ET OCCIDIT
PISCES EORUM. At vero nec illud silentio praetereundum est, quod
salvator noster ad nuptias invitatus, cum iam vinum defecisset, ro-
535 gatu virginis matris in vinum aquam convertit. Si igitur haec omnia non fantastice sed revera mutata propriam amisere naturam,
constat quia panis et vinum singulari amissa proprietate in Christi
carnem vertuntur et sanguinem.

15. His igitur sic expeditis, illud evangelii videamus, ubi dicitur:
540 NISI QUIS MANDUCAVERIT CARNEM MEAM, ET BIBERIT SAN-
GUINEM MEUM, NON HABEBIT IN SE VITAM. Unde scandalizati
sunt quidam qui eum sequebantur, et dixerunt ad semetipsos: DU-
RUS EST HIC SERMO, ET QUIS POTEST EUM AUDIRE? Putabant

---

533 quod] quia *A*.

531–33 Convertit . . . eorum] Ps. 105:29.   540–41 nisi . . . vitam] Ioh. 6:53.
542–43 durus . . . audire] Ioh. 6:60.

in reality, as the very angel of Satan transforms himself into an angel of light; and often many things are changed by craftsmen in such a way that, although they have not lost their own nature, yet they are believed to be something else altogether. Further, substance changes in reality and not in seeming as wine changes into vinegar; for even if it were to be another thing, nevertheless the seeming cannot easily be distinguished except by smelling or tasting; yet the thing is so far removed from it that the one has a warm nature and the other a cold. Therefore, of these three changes, which do the bread and the wine, when transformed in the sacrifice, undergo? Why, it is the one that we said takes place in seeming and in reality. *For if there were not a horror of blood,* as the blessed Ambrose said, *the true form of flesh and blood would be obvious.* But lest anyone should perhaps suppose that after this change the substance of the bread and the wine still remained, let us bring in other changes that have been done as proof of divine power. For we have been told that Lot's wife was turned into a statue of salt, which in fact altogether lost the proper quality of flesh. The rod of Moses, changed into a serpent, was turned from a serpent into a rod again; but just as, being changed into a rod, it lost the substance of the serpent, so also, when it was changed into a serpent, it lost the nature of wood. At the Lord's command Moses changed the rivers of Egypt into blood; in the case of these he took away the nature of water as well; for if the nature of water had not been lost, the fishes would by no means have died; for they cannot endure the nature of blood, being creatures whose generation took its beginning from the waters. The prophet says, HE TURNED THEIR WATERS INTO BLOOD, AND SLEW THEIR FISHES. But in truth we should not pass over in silence the fact that our Savior, being invited to a wedding, when the wine had run out, at the request of the Virgin his mother, converted water into wine. If then all these things, being changed not in fantasy but in truth and reality, lost their own nature, it is well established that the bread and the wine, losing their individual properties, are turned into Christ's flesh and blood.

15. Therefore, having so explained these matters, let us look at the passage in the Gospels that contains the saying, UNLESS ONE EATS MY FLESH AND DRINKS MY BLOOD, HE SHALL NOT HAVE LIFE IN HIM. Whence certain ones who were following him were scandalized, and they said among themselves: THIS SAYING IS HARSH, AND WHO CAN COMPLY WITH IT? For they thought,

enim, dicit beatus Augustinus, hoc dicere Iesum, quod eum pos-
545 sent concisum sicut agnum quoquere et manducare; abhorrentes a
verbis eius, recesserunt, et amplius eum non sunt secuti. Et alibi id
ipsum exponens ait: *Prout voluerunt, ita intellexerunt ex more
hominum, quia poterat Iesus, aut hoc disponeret Iesus, carnem, qua in-
dutum erat Verbum, velut concisam distribuere credentibus in se.* Idip-
550 sum et alibi: *Quomodo,* inquit, *illi intellexerunt carnem? Quippe sic
intellexerunt, quomodo in cadavere dilaniatur, aut in macello vendi-
tur, non quomodo spiritu vegetatur.* Illi utique dixerunt: DURUS EST
HIC SERMO, qui durum et lapideum cor habentes nil spiritualiter
intelligere potuerunt. Unde consequenter ipse dominus ait: SPIRI-
555 TUS EST QUI VIVIFICAT; CARO AUTEM NICHIL PRODEST. VERBA,
QUAE EGO LOCUTUS SUM VOBIS, SPIRITUS ET VITA SUNT. Quod
Augustinus exponens dixit: *Quid est,* SPIRITUS ET VITA SUNT?
Spiritualiter intellegenda sunt. Intellexisti spiritualiter? SPIRITUS ET
VITA SUNT. *Intellexisti carnaliter? Etiam sic illa* SPIRITUS ET VITA
560 SUNT, *sed tibi non sunt.* Sed dicis: Quid est, carnaliter intelligere?
Audisti superius. Illi enim carnaliter intellegebant, qui scandalizati
dixerunt: DURUS EST HIC SERMO. Illi vero spiritualiter intelligunt,
qui divina virtute et caelesti benedictione panis atque vini substantiam Christi carnem et sanguinem fieri credunt, et hoc cum ore
565 carnis ad redemptionem sumunt, ad imitationem quoque ore
cordis intenta mente suscipiunt. Qui etiam hoc certissime sciunt,
quod Christi caro et sanguis numquam corporaliter manducaretur
vel biberetur, nisi prius in eius carnem et sanguinem panis et vinum
mutaretur. Nam ipse dominus et salvator noster, prius manibus suis
570 accipiens panem, gratias agens benedixit et fregit, et post modum
dixit: ACCIPITE ET COMEDITE: HOC EST CORPUS MEUM. Ac si
diceret: Panem quidem mutavi in carnem, ut iuxta id, quod
promiseram, [61ʳ] meam carnem edatis. Quod ne me fortasse meo
ore loqui arbitreris, ipsum Augustinum audi dicentem: SPIRITUS
575 EST, inquit, QUI VIVIFICAT, CARO AUTEM NICHIL PRODEST.
VERBA, QUAE LOCUTUS SUM VOBIS, SPIRITUS ET VITA SUNT.

---

548 aut] ut *A*.   550 sic] si *A*.   564 ore] cruore *A*, cum ore *coniecit Morin*.   568–69 nisi
. . . mutaretur] nisi prius in eius carnem et sanguinem et vinum mutaretur *A*, nisi prius in eius
carnem et sanguinem et vinum mutaretur et panis *coniecit Morin*, nisi prius in eius carnem et
sanguinem panis et vinum mutaretur *vel* mutarentur *coniecit FN*.   572 id] *om. A, add. A*¹.

547–49 Prout . . . se] Aug. *Tract. 27 in Ioh.* c. 2, *CC* 36, p. 270 [*PL* 35: 1616].   550–52 Quomodo
. . . vegetatur] Aug. *Tract. 27 in Ioh.* c. 5, *CC* 36, p. 272 [*PL* 35: 1617].   554–56 Spiritus . . . vita
sunt] Ioh. 6:14.   557–60 Quid . . . non sunt] Aug. *Tract. 27 in Ioh.* c. 6, *CC* 36, p. 273 [*PL* 35:
1618].   562 durus . . . sermo] Ioh. 6:60.   571 accipite . . . meum] Matt. 26:26.   574–81
spiritus . . . intellegi] Aug. *In Psalmum 98 Enarratio,* c. 9 [*PL* 37:1265].

the blessed Augustine says, that Jesus was saying this because they could cut him up and cook him like lamb and eat him; shrinking from his words, they withdrew and followed him no longer. And elsewhere, in expounding the same passage, he says, *They understood, as they wished to in accordance with the way of men, that Jesus was able to or that Jesus proposed to, so to speak, cut up and distribute the flesh in which the Word was clothed to those who believed in him.* And he says the very same thing elsewhere: *How did they understand "flesh"? Why, they understood it as torn in strips from a cadaver, or sold in a market, not as it is given life by the spirit.* In fact, they said, THIS WORD IS HARD, who, having a hard and stony heart, could do nothing spiritually. As a consequence, the Lord himself says, IT IS THE SPIRIT THAT GIVES LIFE, THE FLESH IS OF NO EFFECT. THE WORDS THAT I HAVE SAID TO YOU ARE SPIRIT AND LIFE. Augustine said in exposition of this, *What is this:* ARE SPIRIT AND LIFE? *They are to be understood spiritually. Did you understand them spiritually?* THEY ARE SPIRIT AND LIFE. *Did you understand them carnally? Even so those are* SPIRIT AND LIFE, *but not for you.* But you say, "What is this, to understand carnally?" You have heard it above. For those were understanding carnally, who being offended said, THIS WORD IS HARSH. But those understand spiritually who through the divine power and celestial benediction believe that the substance of the bread and wine becomes the flesh and blood of Christ, and who with the lips of the flesh take this for their redemption and who with the lips of the heart through an attentive mind also take it for their imitation. They also know this as most certain, that Christ's flesh and blood would never be eaten or drunk corporeally, if both the bread and the wine were not first changed into his flesh and blood. For our Lord and Savior himself, first taking the bread in his hands, giving thanks, blessed and broke it and afterwards said, TAKE AND EAT; THIS IS MY BODY. As if he were saying, "I have indeed turned bread into flesh, that according to what I had promised, you might eat my flesh." That you may not think that I am perhaps saying this with my own lips, listen to what Augustine himself says: IT IS THE SPIRIT THAT GIVES LIFE, BUT THE FLESH IS OF NO AVAIL. THE WORDS WHICH I HAVE SPOKEN TO YOU ARE SPIRIT AND LIFE.

Spiritualiter intelligite quod locutus sum. Non hoc corpus, quod vide-
tis, manducaturi estis, et bibituri illum sanguinem quem fusuri sunt qui
me crucifigent. Sacramentum aliquod vobis commendavi; spiritualiter
580 *intellectum vivificabit vos. Etsi necesse est visibiliter illud celebrari,*
oportet tamen invisibiliter intellegi. Hoc autem invenies in psalmo
ubi dicitur: ADORATE SCABELLUM PEDUM EIUS, QUONIAM
SANCTUM EST. Haec autem verba talia sunt, ac si diceret: Scandalizati estis, quia dixi: NISI QUIS MANDUCAVERIT CARNEM
585 MEAM, ET BIBERIT SANGUINEM MEUM, NON HABEBIT VITAM IN
SE. HOC, inquit, VOS SCANDALIZAT. Non fiet ut putatis; non dilaniabitur, non concidetur, non in frusta diminuetur caro mea. Nolite aestimare, quod more ferarum meam carnem devoretis, vel
crudelitate bestiae meum sanguinem bibatis. Nolite hoc putare.
590 Aliud est quod dico: VERBA QUAE LOCUTUS SUM VOBIS, SPIRI-
TUS ET VITA SUNT. Spiritualiter intellegite, si vitam habere vultis.
Sacramentum enim aliquod commendavi vobis. Quid est, commendavi? Insinuavi, intimavi, indidi, laudavi, et ut post me in mei
memoriam omni tempore fieret praecepi. Quod est hoc sacramen-
595 tum? Illud quidem, quod nunc in sancta ecclesia et visibiliter fit, et
invisibiliter intelligitur. Visibiliter, nimirum quia et sacerdotem et
altare, et panem et vinum unde fit videmus. Invisibiliter autem,
quoniam nec quomodo mutetur, nec a quo mutetur, videre possumus. DEUM NEMO VIDIT UMQUAM. Sed, ut Iohannes Con-
600 stantinopolitanus episcopus ait: *ore sacerdotis verba proferuntur, dei*
virtute consecrantur. Similiter Ambrosius: *Consecratio,* inquit,
quibus verbis est, et cuius sermonibus? Domini Iesu. Sermo Christi hoc
conficit sacramentum. Et paulo post: *Vides igitur quemadmodum*

---

584 quis] *om. A, add. A*[1].   586 fiet] fiat *A, tacitus emendavit Morin.*   587 in frusta] frustra *A,*
in frusta *coniecit Morin.*   596 sacerdotem] sacerdotes *A, Morin,* sacerdotem *A*[1].   601
consecrantur] dei *A,* consecrantur *A*[1].

582–83 adorate . . . est] Ps. 99:5.   584–86 nisi . . . scandalizat] Ioh. 6:53, 61.   590–91 Verba
. . . sunt] Ioh. 6:63.   599 Deum . . . umquam] Ioh. 1:18 or 4:12.   600–601 ore . . .
consecrantur] Ioh. Chrys. *De proditione Iudae,* see above ll. 187–188. This phrase also in Gezo
Dertonensis, *Lib. de Corpore et Sanguine Christi PL* 137: 391C].   601–3 Consecratio . . .
sacramentum] Ambros. *De sacram.* 4.4.14, *CSEL* 73, p. 52 [*PL* 16: 459A].   603–5 Vides . . .
naturae] Ambros. *De sacram.* 4.4.17, *CSEL* 73, p. 53 [*PL* 16: 461A].

Understand spiritually what I have said. You are not going to eat this body, which you see, and drink that blood which those who will crucify me will shed. I have commended to you some sacrament; spiritually understood, it will give you life. Even if that must of necessity be celebrated visibly, yet it should be understood invisibly. This you will also find in the Psalm, in which it is said, ADORE THE STOOL BENEATH HIS FEET, FOR IT IS HOLY. These words are as if he were saying, "You are offended that I have said, UNLESS ONE SHALL EAT MY FLESH, AND DRINK MY BLOOD, HE SHALL HAVE NO LIFE IN HIM. *This* (he says) OFFENDS YOU. It will not be as you suppose; my flesh will not be torn, will not be cut up, will not be divided into bits. Do not imagine that you devour my flesh in the manner of wild animals or drink my blood with the cruelty of a beast. Do not suppose this. There is another thing that I say: THE WORDS THAT I HAVE SPOKEN TO YOU ARE SPIRIT AND LIFE. Understand them spiritually, if you wish to have life. For I have commended a sacrament to you. What is this, I have 'commended'? I have instilled it, I have impressed it, I have inserted it, I have praised it, and I have bidden it to be observed throughout all time after me, in remembrance of me." What is this "sacrament"? Why, that which now is both visibly carried out in the holy church and invisibly understood. Visibly, precisely because we see both the priests and the altar, and the bread and wine from which it is made. But invisibly, because we can see neither how it is changed nor by whom it is changed. NONE HAS EVER SEEN GOD. But, as John, Bishop of Constantinople, says, *The words are brought forth by the lips of the priest, but consecrated by the power of God.* Similarly, Ambrose says, *In what words and in whose speech is the consecration [done]? Our Lord Jesus's. It is the speech of Christ that performs this sacrament.* And, a little later, *You see, then, how*

sermo Christi creaturam mutare consueverit, et mutet, quando vult, in-
605 *stituta naturae.*

16. Ex his ergo manifestum est quoniam Christi caro numquam corporaliter commederetur, nisi panis substantia spiritualiter, id est, spiritu operante in eam mutaretur. Sed si adhuc dubitas, audi Hieronimum: *Dupliciter,* inquit, *sanguis Christi et caro intelligitur:*
610 *vel spiritualis illa atque divina, de qua ipse dicit* (Ioan. 6:56) CARO MEA VERE EST CIBUS, ET SANGUIS MEUS VERE EST POTUS, *et* (Ioan. 6:54) NISI MANDUCAVERITIS CARNEM MEAM, ET BIBERITIS SANGUINEM MEUM, NON HABEBITIS VITAM AETERNAM; *vel caro et sanguis, quae crucifixa est, et qui militis effusus est lancea.* Hoc
615 autem in eius expositione super epistolam ad Ephesios repperire poteris. Id autem intuere, quomodo divisionem fecerit inter eam Christi carnem quae manducatur, et illam quae in cruce pependit. Tale est enim, ac si diceret: Haec manducatur, illa non manducatur. Manducatur utique illa, quae spiritualis est atque divina, id est,
620 quae cotidie immolatur, quae spiritualiter consecratur, quae divina benedictione in propriam Christi carnem mutatur. Cum ergo ista comeditur, nonne et illa sumitur, quae crucifixa est? nonne et ille sanguis bibitur, qui militis lancea effusus est? Dicat Ambrosius: *Ante verba Christi,* inquit, *calix est vini et aquae plenus; ubi verba*
625 *Christi operata fuerint, ibi sanguis efficitur, qui plebem redemit.* Quis, inquam, sanguis plebem redemit? Ille utique, qui militis effusus est lancea. Sed, ut audis, ille est in calice, qui plebem redemit. Liquet igitur [61ᵛ] quod illum bibamus, qui militis effusus est lancea. Unde Gregorius: *Quis,* inquit, *sit sanguis agni, iam non audiendo,*
630 *sed bibendo didicistis.* Et Remigius: *Non sunt,* inquit, *duo corpora, illa caro quam Christus assumpsit, et iste panis, sed unum corpus Christi; in tantum ut, dum ille frangitur et comeditur, Christus immolatur et*

---

607 corporaliter] carnaliter *A, corr. A¹.*   615 ad Ephesios] *om. A, coniecit Morin.*   616 quomodo] quod modo *A.*   629 sit] scit *A.*

609–14 Dupliciter . . . lancea] Hieron. *Comment. in epistolam ad Ephesios* 1:7 [*PL* 26: 481A].
624–25 Ante . . . redemit] Ambros. *De sacram.* 4.5.23, *CSEL* 73, p. 56 [*PL* 16: 463B].
629–30 Quis . . . didicistis] Greg. M. *Homiliarum in evangelia libri duo,* lib. 2, hom. 22 [*PL* 76: 1178B].   630–33 Non . . . manet] Haimo *In epistolam I ad Corinthios* [*PL* 117: 572C].

the speech of Christ habitually changes creation and changes, when he will, the dispositions of nature.

16. On this basis then, it is clear that Christ's flesh would never be eaten corporeally, unless the substance of the bread were changed into it spiritually, that is, by the working of the Spirit. But if you still have doubts, hear Jerome: *The blood and flesh of Christ is understood in two-fold fashion: either that spiritual and divine one of which he himself speaks,* MY FLESH IS TRULY FOOD, AND MY BLOOD IS TRULY DRINK, *and* UNLESS YOU EAT MY FLESH, AND DRINK MY BLOOD, YOU WILL NOT HAVE ETERNAL LIFE; *or the flesh and blood which was crucified, and which was shed by the soldier's lance.* You will be able to find this also in his exposition of the Epistle to the Ephesians. Observe this as well, how he made a distinction between that flesh of Christ which is eaten, and that which hung on the cross. For such a statement is as if he were to say, "This one is eaten, that one is not eaten." That is, that one is eaten which is spiritual and divine, that is, which is daily sacrificed, which is spiritually consecrated, which by divine blessing is changed into Christ's true flesh. Therefore, since this is eaten, is not that also, which was crucified, consumed? Is not also that blood drunk, which was shed by the soldier's lance? Let Ambrose speak: *Before the words of Christ* (he said), *the cup is full of wine and water; but when the words of Christ have acted, then it is made the blood that redeemed the people.* What blood, I say, redeemed the people? Why, that blood that was shed by the soldier's lance. But, as you hear, it is that in the chalice, which redeemed the people. Therefore it is obvious that we drink that which was shed by the soldier's lance. Whence Gregory says, *You have now learned, not through hearing, but through drinking, what is the blood of the lamb.* And Remigius says, *There are not two bodies, that flesh which Christ took on, and this bread, but one body of Christ; so far is this true that, while that is broken and eaten, Christ is sacrificed and*

sumitur, et tamen vivus et integer manet. Sed quid Iohannes Constantinopolitanus episcopus ait? *Iste est,* inquit, *sanguis,—dic,*
635 *Iuda—, quem XXX denariis vendidisti; iste est sanguis, de quo ante
cum Fariseis pactum fecisti. O Christi misericordia! o Iudae dementia!
Ille cum XXX denariis paciscebatur ut venderet, et Christus ei sanguinem quem vendidit offerebat.* Unus enim idemque est, et quem
Iudas vendidit, et qui militis effusus est lancea.

640   17. Ecce quattuor isti doctores quasi uno ore confirmant quod
illum sanguinem bibamus, qui militis effusus est lancea. Hieronimus autem et Augustinus, ut modo superius audivimus, aliud
sonare videntur. Quid igitur dicemus? Numquid inter eos, quos
unus spiritus docet, discordia esse potuit? Dicunt enim illi quia
645 bibis; dicunt isti: Non bibis. Bibis igitur, et non bibis. Quod
utrumque verum est. Bibitur enim ille per hunc, qui numquam corporaliter biberetur secundum se. Mutatur iste in illum; bibitur ille
in isto; et cum uterque idem sit, non potest fieri quin ipse bibatur.
Unde beatus Gregorius ait: *Qui licet* (Rom. 6:9) SURGENS A MOR-
650 TUIS IAM NON MORITUR, ET MORS ILLI ULTRA NON DOM-
INABITUR, *tamen in se ipso immortaliter atque incorruptibiliter
vivens, pro nobis iterum in hoc misterio sacrae oblationis immolatur.*
His enim paucis verbis cuncta solvuntur; his omnes in unam ean-
demque sententiam rediguntur. Quomodo autem iste mutetur,
655 quomodo ille vivens immoletur, quomodo in isto manducetur, noli
interrogare, si non vis errare. Recordare quid Iohannes ille dixerit,
quo non surrexit maior inter natos mulierum: ECCE, inquit, VENIT
POST ME, CUIUS NON SUM DIGNUS SOLVERE CORRIGIAM CAL-
CIAMENTI. Et apostolus: O ALTITUDO DIVITIARUM SAPIENTIAE
660 ET SCIENTIAE DEI; QUAM INCOMPREHENSIBILIA SUNT IUDICIA
EIUS, ET INVESTIGABILES VIAE EIUS. Et psalmista: IUDICIA TUA
ABYSSUS MULTA. Propter hoc etiam per Moysen dictum est: SI
QUID RESIDUUM FUERIT, IGNE COMBURATUR. Hoc etenim est
MUTATIO DEXTERAE EXCELSI. Mutatur enim quomodo vult, im-

---

647 biberetur] liberetur *A, corr. Morin.*   656 quid] quod *A, corr. Morin.*

634–38 Iste est . . . offerebat] Ioh. Chrys. as above, ll. 176–194.   649–52 Qui . . . immolatur]
Greg. M. *Dialogi* 4.58 [*PL* 77: 425C].   657–59 Ecce . . . calciamenti] Ioh. 1:27.   659–61 O
. . . viae eius] Rom. 11:33.   661–62 Iudicia . . . multa] Ps. 36:6.   662–63 si . . . comburatur]
Exod. 12:10.   664 mutatio . . . excelsi] Ps. 76:11.

taken, and yet he remains living and whole. But what does John the bishop of Constantinople say?: *This is* (he says) *the blood—speak, O Judas—which you sold for thirty denarii; this is the blood for which you first bargained with the Pharisees. Oh the mercy of Christ! Oh the madness of Judas! He was bargaining to sell it for thirty denarii, and Christ was offering him the blood that he sold.* For it is one and the same, both the blood which Judas sold and that which was shed by the soldier's lance.

17. Behold, these four doctors, as though with one voice, confirm that we drink that blood that was shed by the soldier's lance. Jerome and Augustine, however, as we have just heard above, seem to utter something that sounds different. What then shall we say? Surely there could not be discord, could there, among those who are taught by one Spirit? For those say that you drink it; these say, "You do not drink it." Therefore you drink it, and you do not drink it. Both of these are true. For that one is drunk through this one, which would never be drunk corporeally according to itself. This is changed into that; that is drunk in this; and inasmuch as both are the same, it cannot fail to be true that he himself is drunk. Whence the blessed Gregory says, *Who, though* RISING FROM THE DEAD, NO LONGER DIES, AND DEATH HAS NO MORE DOMINION OVER HIM, *yet, living in his very self immortally and incorruptibly, for us he is again sacrificed in this mystery of the sacred oblation.* For by means of these few words, all problems are solved; by means of these all are brought to one and the same conclusion. Yet how it is changed, how he, living, is sacrificed, how he is eaten in this, do not ask, if you wish to avoid error. Recall what that famous John said, than whom no greater has arisen among the sons of women: BEHOLD (he said), THERE COMES AFTER ME ONE THE FASTENING OF WHOSE SANDALS I AM NOT WORTHY TO LOOSEN. And the Apostle: O THE DEPTH OF THE RICHES OF WISDOM AND KNOWLEDGE OF GOD; HOW UNSEARCHABLE ARE HIS JUDGMENTS, AND UNTRACEABLE ARE HIS WAYS. And the Psalmist: YOUR JUDGMENTS ARE A GREAT DEEP. For this cause also it was said by Moses: IF ANYTHING REMAINS, LET IT BE BURNED IN THE FIRE. For this indeed is CHANGE WROUGHT BY THE RIGHT HAND OF THE ONE ON HIGH. For he is changed as he will, he

665 molatur quomodo vult, manducatur et bibitur quomodo vult. Sed de his hactenus.

18. Nunc autem ipsius evangelii verba brevi quasi epilogo repetamus, et solas quae obici possunt obiectiones determinemus. AMEN AMEN DICO VOBIS, NISI MANDUCAVERITIS CARNEM FILII 670 HOMINIS, ET BIBERITIS EIUS SANGUINEM, NON HABEBITIS VITAM IN VOBIS, videlicet vel corde, vel ore et corde. CARO ENIM MEA VERE EST CIBUS, ET SANGUIS MEUS VERE EST POTUS, quoniam immortales et incorruptibiles eos facit, qui eum sumunt, vel corde, vel ore et corde. QUI MANDUCAT MEAM CARNEM, ET 675 BIBIT MEUM SANGUINEM, HABET VITAM AETERNAM, videlicet vel corde, vel ore et corde. SICUT MISIT ME VIVENS PATER, ET EGO VIVO PROPTER PATREM; ET QUI MANDUCAT ME, ET IPSE VIVIT PROPTER ME, videlicet vel corde, vel ore et corde. Bonum est igitur manducare corde, sed melius ore et corde. Qui enim solo 680 ore manducat et bibit, iudicium sibi manducat et bibit. Nos igitur, beati papae Leonis sententiae memores, *sic sacrae mensae communicemus, ut nichil prorsus de veritate Christi corporis et sanguinis ambigamus.*

---

679 manducare corde] manducare *A,* manducare corde *coniecit Morin.*

669–71 Amen . . . vobis] Ioh. 6:53.   671–72 Caro . . . potus] Ioh. 6:55.   674–75 Qui . . . aeternam] Ioh. 6:54.   676–78 Sicut . . . propter me] Ioh. 6:57.   681–83 sic . . . ambigamus] Leo I, *Sermo 91;* see above ll. 465–69.

is sacrificed as he will, he is eaten and drunk as he will. But enough on this subject for this time.

18. And now, for a brief—as it were—epilogue, let us repeat the words of the Gospel itself and put an end to the only objections that can be raised. VERILY, VERILY, I SAY UNTO YOU, UNLESS YOU SHALL EAT THE FLESH OF THE SON OF MAN, AND DRINK HIS BLOOD, YOU WILL NOT HAVE LIFE IN YOU, that is, either with your heart, or with your lips and your heart. FOR MY FLESH IS TRULY FOOD, AND MY BLOOD IS TRULY DRINK, since it makes immortal and incorruptible those who take it, either with their hearts, or with their lips and their hearts. HE WHO EATS MY FLESH, AND DRINKS MY BLOOD HAS ETERNAL LIFE, that is, either with heart, or with lips and heart. AS THE LIVING FATHER SENT ME, I ALSO LIVE BECAUSE OF THE FATHER; AND HE WHO EATS ME ALSO LIVES BECAUSE OF ME, that is, either with heart, or with lips and heart. It is therefore good to eat with the heart, but better with lips and heart. For he who eats and drinks with the lips alone, eats and drinks judgment upon himself. Let us therefore, being mindful of the words of the blessed Pope Leo, *so partake of the sacred table that we have no doubt at all of the truth of Christ's body and blood.*

APPENDIX

The Dossier of Unconnected
Sententiae Following the Libellus
in the Aberdeen Manuscript

Introduction

In the Aberdonensis there is no explicit or indication of a break for the end of the libellus. The present editors have determined that the treatise ends at line 683, with as a powerful peroratio the "brevis quasi epilogus"; this epilogue, ch. 18, concludes with the reprise of Pope Leo I's words from the beginning of ch. 13 (ll. 465–69), here quoted with *variatio* at the end as an exhortation in the first-person plural. In the Aberdeen manuscript this ending stands on the penultimate line of fol. 61v. What follows is a series of extracts of similar character (see above, pp. 50–52). Beginning on the last line of the page, these are written in the same hand, and Morin—not unreasonably and without studying the internal structure and argument of the libellus—published continuously the additional text that is found on fol. 62 and the first four and one-half lines of fol 63r. There was a certain logic in this decision; although to this point there is no continuous thread of argument, there are short introductory clauses at the beginning of each *sententia*. Though the subject in the latter part focuses upon the Lord's Prayer, an ongoing theme throughout is the "panis cotidianus," and this links these extracts to the subject of the libellus.

We have chosen to print, without apparatus criticus and without translation, all the extracts down through the sixth line of fol. 64r, where a sizable initial marks a definitive break, with the heading "Am-

171

brosius" in larger letters than in the extracts before, and where begins a new subject, the discussion of the *symbolum*. This means the publication of some unpublished parts of the commentary on the Lord's Prayer, which is drawn from Augustine's *De Sermone Domini in Monte* and Pseudo-Augustinian sermons, all of which is or can seem relevant to the Eucharistic Controversy. Identification of the sources is attempted in the text: scriptural citations are identified in parentheses before the quotation; patristic citations are identified in parentheses immediately after the quotation. It seems reasonable to suppose that these extracts, or at least the earlier ones in the series, are the *sententiae* that the author of our libellus mentions in his first chapter as having been deliberately omitted to avoid prolixity. The Aberdonensis has the distinction of being for us (as far as is now known) the unique manuscript of the libellus, whose singular value we have attempted to demonstrate. It has also preserved, it seems, some part of the materials gathered by the author in preparation for his work on the Eucharistic Controversy. We have concluded that these latter should be published, even in this summary form.

The punctuation of the manuscript has been modified for sense. Spellings are left as in the manuscript. It should be noted that the first extract here, though introduced by a clause stressing agreement with what precedes (Cui . . . concordans) is on a different subject; at this point also there is a serious misattribution. The *sententiae* that follow are characterized by gross textual errors, which we retain in this brief edition; obviously the *sententiae praetermissae* did not receive the careful checking that was given to the *sententiae* included in the libellus.

Cui et Hieronimus in libro ad Edibiam concordans ait: *Rogo,*
dilectissimi fratres [62r] *mei, rogo, perpendite quam debitores sumus*
beate dei genitrici, quantasque illi post dominum de nostra redemptione
gratias agere debeamus. Illud siquidem corpus Christi, quod beatissima
5 *virgo genuit, quod gremio fovit, quod fasciis cinxit, illud, inquam, non*
aliud, nunc de sacro altari percipimus, eiusque sanguine in sacramento
redemptionis haurimus: hoc catholica fides habet, hoc sancta ecclesia
universaliter docet (Petr. Dam., *Sermo XLV* [*PL* 144: 743A-B]). Audi
etiam quid Ambrosius in sexto sacramentorum libro dixerit: *Sicut*
10 *verus est,* inquit, *dei filius dominus noster Iesus Christus, non quem ad*
modum homines per gratiam, sed quasi filius ex substantia patris, ita
vero caro, sicut ipse dixit, quam accipimus, te verus est potus (Ambr.,
De Sacramentis 6.1.1 [*CSEL* 73:72]). Et paulo post: *Deinde, ubi non*
tulerunt sermonem Christi discipuli eius, sed audientes quod carnem
15 *suam daret manducare, et sanguinem suum daret bibendum, recede-*
bant; solus tamen Petrus dixit: (Ioh. 6:69) VERBA VITAE AETERNAE
HABES, *et ego a te quomodo recedam? Ne igitur plures hoc dicerent, ve-*
luti quidam esset honor cruoris, sed manere gratia redemptionis, ideo in
similitudinem quidem accipi sacramentum, sed vere naturae gratiam
20 *virtutemque consequeris.* (Ioh. 6:51) EGO SUM, inquit, PANIS VIVUS
QUI DE CAELO DESCENDI. *Sed caro non descendit de caelo; hoc est,*
carnem in terris assumpsit ex virgine. Quomodo descendit panis de
caelo, et panis vivus? Quia idem dominus noster Iesus Christus consors
est et divinitatis et corporis; et tu, qui accipis carnem, divinae eius sub-
25 *stantiae in illo participaris alimento* (Ambr., *De Sacramentis* 6.1.3–4
[*CSEL* 73:73]). His igitur in verbis verissime deprehendi potest,
quoniam illam carnem comedimus, quam de virgine Christus assumpsit. Audi quid et in alio loco Ambrosius ait: *Ista autem esca*
quam accipis, iste panis vivus qui de caelo descendit, vitae aeternae sub-
30 *stantiam subministrat; et quicumque hunc manducaverit, non mori-*
etur in aeternum; et corpus est Christi. Considera nunc utrum praes-
tantior sit panis angelorum, an caro Christi, quae utique corpus est
vitae. Manna illud e caelo, hoc supra caelum; illud caeli, hoc domini
caelorum: illud corruptioni obnoxium, si in diem alterum reservatur,
35 *hoc alienum ab omni corruptione; quoniam, quicumque hoc religiose*
gustaverit, corruptionem sentire non poterit (Ambr., *De Mysteriis*
9.47–48 [*CSEL* 73:109]).

Item in eodem: *Fortasse dicas: aliud video; quomodo tu mihi asseris quia Christi corpus accipiam? Et hoc nobis adhuc superest ut probemus.*
40 *Quantis igitur utimur exemplis, ut probemus non hoc esse quia natura formavit, sed quia benedictio consecravit; maioremque vim esse benedictionis quam naturae; quia benedictione etiam natura [naturae A] ipsa mutatur* (Ambr., *De Mysteriis* 9.50 [*CSEL* 73:110]). Deinde a virga Moysi incipiens multa enumerat, in quibus vim propriam
45 natura perdidit [ostendit *A, corr. A¹*]. Unde et subinferens ait: *Quod* [Quid *A, corr. A¹*] *si tantum valuit sermo Heliae, ut ignem de caelo deponeret, non valebit Christi sermo, ut species mutet elementorum? De totius mundi operibus legisti quia* (Ps. 32:9) IPSE DIXIT ET FACTA SUNT, IPSE MANDAVIT ET CREATA SUNT. *Sermo Christi,*
50 *qui potuit ex nichilo facere quod non erat, non potest ea quae sunt in id mutare quod non erant? Nonne minus est novas rebus dare, quam mutare naturas* (Ambr., *De Mysteriis* 9.52 [*CSEL* 73:112])? Et paulo post Ambrosius: *Liquet igitur quod praeter naturae ordinem virgo generavit. Et hoc quia efficimur corpus ex virgine est. Quid hic quaeris*
55 *naturae ordinem in Christi corpore, cum praeter naturam sit ipse dominus Iesus partus ex virgine? Vera utique caro Christi, quae crucifixa est, quae sepulta est: vere ergo carnis Iesu sacramentum est. Ipse clamat dominus Iesus:* (I Cor. 11:24) HOC CORPUS MEUM EST. *Ante benedictionem verborum* [62v] *caelestium, alia species nominatur; post*
60 *consecrationem corpus significatur. Ipse dicit sanguinem suum; ante consecrationem aliud dicitur, post consecrationem sanguis nuncupatur* (Ambr., *De Mysteriis* 9.53–54 [*CSEL* 73:112–13]). Hoc autem in loco et dicitur, et significatur, et nuncupatur, pro esse ponitur; ut si dicatur: Ante consecrationem aliud dicitur, et aliud est;
65 post consecrationem vero et sanguis nuncupatur, et sanguis est. Idem autem in sequentibus sic ait: *Illo,* inquit, *sacramento Christus est, quia corpus est Christi. Non ergo corporalis esca, sed spiritualis est. Unde apostolus de typo eius ait quia* (I Cor. 10:1,3-4) PATRES NOSTRI ESCAM SPIRITUALEM MANDUCAVERUNT, ET
70 POTUM SPIRITUALEM BIBERUNT. *Corpus enim domini corpus est spirituale; corpus Christi corpus est divini spiritus; quia spiritus Christus, ut legimus:* (Cf. Lam. 4:20) SPIRITUS ANTE FACIEM NOSTRAM CHRISTUS DOMINUS (Ambr., *De Mysteriis* 9.58 [*CSEL* 73:115]).

75 (Luc. 11:3) PANEM NOSTRUM COTIDIANUM DA NOBIS HODIE.
Memini, inquit, *sermonis mei, cum* [cum *A,* dum *A¹*] *de sacramentis
tractarem. Dixi vobis quod ante verba Christi, quod offertur, panes dicatur; ubi Christi verba deprompta fuerint, iam non panis dicitur, sed
corpus appellatur. Cur ergo in oratione dominica, quae postea sequitur,*
80 *ait:* (Luc. 11:3) PANEM NOSTRUM [PANEM NOSTRUM *om. A*]?
Panem quidem dixit, sed epiusion dixit, hoc est, supersubstantiales
[supersup- *A,* supersubstantiales *A¹*]. *Non iste panis est, qui vadit,
sed ille panis vitae aeternae, qui animae nostrae substantiam fulcit.
Ideo graece* ἐπιούσιος [ЄПНЦОНШΝ *A*] *dicitur: latinis autem hunc*
85 *panem cotidianum dixit; quia graeci dicunt* τὴν ἐπιοῦσαν ἡμέραν
[TЄΝΟЄΠΙΟΥΑΝЄΑ ΑΗΡΑΝ *A*] *aut venientem diem. Ergo et quod
latinus dixit, et quod graecus, utrumque videtur utile. Graecus
utrumque uno sermone significavit; latinus cotidianum dixit. Si cotidianus est panis, cur post annum illum sumis, quemadmodum graeci in*
90 *oriente facere consueverunt? Accipe cotidie, quod cotidie tibi prosit; sic
vive, ut cotidie merearis accipere* (Ambr., *De Sacramentis* 5.4.24-25
[*CSEL* 73:68–69]). Dicitur autem et in sinodo Efesina, ut, *cum ad
misticas benedictiones accedimus, non carnem communem, nec alicuius
viri sanctificati, nos sumere credamus, sed vere vivificatricem, et ipsius*
95 *Verbi propriam factam* (Cf. Collectio Canonum [*PL* 84:155B-C]).
Unde et Augustinus: *Hoc,* inquit, *in pane accipe quod in cruce pependit; hoc bibe in calice quod manavit e latere* (Cf. Aug., *Serm.* [*Miscellanea Agostiniana* I:19]). Audi etiam quod Eusebius Emisenus dicat, *Vere unica et perfecta hostia, fide aestimanda, non specie; neque*
100 *exteriori censenda visu, sed interiori effectu. Unde caelestis confirmat
auctoritas:* (Ioh. 6:56) QUIA CARO MEA VERE EST CIBUS, ET SAN-
GUIS MEUS VERE EST POTUS. *Recedat ergo omne infidelitatis am-
biguum, quandoquidem, qui auctor est muneris, ipse etiam testis est
veritatis. Nam invisibilis sacerdos visibiles creaturas in substantiam*
105 *corporis et sanguinis sui verbo suo secreta potestate convertit* [conver-
titur *A, corr. A¹?*] *dicens:* (Matt. 26:26) ACCIPITE ET COMEDITE,
HOC EST CORPUS MEUM (Ps.-Eusebius Emesinus, *Epist.*
XXXVIII [*PL* 30:272A-B (280D)]). *Sicut caro Christi, quam assumpsit in utero virginali, verus corpus eius est, et pro nostra salute oc-*
110 *cisum, ita panis quem Christus tradidit discipulis suis, omnibusque
praedestinatis ad vitam aeternam, et quem cotidie consecrant sacerdotes*

in aecclesia cum virtute divinitatis, quem illum replet, verum corpus est Christi; nec sunt duo corpora, illa caro quam assumpsit, et iste panis, sed unum verum corpus; in tantum ut, dum illud frangitur et
115 *comeditur, et tamen vivus manet. Et sicut illud corpus quod in cruce deposuit, pro nostra salute et immolatione est immolatum, ita cotidie ad nostram salutem et redemptionem iste panis deo offertur; qui licet panis videatur, ne nostra fragilitas aborreret, tamen verum corpus est Christi* (Cf. Haimo, *Expos. in Epist. I ad Cor.* [*PL* 117: 572C]).
120 Similiter et de calice.

(I Cor. 11:27) ITAQUE QUICUMQUE MANDUCAVERIT PANEM VEL BIBERIT CALICEM DOMINI INDIGNE, REUS ERIT [63r] CORPORIS ET SANGUINIS DOMINI: *id est, poenas aeternas inde exsolvet, nisi paenitentia digna hoc expiaverit,* INDIGNE *dicit, id est, ordine*
125 *non observato. Videat qualiter misterium illud celebret vel sumat, sicut traditum est a sanctis patribus, qui nullam differentiam inter illud corpus et reliquos cybos, vel qui gravioribus criminibus sunt commaculati accipere praesumunt* (Cf. Haimo, *Expos. in Epist. I ad Cor.* [*PL* 117:573D-574A]).
130 *Nolo vos ignorantes reddere quod nemo in spiritu Dei loquens dicit anathema Iesu, id est nemo spiritum sanctum habens et per spiritum sanctum loquens qui linguas infantium fecit dissertas anathema Iesu, id est separatus a Deo patre et spiritu sancto, vel aliqua parte inferior quod hereticorum vesania dicere non timuit, ideo anathemate, id est*
135 *separatione a Deo et aecclesia perculsi sunt* (Cf. Haimo, *Expos. in Epist. I ad Cor.* [*PL* 117: 576A-B]).

Et nemo potest dicere, dominus Iesu, nisi in spiritu sancto, id est corde credere, ore confiteri, et digna opera fidei exercere, Iesum diligendo deum asserere nisi gratiam sancti spiritus interfuerit edoctus (Cf. Haimo,
140 *Expos. in Epist. I ad Cor.* [*PL* 117: 576B]).

Quis hic oritur cum dominus dicat: de corde exeunt cogitationes male, homicidia, adulteria, et cetera, et cum nullum fiat peccatum nisi corpore delectante, animaque consentiente, cur apostolus Paulus omnia peccata extra corpus esse, solumque fornicationis peccatum in corpore consistere
145 *dicat? Ad exaggerendum tantum malum hoc apostolus dixit, quoniam comparatione istius peccati omnia peccata quasi extra corpus sunt. Dum enim facit furtum, homicidium, aut tale aliquid, dum illud agit, aliud potest cogitare. Verbi gratia, vult facere furtum, cogitat se acturum*

paenitentiam. Sic de ceteris. Dum autem fornicator, ita prae omnibus
150 *peccatis tota mens absorbetur in [cognitione?] totumque animum*
voluptas corporis ita facit captivum atque servum sibi ut totus sit homo
carneus, nil valens cogitare praeter quod delectatio carnis agit (Cf.
Haimo, *Expos. in Epist. I ad Cor.* [*PL* 117: 542C-D]).

Reprobum sensum hoc est cecitas mentis in eam quisquis datus fuerit,
155 *ab interiori dei luce secluditur* (Cf. Ps.-Rufin., *In Psalm. 6* [*PL*
21:666C]). *Sequentium rerum certitudo est praeteritarum exhibitio*
(Cf. Greg. M., *XL Hom. in Evang.* I.1 [*PL* 76:1437]).

Predestinatio est preparatio gratiae (Cf. Haimo, *Expos. in Epist.*
ad Rom. cap. 11 [*PL* 117:456C]). *Solum ordinatio et in bonis et in malis*
160 (Unidentified).

(Matt. 6:9) PATER NOSTER QUI ES, *id est hoc nomine et caritas*
excitatur. Quid enim carius filiis esse debet quam pater? Et supplex
affectus cum homines dicunt Deo PATER NOSTER, *et quaedam inpe-*
trandi presumptio quae petituri sumus cum prius quam aliquid
165 *petamus tam magnum donum accipimus, ut sinamur dicere:* PATER
NOSTER. *Quid enim non det filiis petentibus, cum hoc ipsum iam*
dederit ut filii essent? Postremo quam cura animum tangit, ut qui dicit
PATER NOSTER *tanto patre non sit indignus* (Cf. Aug., *De Sermone*
Domini in Monte II.4.16 [*CC* 35:107]). *Ammonentur etiam hic divites*
170 *vel genere nobiles vel qui Christiani facti fuerint non superbire adver-*
sus pueros et ignobiles, quoniam similiter dicunt Deo PATER NOSTER;
quod non possunt vere ac pie dicere nisi se fratres esse cognoscant.
Utatur ergo voce novi testamenti populus novus ad aeternam heredi-
tatem vocatus et dicat, PATER NOSTER QUI ES IN CAELIS, *id est, in*
175 *sanctis et iustis* (Cf. Aug., *De Sermone Domini in Monte* II.4.16 [*CC*
35:107]). *Nam si in superioribus partibus mundi locus Dei creditur esse*
tantum melioris meriti. Sunt aves quarum una est deo vicinior. In
caelis autem in cordibus iustorum dictum est tamquam in templo suo
et accommodatissima est ista similitudo ut spiritualiter tantum inter-
180 *esse videatur inter iustos et peccatores quantum temporaliter inter*
caelum et terram; peccator enim terra dictum est, cuius rei significan-
dae gratia cum ad orationem stamus, ad orationem convertimur [ad
orationem convertimur *A*, ad orientem convertimur *A²*]. *Unde*
celum surgit non ut ibi surgit, relictis ceteris mundi partibus, sed ut
185 *ammoneamur ad naturam excellentiorem, id est ad Deum, se convert-*

ere (Cf. Aug., *De Sermone Domini in Monte* II.5.17-18 [*CC* 35:107-108]).

AMBROSIUS. *Caelum ubi cessavit, ubi flagitia feriantur* (Cf. Ambr., *De Sacramentis* V.4.20 [*CSEL* 73:67]). *Iam videramus quae*
190 *sunt petenda. Dictum est enim qui sit qui petitur, et ubi habitat.* (Matt. 6:9) SANCTIFICETUR NOMEN TUUM. *Quod non sic petitur quasi non sit sanctum Dei nomen, [63v] sed ut sanctum habeatur ab omnibus id est ita ut innotescat Deus, ut non extimentur aliqua sanctis quod magis ostendere timeant* (Cf. Aug., *De Sermone Domini in Monte*
195 II.5.19 [*CC* 35:109]).

AMBROSIUS. *Sanctificetur in nobis ut ad nos possit eius sanctificatio pervenire* (Cf. Ambr., *De Sacramentis* V.21 [*CSEL* 73:67]). (Matt. 6:10) ADVENIAT REGNUM TUUM, *id est manifestetur omnibus. Sicut enim presens lux etiam absens est cecis, ita Dei regnum quamvis de-*
200 *scendat de terris, tamen absens est ignorantibus* (Cf. Aug., *De Sermone Domini in Monte* II.6.20 [*CC* 35:109–10]). *Vel ita:* ADVENIAT REGNUM TUUM, *ut per iusticiam et sanctitatem in nobis regnare digneris. Vel ita: hoc optamus ut finem nostris faciat malis, et veniens de caelo nos assumat in regnum. Hoc enim dicto ammonemur ubi ve-*
205 *ram nostram substantiam sperare videamus* (Cf. Ps.-Aug., *Serm.* 65 [*PL* 39:1870]). (Matt. 6:10) FIAT VOLUNTAS TUA SICUT IN CAELO, *id est, sicut in angelis qui sunt in celo fiat voluntas tua, ut omnino tibi adhereant, teque perfruantur nullo errore obviante sapientiam eorum, nulla miseria impediente* [impediente *corr.* ex ? *A*[1]] *beatitudinem*
210 *eorum, ita fiat in sanctis tuis qui sunt in terra et de terra, quod ad corpus attinet, facti sunt; et quamvis in caelestem habitationem atque immutabilem tamen de terra assumendi sunt. Ad hoc respicit etiam illa angelorum praedicatio:* (Luc. 2:14) GLORIA IN EXCELSIS DEO, ET IN TERRA PAX HOMINIBUS BONAE VOLUNTATIS, *ut cum prae-*
215 *cesserit bona voluntas nostra quae vocantem sequitur, efficiatur in nobis voluntas dei sicuti est in caelo id est in angelis, ut nulla adversitas resistat nostrae beatitudini, quae est pax. Item* FIAT VOLUNTAS TUA SICUT ET IN CAELO ET IN TERRA, *id est, obaediatur praeceptis tuis sicut ab angelis ita ab omnibus, quod ergo faciunt voluntatem*
220 *Dei; in illis fit voluntas Dei, non quia ipsi faciunt ut velit Deus, sed quod faciunt quod ille vult, id est, faciunt voluntatem eius. Item:* FIAT VOLUNTAS TUA SICUT IN CAELO ET IN TERRA, *id est, sicut in iustis et sanctis ita etiam in peccatoribus, vel ut* [velut *A, corr. A*[2]]

ad te convertantur, vel ut sua cuique tribuantur [buantur *A*, tribuan-
225 tur *A*¹] *quod fiet extremo iuditio vel ita sicut in spiritu et in carne* (Cf.
Aug., *De Sermone Domini in Monte* II.6.21-22 [*CC* 35:111–12]).
*Aliter, sicut in domino nostro Iesu Christo ita et in aecclesia. Caelum
enim et terra convenienter intelligitur quasi vir et femina, quoniam
terra caelo fecunditate fit fructifera* (Cf. Aug., *De Sermone Domini*
230 *in Monte* II.6.23–24 [*CC* 35:113]). (Luc. 11:3) PANEM NOSTRUM
COTIDIANUM DA NOBIS. *Si panem necessarium corpori intelligas,
divina sapientia sapienter docuit et solum panem et hodie nos petere.
Hoc enim dicto et avaritia cum aviditate tollitur, et humanae vitae
insinuatur in terris* (Cf. Ps.-Aug., *Serm. 65* [*PL* 39:1870]). Illud
235 (Matt. 6:34) NOLITE SOLLICITI ESSE IN CRASTINUM, *si et duplex
in Christo Domino qui panis vivus de caelo descendit. Hic intelligitur
sacramentum unum visibile quod ab altaris per manum sacerdotis
ore corporis visibiliter sumpsimus, alterum invisibile quod sola ratione et intellectu mentis qui possunt accipiunt. Quod panis substan-
240 tialis secundum Matheum dicitur eo quod melior sit omni cybo corpo-
rali. Hodie autem id est semper petitur, dum hodie cognominatur*
(Unidentified*). Cotidianum igitur panem petimus spiritualem, id
est, divina praecepta quae cotidie oportet praemeditari et operari.
Operamini, inquit, escam quae non corrumpitur, ut animus quem
245 temporalibus affectibus, quasi dispendium, ab intentione Dei patitur,
praeceptorum cibo reficiatur* (Cf. Aug., *De Sermone Domini in Monte*
II.7.27 [*CC* 35:115–16]). (Matt. 6:12) ET DIMITTE NOBIS DEBITA
NOSTRA, *id est, peccata habes debitorem qui in te peccavit, qui forte
iniuriam fecit. Dimitte illi, ne dum negas pietatem fieri, claudas tibi in-
250 dulgentiam patris* (Cf. Ps.-Aug., *Serm. 65* [*PL* 39:1871]). (Matt.
6:13) ET NE NOS INDUCAS IN TEMPTATIONEM, *id est, ne induci
nos patiaris in temptationem. Aliud est induci in temptationem, aliud
temptari. Nam sine temptatione probatus esse nullus potest* (Cf. Aug.,
De Sermone Domini in Monte II.9.30 [*CC* 35:119]). *Nam ergo hic
255 oramus ut non temptemur, sed ut non inferamur in temptationem,
tamquam si quispiam necesse est igne examinari non orat ut igne non
tangatur sed ut non uretur* (Cf. Aug., *De Sermone Domini in Monte*
II.9.32 [*CC* 35:120–21]). *Inducimur enim in temptationem, si talis in-
cedit quod ferre non possumus* (Cf. Aug., *De Sermone Domini in
260 Monte* II.9.34 [*CC* 35:125]). (Matt. 6:13) SED LIBERA NOS [64r] A
MALO. *Orandum est et ut non solum non inducamur in malis, quod*

cum factum fuerit, nichil permanebit formidolosum (Cf. Aug., *De Sermone Domini in Monte* II.9.35 [*CC* 35:125]). *Sed harum specie peticionum res quam quasi in hac vita exordium capiant, tamen* 265 *in aeternum manebunt. Nam et sanctificatio sempiterna Dei erit, et regni eius non erit finis. Et beatitudini nostrae in qua corpus nostra spirituum tamquam caelo summa pace consentiet eterna vita permittitur. Reliqua vero quattuor ad temporalem vitam pertinere videntur* (Cf. Aug., *De Sermone Domini in Monte* II.10.36 [*CC* 270 35:126–27]).

BIBLIOGRAPHY

PRIMARY SOURCES

Adelmannus Leodiensis (Adelmann of Liège), *Epistola ad Berengarium*, in *Serta Mediaevalia* [CCCM, 171], pp. 167–201.

Albericus Casinensis (Alberic of Monte Cassino), *Flores Rhetorici*, ed. Don Mauro Inguanez and H. M. Willard, *Miscellanea Cassinese* 14 (Monte Cassino, 1938).

——. *Passio S. Cesari*, ed. in *Bibliotheca Casinensis* 3 (1877), *Florilegium*, pp. 150–58; the prologue, apologia, and five-fold acrostic verses ed. in J. Mallet and A. Thibaut, *Les manuscrits en écriture bénéventaine de la bibliothèque capitulaire de Bénévent* (Paris, 1984), pp. 246–47.

——. *Passio S. Modesti*, ed. A. Poncelet in *Anal. Bolland.* 51 (1933): 369–74.

——. *Vita S. Aspren*, ed. A. Lentini, in "Alberico di Montecassino nel quadro della Riforma Gregoriana," *Studi Gregoriani* 4 (1952): 89–109.

——. *Vita S. Dominici*, ed. F. Dolbeau, in "Le dossier de saint Dominique de Sora d'Albéric du Mont-Cassin à Jacques de Voragine," *Mélanges de l'École française de Rome: Moyen-age-Temps modernes*, 102 (1990): 7–78.

——. *Vita S. Scolasticae*, ed. A. Lentini, in "L'omilia e la vita di S. Scolastica di Alberico Cassinese," *Benedictina* 3 (1949): 217–38.

Ascelinus Carnotensis (Ascelin of Chartres), *Epistola ad Berengarium*, in *Serta Mediaevalia* [CCCM, 171], pp. 150–54.

Beno, *Gesta Romanae Ecclesiae contra Hildebrandum, MGH, Libelli de Lite* 2.366–422.

Beringerius Turonensis (Berengar of Tours), *Iuramentum*, ed. R. B. C. Huygens, in *Serta Mediaevalia* [CCCM, 171], pp. 256–70.

——. *Rescriptum contra Lanfrannum*, ed. R. B. C. Huygens [Corpus Christianorum, Cont. Mediaevalis, nos. 84 and 84a] (Turnhout, 1988).

Bernoldus Constantiensis (Bernold of Constance), *Chronicon*, ed. G. Waitz, *MGH SS* 5.385–487.

——. *De Veritate Corporis et Sanguinis Domini, PL* 148: 1453B–1460A; also in *Serta Mediaevalia* [CCCM,171], pp. 247–55.

Bertoldus Augiensis (Bertold of Reichenau), *Chronicon*, ed. G. H. Pertz, *MGH SS* 5.264–326.

Briefsammlungen der Zeit Heinrichs IV., ed. C. Erdmann and N. Fickermann, *MGH Ep.* (Weimar, 1950), pp. 149–52.

Chronica Monasterii Casinensis, ed. H. Hoffmann, *MGH, SS* 34 (Hannover, 1980).

Cicero, *Topica,* tr. H. M. Hubbell, Loeb Classical Library (Cambridge Mass., 1949).

Codex Benedictus: an eleventh-century lectionary from Monte Cassino (New York, 1982).

Durandus Troarnensis (Durand of Troarn), *Liber de corpore et sanguine Christi contra Berengarium et ejus sectatores, PL* 149: 1373–1424.

Garlandus Compotista, *Dialectica,* ed. L. M. de Rijk (Assen, 1959).

Guitmundus Aversanus (Guitmund of Aversa), *De Corporis et Sanguinis Christi, PL* 149: 1427–1508.

Herigerus Lobiensis (Heriger of Lobbes), *Libellus de Corpore et Sanguine Domini, PL* 139: 177–88.

Hildeberti Cenomanensis Episcopi Carmina Minora (Hildebert of Le Mans), ed. A. Brian Scott (Leipzig, 1969).

Hugo Lingonensis (Hugh of Langres), *De Corpore et Sanguine Christi contra Berengarium, PL* 142: 1325–31.

Iohannes Fiscamnensis (John of Fécamp), *Albini Confessio Fidei, PL* 101: 1027–98.

Lanfrancus Beccensis/Ticinensis (Lanfranc of Bec), *Liber de Corpore et Sanguine Domini, PL* 150: 407–42.

Laurentius Monachus Casinensis Archiepiscopus Amalfitanus Opera (Lawrence of Amalfi), ed. Francis Newton, MGH, *Quellen zur Geistesgeschichte des Mittelalters,* vol. 7 (Weimar, 1973).

Manegoldus Lautenbacensis (Manegold of Lautenbach), *Liber ad Gebhardum,* MGH *Libelli de Lite* 1.300–430.

Matronola, M. *Un testo inedito di Berengario di Tours e il Concilio Romano del 1079* [*Orbis Romanus* 6] (Milan, 1936).

Maurer, Rudolf. "Berengarii ut videtur De eucharistia (Wiederauffindung eines seit Mabillon verschollenen Fragmentes)," *Wiener Studien* 103 (1990): 199–205.

Meyvaert, P. "Bérenger de Tours contre Albéric du Mont-Cassin," *Revue Bénédictine* 70 (1960): 324–32.

Morin, G. "Bérenger contre Bérenger. Un document inédit des luttes théologiques du XIe siècle," *Recherches de Théologie ancienne et médiévale* 4 (1932): 109–33.

Orabona, Luciano. *Guitmondo di Aversa. La Verità dell'Eucaristia* [Chiese del Mezzogiorno. Fonti e Studi, 6] (Naples, 1995).

Ordericus Vitalis (Orderic Vitalis). *The Ecclesiastical History,* ed. M. Chibnall (Oxford, 1969–1980).

Pascasius Radbertus, *De Corpore et Sanguine Domini,* ed. B. Paulus [CCCM, 16] (Turnhout, 1969).

Petrus Damianus (Peter Damian), *Briefe des Petri Damiani,* ed. Kurt Reindel [MGH Briefe der Deutschen Kaiserzeit 4.1–4] (Weimar, 1983–1993).

Petrus Diaconus (Peter the Deacon), *Ortus et Vita Iustorum Cenobii Casinensis,* ed. Robert H. Rodgers [University of California Publications: Classical Studies, vol. 10] (Berkeley and Los Angeles, 1972).

Ratramnus Corbeiensis. *De Corpore et sanguine Domini.* ed. J. N. Bakhuizen van den Brink [Verhandlingen der Koninklijke Nederlandse Akademie van Wetenschappen, Afd. Letterkkunde, nieuwe reeks, deel. 87] (Amsterdam/London, 1974).

Register Gregors VII, ed. Erich Caspar, *MGH Epp. sel.* 2nd ed. (Berlin, 1955).

Rhetorica Ad Herennium, ed. F. Marx (Leipzig, 1923).

Rockinger, L. *Briefsteller und Formelbücher des eilften bis vierzehnten Jahrhunderts. Quellen und Erörterungen zur bayerischen und deutschen Geschichte* 9, 1 (Munich, 1863).

Serta Mediaevalia. Textus varii saeculorum X–XIII Tractatus et epistulae, ed. R. B. C. Huygens [Corpus Christianorum, Cont. Mediaevalis, no. 171] (Turnhout, 2000).

Sigebertus Gemblacensis (Sigebert of Gembloux), *Apologia contra eos qui calumniantur missas coniugatorum sacerdotem,* MGH, *Libelli de Lite,* 2.436–88.

Wido Ferrariensis (Wido of Ferrara), *De schismate Hildebrandi,* MGH, *Libelli de Lite,* 1.529–67.

SECONDARY WORKS

Alverny, M.-T. d'. "Translations and Translators," in *Renaissance and Renewal in the Twelfth Century,* ed. Robert L. Benson and Giles Constable (Cambridge, Mass., 1982), pp. 421–62.

Auctoritas und Ratio. Studien zu Berengar von Tours, ed. Peter Ganz, R. B. C. Huygens, and Friedrich Niewöhner [Wolfenbütteler Mittelalter-Studien, bd. 2] (Wiesbaden, 1990).

Bäumer, S. "Der Micrologus ein Werk Bernolds von Konstanz," *Neues Archiv der Gesellschaft für ältere deutsche Geschichte* 18 (1893): 431–46.

Bibliotheca Casinensis (Monte Cassino, 1874–1894).

Biffi, Inos. "Guitmondo e Anselmo alla scuola di Lanfranco e le arti liberali," in *Guitmondo di Aversa,* vol. 1, pp. 59–78.

Bloch, H. *Monte Cassino in the Middle Ages* (Cambridge, Mass., 1986)

——. "Monte Cassino's Teachers and Library in the High Middle Ages," *Settimane di studio del Centro italiano di studi sull'alto Medioevo* 19 (Spoleto, 1972), pp. 563–613.

Borino, G. "Odelrico vescovo di Padova (1064–80). Legato di Gregorio VII in Germania (1079)," *Miscellanea in onore di Roberto Cessi,* vol. 1, pp. 63–79 [Storia e letteratura: 71] (Rome, 1958).

——. "Per la storia della riforma della Chiesa nel secolo XI," *Archivio della società romana di storia patria* 38 (1915): 60.

Bouhot, Jean-Paul. *Ratramne de Corbie. Histoire littéraire et controverses doctrinales* (Paris, 1976).

Brown, Virginia. "A New Commentary on Matthew in Beneventan Script at Venosa," *Mediaeval Studies* 49 (1987): 443–65.

Cantelli, Silvia. "Il commento al Cantico dei Cantici di Giovanni da Mantova," *Studi medievali* 3a ser., 26,1 (1985): 101–84.

Cantin, André. "Bérenger, lecteur du *De ordine* de saint Augustin, ou, comment se préparait, au milieu du XIe siècle, une domination de la *ratio* sur la science sacrée," in *Auctoritas und Ratio. Studien zu Berengar von Tours,* ed. Peter Ganz, R. B. C. Huygens, and Friedrich Niewöhner [Wolfenbütteler Mittelalter-Studien, bd. 2] (Wiesbaden, 1990), pp. 89–107.

Capitani, O. "La lettera di Goffredo II Martello a Ildebrando (1059)," *Studi Gregoriani* 5 (1956): 19–31.

——. "L' ovvero dell'utilità delle monografie," *Studi medievali* 3rd ser., 16 (1975): 353–78.

——. "Per la storia dei rapporti tra Gregorio VII e Berengario di Tours," *Studi Gregoriani* 6 (1959–61): 99–145.

——. "Problemi della cultura europea nel secolo XI—Prolusione," in *Guitmondo di Aversa,* vol. 1, pp. 39–57.

——. "Status questionis dei falsi berengariani: note sulla prima fase della disputa," *Fälschungen im Mittelalter* [*MGH* Schriften 33.2] (Hannover, 1985).

——. "Studi per Berengario di Tours," *Bullettino dell'Istituto Storico italiano e archivio muratoriano,* 69 (1957): 67–173.

Cappuyns, M. Review of Matronola, *Un testo inedito di Berengario di Tours, Bulletin de Théologie Ancienne et Médiévale* 3 (1937–1940): 241–42.

Carli, Matilde Tirelli. "La donazione di Matilde di Canossa all'Episcopato pisano," *Boll. Storico Pisano* 46 (1977): 139–59.

Catalogue des manuscrits en écriture latine portant des indications de date, de lieu, ou de copiste, vol. 2, ed. M.-Th. d'Alverny, M.-C. Garand, M. Mabille, and J. Metman (Paris, 1962).

Chadwick, Henry. "Ego Berengarius," *Journal of Theological Studies* n.s. 40 (1989): 414–45.

——. "Symbol and Reality: Berengar and the Appeal to the Fathers," in *Auctoritas und Ratio. Studien zu Berengar von Tours,* ed. Peter Ganz, R. B. C. Huygens, and Friedrich Niewöhner [Wolfenbütteler Mittelalter-Studien, bd. 2] (Wiesbaden, 1990), pp. 25–45.

Chazelle, Celia. *The Crucified God in the Carolingian Era. Theology and Art of Christ's Passion* (Cambridge, 2001).

——. "Figure, Character, and the Glorified Body in the Carolingian Eucharistic Controversy," *Traditio* 47 (1992): 1–36.

Chenu, M.-D. *La théologie au douzième siècle,* 3rd ed. (Paris, 1976) [partially translated in *Nature, Man, and Society in the Twelfth Century,* ed. and trans. Jerome Taylor and Lester K. Little (Chicago, 1968)].

Cilento, Nicola. "La riforma gregoriana, Bisanzio e l'Italia meridionale," *Studi gregoriani* 13 (1989): 353–72.

Coffey, Thomas F. "The Homily of Alberic the Deacon on Saint Scholastica," in *Diakonia. Studies in Honor of Robert T. Meyer,* ed. by Thomas Halton and Joseph P. Williman (Washington, D.C., 1986), pp. 289–301.

Cowdrey, H. E. J. *The Age of Abbot Desiderius* (Oxford, 1983).

——. "The Enigma of Archbishop Lanfranc," *Haskins Society Journal* 6 (1994): 129–52. [repr. in *Popes and Church Reform in the 11th Century* (Aldershot, 2000)]

——. ed. and trans., *The Epistolae Vagantes of Pope Gregory VII* (Oxford, 1972).

——. "The Papacy and the Berengarian Controversy," in *Auctoritas und Ratio. Studien zu Berengar von Tours,* ed. Peter Ganz, R. B. C. Huygens, and Friedrich Niewöhner [Wolfenbütteler Mittelalter-Studien, bd. 2] (Wiesbaden, 1990), pp. 109–36. [repr. in *Popes and Church Reform in the 11th Century* (Aldershot, 2000)]

——. *Pope Gregory VII 1073–1085* (Oxford, 1998).

——. *Popes and Church Reform in the 11th Century* (Aldershot, 2000).

Dell'Omo, M. "Guitmund v. Aversa," in *Lexikon des Mittelalters* 4 (Munich/ Zurich, 1989), 1789.

——. "Per la storia dei monaci-vescovi nell'Italia normanna del secolo XI: Ricerche biografiche su Guitmondo di La Croix-Saint-Leufroy, vescovo di Aversa," *Benedictina* 40 (1993): 1, 9–34.

Dizionario biografico degli italiani (Roma, 1960–).

Dolbeau, François. "Le dossier de saint Dominique de Sora d'Albéric du Mont-Cassin à Jacques de Voragine," *Mélanges de l'École française de Rome: Moyen âge-Temps modernes,* 102 (1990): 7–78.

——. "Recherches sur les oeuvres littéraires du Pape Gelase II," *Analecta Bollandiana* 107 (1989): 65–127.

Engels, O. "Alberich von Monte Cassino und sein Schüler Johannes von Gaeta," *Studien und Mitteilungen zur Geschichte des Benediktinen-Ordens* 66 (1955): 35–50.

Erdmann, C. "Gregor VII. und Berengar von Tours," *Quellen und Forschungen aus ital. Archiven un Bibliotheken* 28 (1937–38): 48–74.

Foggi, Fabrizio. "Pisa e Enrico IV," *Bollettino storico Pisano* 1988 (57): 1–10.

Franklin, Carmella V. "The restored *Life and Miracles of St. Dominic of Sora* by Alberic of Monte Cassino," *Mediaeval Studies* 55 (1993): 285–345.

Ganz, David. *Corbie in the Carolingian Renaissance* (Sigmaringen, 1990).

Gehl, Paul F., Monastic Rhetoric and Grammar in the Age of Desiderius: The Works of Alberic of Montecassino (Diss., University of Chicago, 1976).

———. "Vat. Ottobonianus lat. 1354: Apropos of Catalogue Notices and the History of Grammatical Pedagogy," *Revue d'histoire des textes* 8 (1978): 303–97.

Geiselmann, J. *Die Eucharistielehre der Vorscholastik* (Paderborn, 1926).

———. "Ein neuentdecktes Werk von Berengar von Tours über das Abendmahl?" *Theologische Quartalschrift* 118 (1937): 1–31, 133–72.

Gibson, Craig A., and Newton, Francis. "Pandulf of Capua's *De Calculatione:* An Illustrated Abacus Treatise and Some Evidence for the Hindu-Arabic Numerals in Eleventh-Century South Italy," *Mediaeval Studies* 57 (1995): 293–335.

Gibson, M. "The Early Scholastic 'Glosule' to Priscian, 'Institutiones Grammaticae': the Text and Its Influence," *Studi Medievali* 20,1 (1979): 235–54.

———. *Lanfranc of Bec* (Oxford, 1978).

———. "Letters and Charters Relating to Berengar of Tours," in *Auctoritas und Ratio. Studien zu Berengar von Tours*, ed. Peter Ganz, R. B. C. Huygens, and Friedrich Niewöhner [Wolfenbütteler Mittelalter-Studien, bd. 2] (Wiesbaden, 1990), pp. 5–23.

Glossarium Mediae et Infimae Latinitatis, ed. Charles du Fresne du Cange (1883–1887, rep. Graz, 1954).

Green, Monica H. "The *De genecia* Attributed to Constantine the African," *Speculum* 62 (1987): 299–324.

Guitmondo di Aversa. La Cultura europea e la riforma gregoriana nel Mezzogiorno, 3 vols., ed. Luciano Orabona [Chiese del Mezzogiorno. Fonti e Studi, vols. 13–15] (Naples, 2000).

Hagendahl, H. "Le manuel de rhétorique d'Albericus Casinensis," *Classica et Mediaevalia* 17 (1956): 56–70.

Häring, N. M. "Berengar's Definitions of *Sacramentum* and Their Influence on Mediaeval Sacramentology," *Mediaeval Studies* 10 (1948): 109–46.

Hödl, Ludwig. "Die theologische Auseinandersetzung mit Berengar von Tours im frühscholastischen Eucharistietraktat *De corpore Domini*," in *Auctoritas und Ratio. Studien zu Berengar von Tours*, ed. Peter Ganz, R. B .C. Huygens, and Friedrich Niewöhner [Wolfenbütteler Mittelalter-Studien, bd. 2] (Wiesbaden, 1990), pp. 69–88.

Holopainen, Toivo J. *Dialectic and Theology in the Eleventh Century* [Studien und Texte zur Geistesgeschichte des Mittelalters, bd. 54] (Leiden/New York/Cologne, 1996).

Holtzmann, W. "Laurentius von Amalfi. Ein Lehrer Hildebrands," *Studi Gregoriani* 1 (1947): 207–37, repr. in Holtzmann's *Beiträge zur Reichs- und Papstgeschichte des hohen Mittelalters* [Bonner historische Forschungen 8] (Bonn, 1957), pp. 9–33.

Houben, H. *Il "libro del capitolo" del monastero della SS. Trinità di Venosa (cod. Cas. 334): una testimonianza del Mezzogiorno normanno* (Galatina [Lecce], 1984).

Howe, John. *Church Reform and Social Change in Eleventh-Century Italy: Dominic of Sora and His Patrons* (Philadelphia, 1997).

———. "Peter Damian and Monte Cassino," *Revue Bénédictine* 107 (1997): 330–51.

Hunt, R. W. "Studies on Priscian in the Eleventh and Twelfth Centuries," *Medieval and Renaissance Studies* 1 (1941–43): 194–231; 2 (1950): 1–56.

Huygens, R. B. C. "A propos de Bérenger et son traité de l'eucharistie," *Revue Bénédictine* 76 (1966): 133–39.

———. "Textes latins du XIe au XIIIe siècle," *Studi medievali* 3rd s. 8 (1967): 476–89.

Inguanez, M. *Codicum Casinensium Manuscriptorum Catalogus,* 3 vols. (Monte Cassino, 1914–41).

Iogna-Prat, Dominique. "L'oeuvre d'Haymon d'Auxerre. État de la question," in *L'école carolingienne d'Auxerre de Murethach à Rémi 830–908,* ed. Dominique Iogna-Prat, Colette Jeudy, Guy Lobrichon (Paris, 1991).

James, M. R. *A Catalogue of the Medieval Manuscripts in the University Library, Aberdeen* (Cambridge, 1932).

Kamp, Norbert. "Le fonti per una biografia di Guitmondo di Aversa." in *Guitmondo di Aversa,* vol. 1, pp. 129–57.

Klewitz, H.-W. *Reformpapsttum und Kardinalkolleg* (Darmstadt, 1957).

Lange, Klaus. "Geistliche Speise. Untersuchungen zur Metaphorik der Bibelhermeneutik," *Zeitschrift für deutsches Altertum und deutsche Literatur* 95 (1966): 81–123.

Lentini, A. "Alberico di Montecassino nel quadro della Riforma Gregoriana," *Studi Gregoriani* 4 (1952): 55–109.

———. "L'omilia e la vita di S. Scolastica di Alberico Cassinese," *Benedictina* 3 (1949): 217–38.

———. "La 'Vita S. Dominici' di Alberico Cassinese," *Benedictina* 5 (1951): 57–77.

Lentini, A., and Avagliano, F. *I carmi di Alfano I arcivescovo di Salerno* (Monte Cassino, 1974).

Licitra, V. "Il mito di Alberico di Montecassino iniziatore dell'Ars dictaminis," *Studi Medievali* 3rd ser., 18,2 (1977): 609–28.

Lowe, E. A. *Beneventan Script,* 2nd ed. Virginia Brown (Rome, 1980).

MacDonald, A. J. *Berengar and the Reform of Sacramental Doctrine* (London, 1930).

———. "Berengariana," *Journal of Theological Studies* 33 (1932): 181–86.

Macy, Gary. "Berengar's Legacy as Heresiarch," in *Auctoritas und Ratio. Studien zu Berengar von Tours,* ed. Peter Ganz, R. B. C. Huygens, and Friedrich Niewöhner [Wolfenbütteler Mittelalter-Studien, bd. 2] (Wiesbaden, 1990), pp. 47–67.

188 ✦ Bibliography

——. The Theologies of the Eucharist in the Early Scholastic Period. A Study of the Salvific Function of the Sacrament According to the Theologians c. 1080–c. 1220 (Oxford, 1984).

Mallet, J., and Thibaut, A. Les manuscrits en écriture bénéventaine de la Bibliothèque Capitulaire de Bénévent, vol. 1 (Paris, 1984).

Martinet, Suzanne. "Les arts libéraux à Laon au IXᵉ siècle," in Enseignement et vie intellectuelle (IXe–XVe siècle) [Actes du 95e Congrès national des sociétés savantes] (Reims, 1970), pp. 55–62.

Mittellateinisches Wörterbuch bis zum ausgehenden 13. Jahrhundert (Munich, 1967).

Montclos, J. de. Lanfranc et Bérenger. La controverse eucharistique du XIe siècle [Spicilegium Sacrum Lovaniense. Études et documents, 37] (Louvain, 1971).

Morris, Colin. The Papal Monarchy. The Western Church from 1050 to 1250 (Oxford, 1989).

Nelis, Suzanne J. "What Lanfranc Taught, What Anselm Learned," Haskins Society Journal 2 (1990): 75–82.

Newton, Francis. "Due tipi di manoscritti ed il rinnovamento culturale nell'epoca di Desiderio," in F. Avagliano and O. Pecere, eds. L'età dell'abate Desiderio. III.1: storia arte e cultura, Atti del IV Convegno di studi sul medioevo meridionale (Monte Cassino, 4–8 ottobre, 1987), Miscellanea Cassinese 67 (1992): 467–81.

——. The Monte Cassino Scriptorium and Library Under Abbots Desiderius and Oderisius I (1058–1105), (Cambridge/New York, 1999).

——. "A Newly-Discovered Poem on Saint Maur by Lawrence of Amalfi," Benedictina 20,1 (1973): 91–107.

——. "A Third and Older Cassinese Lectionary for the Feasts of Saints Benedict, Maur, and Scholastica," Miscellanea Cassinese 47 (1983), 45–75.

Patt, William D. "The early 'Ars Dictaminis' as Response to a Changing Society," Viator 9 (1978): 133–55.

Radding, Charles M. "The Geography of Learning in Early Eleventh-Century Europe: Lanfranc of Bec and Berengar of Tours Revisited," Bullettino dell'Istituto Storico Italiano per il Medio Evo e Archivio Muratoriano 98 (1992): 145–72.

Radding, Charles M., and Clark, William W. Medieval Architecture, Medieval Learning. Builders and Masters in the Age of Romanesque and Gothic (New Haven, 1992).

Reiche, Rainer. Ein Rheinisches Schulbuch aus den 11. Jahrhundert [Münchener Beiträge zur Mediävistik und Renaissanceforschung, 24] (Munich, 1976).

Robinson, I. S. Authority and Resistance in the Investiture Contest (New York, 1973).

——. "Colores rhetorici in the Investiture Contest," Traditio 32 (1976): 209–38.

——. "The Friendship Network of Gregory VII," History 63 (1978): 1–22.

——. The Papacy 1073–1198 (Cambridge, 1990).

———. "Pope Gregory VII, the Princes, and the Pactum 1077–1080," *English Historical Review* 94 (1979): 721–56.

Ropa, Giampaolo. "Testimonianze di vita culturale nei monasteri matildici nei secoli xi–xii," in *Studi Matildici. Atti e memorie del II convegno di studi matildici. Modena-Reggio E., 1–2–3 maggio 1970* (Modena, 1971), pp. 231–80.

Rubin, Miriam. *Corpus Christi.* (Cambridge, 1991).

Somerville, R. "The Case Against Berengar of Tours—A New Text," *Studi Gregoriani* 9 (1972): 55–75.

———. "The Councils of Gregory VII," *Studi Gregoriani* 13 (1989): 33–53.

Southern, R. W. "Lanfranc of Bec and Berengar of Tours," in *Studies in Medieval History Presented to Frederick Maurice Powicke,* ed. R. W. Hunt, W. A. Pantin, and R. W. Southern (Oxford, 1948), pp. 27–48.

———. *Making of the Middle Ages* (New Haven, 1953).

———. *Saint Anselm and His Biographer. A Study of Monastic Life and Thought 1059–c.1130* (Cambridge, 1963).

———. *Saint Anselm. A Portrait in a Landscape* (Cambridge, 1990).

Stock, Brian. *The Implications of Literacy* (Princeton, 1983).

Supino Martini, P. *Roma e l'area grafica romanesca (secoli x–xii)* [Biblioteca di Scrittura e Civiltà I] (Alessandria, 1987).

Toubert, Hélène. *Un art dirigé. Réforme grégorienne et iconographie* (Paris, 1990), p. 163.

Violante, C. "Le concessioni ponteficie alla Chiesa di Pisa riguardanti la Corsica alla fine del secolo XI," *Bullettino dell'Istituto Storico Italiano per il Medio Evo* 75 (1963): 43–56.

———. "Cronotasi dei vescovi e degli arcivescovi di Pisa dalle origini all'inizio del secolo XIII. Primo contributo ad una nuova 'Italia Sacra,'" in *Miscellanea Gilles Gérard Meersseman,* vol. 1 (Padua, 1970), pp. 3–56.

Vogel, Jörgen. *Gregor VII. und Heinrich IV. nach Canossa* [Arbeiten zur Frühmittelalterforschung, 9] (Berlin/New York, 1983).

Witt, Ronald. "Medieval 'Ars Dictaminis' and the Beginnings of Humanism: A New Construction of the Problem," *Renaissance Quarterly* 35 (1982): 1–35.

———. "Medieval Italian Culture and the Origins of Humanism," in *Renaissance Humanism. Foundations, Forms, and Legacy,* vol. 1, ed. Albert Rabil, Jr. (Philadelphia, 1988), pp. 28–71.

INDEX

References are to the page number. In the case of the entries for "vocabulary of notable words in dossier" and "vocabulary of notable words in libellus," the first number is that of the page, and the number in parentheses is that of the line of the text.

146(324); *series,* 128(38); *sillogismus,*
152(422); *similitudo,* 146(323);
sonare, 166(643); *species/res,*
156(506)–158(518); *spiritualiter,*
160(553), 160(562), 162(591), 164(607),
164(620); *statua,* 158(523); *subaudire,*
142(267); *subdere,* 140(241); *subinferre,*
142(263), 150(391); *substantia,*

156(505–6), 158(521), 158(526),
160(563), 164(607); *sufficere,* 148(359);
superius, 166(642); *tipice,* 126(31);
tipicus, 134 (152, 153, 156);
transfigurare, 158(510); *visibiliter,*
162(595–96)

Zenobius, St., bishop of Florence, 39